Advanced *Masterclass*

CAE

NEW EDITION

Teacher's Book

Tricia Aspinall

Annette Capel

with Structure
sections by
Kathy Gude

OXFORD
UNIVERSITY PRESS

Oxford University Press, Walton Street, Oxford OX2 6DP

Oxford   New York

Athens   Auckland   Bangkok   Bogotá
Buenos Aires   Calcutta   Cape Town   Chennai
Dar es Salaam   Delhi   Florence   Hong Kong
Istanbul   Karachi   Kuala Lumpur   Madrid
Melbourne   Mexico City   Mumbai   Nairobi
Paris   São Paulo   Singapore   Taipei   Tokyo
Toronto   Warsaw

and associated companies in
Berlin   Ibadan

OXFORD and OXFORD ENGLISH
are trade marks of Oxford University Press

ISBN 0 19 453428 6

Photocopying

Printed in Hong Kong

Acknowledgements

The authors and publisher are grateful to those who
have given permission to reproduce the following
extracts and adaptations of copyright material:
p124 Adapted from 'Dream On', by permission, Verity
Watkins/19 Magazine/Robert Harding Syndication
p130 Adapted from 'Power of Persuasion', Executive PA
Magazine, with kind permission of Hobsons
(Publishers)
p127 Taken from 'Standard Bearer for the New Rites' by
Katharine Whitehorn, in The Sunday Observer, by
permission of The Observer ©
p124 Adapted from 'The Doodle Bug' with permission
of A.P. Watt Ltd on behalf of Libby Purves
p128/131 From 'Heights of Excellence' and 'Prolonging
Active Life' by Susan Aldridge, © The Guardian, by
permission
University of Cambridge Local Examinations
Syndicate: marking information for CAE Papers 2 and
5, July 1995, © UCLES.

Teacher's Book Contents

INTRODUCTION

Advanced Masterclass gives students comprehensive preparation and training for the Cambridge Certificate in Advanced English examination. The course places particular emphasis on the topics and skills students will meet in the examination. The CAE examination has introduced new question types and ways of testing the English language. *Advanced Masterclass* has paid special attention to those areas by breaking down each task type and giving students plenty of guided practice.

The CAE exam makes particular use of authentic texts and *Advanced Masterclass* has included a wide range of appropriate authentic extracts, taken from magazines, newspapers, brochures and books. As many of these texts are long (up to 1,200 words), students are encouraged to time their reading and to build up their speed.

This course places great emphasis on writing skills. The writing paper in the CAE examination consists of a variety of task types which focus on the need to write for a specific target reader. Students are prepared for these tasks with a step-by-step approach.

Although grammar is not overtly tested in CAE, *Advanced Masterclass* recognizes the importance of structural accuracy and provides revision in all the areas students should be proficient in at this level. Vocabulary is focused on throughout the course as students will need to cope with the lexis presented in the authentic texts.

The main aim of *Advanced Masterclass* is to give students full training in all the exam tasks for the CAE. The course is pitched at the advanced level throughout but there is a progression in the exam tasks leading to full exam-type tasks in the later units and in the Progress tests.

What's in Advanced Masterclass?

The Student's Book

The course consists of 14 units, each of which is divided into four sections. The first three sections cover reading, listening and speaking, and writing; the final section always deals with structure. Vocabulary and style sections appear in appropriate parts of all four sections. Preparation for the English in Use paper appears at the most relevant point within the four sections. The Contents page in the Student's Book gives a brief guide to the unit structure and can be used as a quick reference for students or a syllabus planner for teachers.

The units are each based around a theme which is incorporated in the unit title. The sections within the units also have titles which indicate what aspect of the theme is explored. To stimulate the students, the order of the sections within the units varies. Unit 1, for example, which is an introduction to relevant skills and exam tasks, has the following format:

Unit 1   Loud and Clear

Listening and Speaking	The introduction focuses on a class discussion about high-tech communication aids and moves on to pre-listening activities. Then comes a listening activity which prepares students for an exam-type task. For the speaking activity, students practise talking about themselves and their interests and introducing their partner as in Part 1 of the speaking test. Turn-taking strategies are also provided.
Reading	Students are introduced to the idea of skimming a text quickly for gist through a text on speed reading. Another longer text on the dangers of *doublespeak* is followed by a vocabulary exercise on compound adjectives.
Writing	Students are encouraged to think carefully about what to include in a CAE writing task and in particular to consider who will be the target reader and what register is appropriate. This leads on to choosing suitable vocabulary for particular registers. Students are then

asked to write a postcard to a friend postponing an invitation. Finally there is an exercise asking students to spot punctuation errors.

Structure   This section acts as an introduction to the structure sections in the rest of the course. It focuses on how grammatical structures affect meaning and how incorrect use can lead to a breakdown in communication.

The structure section has been placed at the end of each unit so that it can be used out of sequence or perhaps not at all if the teacher feels the structures being covered are already understood by the students. However, as this is the section which contains most of the grammar clozes in the course, the teacher should give students this task as homework or class work, even if the rest of the section is omitted.

The Teacher's Book

The following features are included in the Teacher's Book:

- keys to all the exercises in the Student's Book
- a full transcript of all the recorded material
- detailed procedural notes indicating how the teachers might use the material in class
- optional activities which include speaking activities and writing tasks
- additional activities designed to give students freer practice in the structure sections
- background notes to the texts including explanations of potentially difficult or culture-specific vocabulary
- photocopiable Unit tests to check students' understanding of each unit and Progress tests to review the language and exam tasks of a group of units.

How long will the lessons take?

Suggestions are given in the procedural notes for how long the main exam tasks will take. On average, each unit represents 6–10 hours of class work and in total the course provides around 120–140 hours of classroom teaching. The exact amount of time will depend on the language level of the class and the balance between class work and homework.

How are the units structured?

Each unit is divided into four sections: Reading, Listening and Speaking, Writing, and Structure. There is an introductory phase to each section which may be a listening activity, a discussion based on a text or a visual stimulus. The aim is to highlight a particular aspect of the unit theme and give each section an initial focus. In addition, there are Vocabulary sections which exploit the texts and provide extension exercises, English in Use exercises which give specific exam practice, and Style sections which concentrate on register and tone.

A more detailed description of the unit sections is given below.

Reading

Texts have been selected from a wide variety of sources and wherever possible these texts have been set up in their original format to add to their authenticity. Some editing has occurred to reduce the length and density of some texts but vocabulary and structure has been left as in the original. In most cases newspaper extracts have been taken from 'quality' newspapers rather than the tabloids.

A particular feature of the Reading sections is the attention paid to helping the students cope with the longer length of texts (450–1,200 words) they will meet in the exam. The number of words in a text is always given and students are encouraged to practise their skimming and scanning skills. In the early units a stopwatch icon (⏱) indicates that the students should time themselves with a view to steadily increasing their reading speed. Most reading texts are illustrated to give context and to provide additional discussion points.

The Reading paper of CAE has three question formats in addition to the four-option multiple-choice. These are the single and double page multiple matching tasks and the gapped text, where a number of paragraphs have to be reinserted into the text. The Reading sections give the students support and practice in these tasks as well as preparation for the more traditional multiple choice. Particular emphasis is therefore given to the following reading skills in this section:

- skimming to form an overall impression
- scanning for specific information
- understanding the gist of a text
- understanding how the text is structured
- deducing meaning from context.

Writing

Each unit concentrates on either Part 1 or Part 2 writing tasks.

Part 1

This part of Paper 2 is compulsory and requires candidates to select and organize information from given stimulus material. In the Student's Book, writing tasks have been carefully graded to ensure that students are thoroughly trained in the processing skills needed for Part 1.

In Unit 5, for example, where the focus is on report writing, students are guided through activities where they are asked to summarize the main points in a sample report, analyse other documents which show the purpose and target reader of the report, and finally complete the concluding paragraph of the sample report.

In later units, complete Part 1 tasks are set. Task types include formal and informal letters, personal notes and reports. Practice is given in producing two pieces of writing based on the same input but using different registers.

Part 2

A similar approach is followed for Part 2 tasks. The writing tasks covered include an article, informal letter, guidebook entry, review, leaflet, character reference and report.

As the students practise each type of writing task, the approach is tailored to fit the differences in register and structure. In Unit 13, where the Part 2 task is to write a character reference, students analyse the sample character reference before reading the task which is to write a character reference for a friend who wants to be a tourist guide. Students are advised to consider the qualities and skills needed for the job and are reminded to include the strengths and weaknesses of the applicant.

Particular pitfalls in writing a character reference are highlighted such as including unnecessary details about the relationship between the writer and the applicant.

Writing sections follow the sequence outlined below.

Part 1
1 Understanding the task, ie reading through the input material and seeing what is required by the task.
2 Selecting ideas, ie deciding what specific information is needed from the input material but taking care to avoid 'lifting' phrases from the texts.
3 Focusing on the reader, ie deciding who the target reader or audience for the writing task is and what register is most appropriate.

4 Planning your answer, ie deciding on the outline for the writing task, how to structure it, thinking about paragraphs and linking devices.
5 Writing and checking the finished task.

Part 2
1 Understanding the task, ie reading the question carefully and deciding what kind of response is required.
2 Brainstorming ideas, ie thinking of relevant ideas to include.
3 Focusing on the reader, ie deciding on an appropriate register and taking care not to introduce irrelevant material.
4 Planning your answer, ie deciding what should be included in the task and how the content should be organized into paragraphs.
5 Writing and checking the finished task.

Sample answers in the units and the Writing Resource (see below) are provided for students as models of the different exam task types. Every answer has been written to exam length and contains relevant organizational and stylistic features that students can refer to.

Most of the training and preparation work should be done in class, but the completion of the writing tasks can usefully be set for homework.

Writing Resource

Students are given additional support for Paper 2 in the form of the Writing Resource at the back of the Student's Book on pages 184–192. This includes an example of a compulsory Part 1 task, and a range of Part 2 tasks. For each task type, useful key points are given followed by a sample question and a model answer. Notes alongside each model answer remind students of the important features which need to be included in a piece of writing of this type.

The symbol (✍) within a writing section indicates to students when it would be useful to refer to the Writing Resource. Teachers may wish to set the tasks as additional assignments for homework.

Listening and Speaking

Listening

Each unit has one or two listening passages in the listening section and there are additional listening activities in some other sections. The material, as in the examination, has been based on authentic situations and sources. Delivery is at normal speed and a range of accents is used.

Each listening section focuses on a different section of the listening paper and in the earlier units includes pre-listening activities to prepare students for the listening skills they will need in the exam. Students are given a variety of test formats which are used in the exam including multiple matching, form-filling, note-taking and multiple choice.

The listening skills developed in these sections include:

- understanding specific information.
- understanding gist.
- understanding attitude and opinion.
- recognising context, topic and theme.

Some transcripts are included in the Student's Book when they are used for specific activities. A complete set is included in the Teacher's Book. Exercises are repeated on the tape when students are asked to listen to recordings for a second time.

Speaking

This section includes Paper 5 preparation and training activities. There are also general speaking activities in the form of class and paired discussions in all sections of the units.

The speaking skills developed in the exam training sections include:

- social interaction
- transactional language
- negotiation
- hypothesis.

A variety of activities are used to practise these skills including ranking, comparing, describing, and contrasting.

As in the exam, the sections aim to create real situations and students are expected to complete tasks rather than assume roles. All four parts of the speaking test are given full coverage and in particular the skills of interacting with their partner and the examiner are discussed in detail.

The exam focus activities are designed to build up the students' confidence in handling a range of stimulus materials and to give them practice working in a pair. Particular attention has been paid to the skills of negotiation and turn-taking. In some cases, students may be examined in a group of three and practice in this format is given in Unit 13.

The stimulus material in the Student's Book is at the back of the book and students are directed to particular pages so that the procedures in the examination can be closely followed.

Structure

This section contains most of the grammatical work in the course (other than that which features in the English in Use sections elsewhere). The grammar cloze (Part 2, Paper 3) appears mostly in this section.

The grammar points which are covered in the Student's Book are not meant to be a comprehensive grammatical syllabus but are there to revise and consolidate what the student already knows and will need to know for the CAE. Although the CAE does not test grammatical structures overtly, it is important to raise the students' level of accuracy so that they perform well in the writing paper and the speaking part of the exam.

After a brief introductory activity, a reading passage reflecting the theme of the unit begins each section and students are given the opportunity to see examples of the target structures in context. Further practice is given in the exercises which follow, where students are encouraged to work out the grammatical rules for themselves. Exercise types include comparing and contrasting sentences, identifying functions, matching halves of sentences or completing gapped sentences.

Additional information about the structure sections is included in the Teacher's Book. **Language activation** tasks have been included at specific points. These have been designed to give students the opportunity to personalize the target language in freer activities.

Vocabulary

There is no doubt that to be successful at CAE students must increase their knowledge of vocabulary substantially and be able to produce a wide range of language in Papers 2 and 5.

Extensive vocabulary development occurs throughout *Advanced Masterclass*. Particular attention is paid to confusable words, prefixes and suffixes, collocation, prepositional phrases and phrasal verbs. Topic-related vocabulary is also featured as well as useful exercises on expressions.

Reading texts are often used as the starting point for focusing on vocabulary. In Unit 5, for example, students are asked to identify words with suffixes and this is followed by a more general exercise in which students are asked to add the appropriate suffix to a word which completes a sentence.

It is particularly important in the CAE examination to be able to deduce meaning from context because the authentic texts are bound to contain some words which students have not met before. Students are trained to tackle unfamiliar vocabulary and understand the gist of texts.

Cartoons are often included next to vocabulary exercises to help students and teachers with particular vocabulary points, and to amuse!

Students planning to take the CAE should read extensively and make a particular effort to read English language newspapers and magazines, which are commonly the source of examination texts.

Vocabulary Resource

The Vocabulary Resource on pages 193–195 provides relevant lists of words and phrases, which students can refer to from the writing and speaking sections in the units. The symbol (📖) refers students to a particular list or lists. The Vocabulary Resource is organized alphabetically under main functional headings, for example *Argument; Comparison and Contrast*. In this way, it ties in with the exam requirements and can be accessed easily by students working on their own.

Style

Some units include a section which focuses on style. These sections aim to encourage students to be aware of the features of different types of texts and the registers used in them.

They include a range of features from specific attributes of formal styles such as the use of the impersonal *'it'* in statements, to the stylistic features commonly found in general interest articles. Students are given practical help in ways to engage the reader's interest through, for example, quotations, expressing opinions, and making references to contemporary life.

Students are also given helpful suggestions on how they can improve the organization of their written work through the appropriate use of cohesive devices and expressions of time. In these sections, students are given examples or referred to examples which occur in the texts, before attempting exercises which give them guided practice.

Exam Factfile and Exam tips

The Exam Factfile on pages 5–8 of the Student's Book provides factual information about the CAE examination. Each of the five papers is covered in detail, with a description of the test focus and references to relevant examples in the units.

The Exam tips in the units themselves give practical advice on how to tackle specific exam tasks and questions.

Unit Tests

These photocopiable tests only appear in the Teacher's Book. They contain vocabulary multiple-choice questions, a structural test in the form of individual sentences or a cloze passage, and an error correction exercise. The tests revise vocabulary and grammatical points covered by the unit and can be done in class or as homework.

A correct answer scores one mark and each unit test carries a total of 30 marks apart from Unit Test 1 which has 25 marks.

Progress Tests

These photocopiable tests only appear in the Teacher's Book. There are three Progress tests designed to be taken after Units 1–5, 6–10, and 11–14. The tests review the language and exam task types from these groups of units. Each Progress test includes one Paper 1 task (multiple matching, multiple choice or a gapped text), Paper 2 Part 2 composition titles, and three Paper 3 tasks.

The Progress tests are marked as in the examination.

Reading
Multiple matching – 1 mark for each item
Multiple-choice – 2 marks for each item
Gapped text – 2 marks for each item

English in Use
Vocabulary cloze – 1 mark for each item
Grammar cloze – 1 mark for each item
Error correction – 1 mark for each item
Register transfer – 1 mark for each item
Phrase gap – 1 mark for each item

Writing
The answer is marked on a scale of 0–5 according to the general impression mark scheme on page 10.

Marking

Paper 2

The general impression mark scheme is used together with a task-specific mark scheme, which focuses on criteria specific to each particular task, including relevance, length, omissions, range of structures / vocabulary and layout; following the conventions of writing letters, reports, etc. is part of task achievement.

5

Totally positive effect on target reader. Minimal errors: resourceful, controlled and natural use of language, showing good range of vocabulary and structure. Completion of task: well-organized, good use of cohesive devices, appropriate register, no relevant omissions.

4

Sufficiently natural. Errors only when more complex language attempted. Some evidence of range of vocabulary and structure. Good attempt at task, only minor omissions. Attention paid to organisation and cohesion; register not always natural but positive effect on reader achieved.

3

Accuracy of language satisfactory; adequate range of vocabulary and structures. Reasonable task achievement. Or, an ambitious attempt at task with good range of vocabulary and structures, causing a number of non impeding errors. There may be minor omissions, but content clearly organized. Would have a positive effect on the target reader.

2

Errors sometimes obscure communication and / or language too elementary. Some attempt at task but notable omissions and / or lack of organization and cohesion would have negative effect on target reader.

1

Serious lack of control and / or frequent basic errors. Narrow range of language. Totally inadequate attempt at task. Very negative effect on target reader.

0

Not sufficient comprehensible language for assessment.

Paper 5

Marks are awarded throughout the test according to the following assessment criteria which together make up the candidate's linguistic profile:

Fluency
Naturalness of rhythm and speed, coherence of spoken interaction: pauses to marshal thoughts rather than language.

Accuracy
Correctness of grammatical structures and vocabulary. (Major errors would be those which obscure the message; slips of the tongue are not penalized).

Range
Evidence of a range of structures and vocabulary to maintain communication in all contexts.

Pronunciation
Control both of individual sounds and of prosodic features such as stress, rhythm, intonation and pitch. First language features may be heard but do not affect communication.

Task Achievement
Participation in the four phases of the test, covering the following areas:

- fullness of contributions;
- appropriacy of contributions to the task;
- independence in carrying out the tasks (ie the degree to which candidates can carry out the task without prompting or redirection by the Interlocutor or the other candidate);
- the organization of contributions;
- flexibility / resourcefulness in task management.

Note
The attempt to complete the tasks is assessed, not arriving at a 'right' answer within the time available.

Interactive Communication
Ability to interact both actively and responsively; demonstrable sensitivity to the norms of turn-taking.

Candidates are assessed on their own individual performance according to the established criteria and are not assessed in relation to each other.

Teaching notes

Unit 1– Unit 14

Loud and Clear

Many of the general exam requirements are presented in this first unit to orientate students towards the CAE. Classes may additionally wish to go through the Exam Factfile in the Student's Book at the beginning of the course.

Listening and Speaking
Face to Face

Introduction Student's Book p 9

1 Ask students whether they have ever seen a video phone and whether any of them uses a mobile phone. Students discuss each of the statements in pairs, for about five minutes. Then initiate a class discussion on the two topics, asking students to think about the role of the listener in each case.

▶ Suggested answers

Video phones will allow the listener to pick up on facial expression and gestures, which may improve communication. Mobile phones give more freedom to the users to communicate where and when they want to; however, there are also public listeners, who may not wish to hear these conversations.

2 Divide students into groups of three and discuss the question. The topic can be broadened to include other high-tech aids, such as the Internet and electronic mail and the implications of 'fingers doing the talking' as opposed to verbal communication.

▶ Suggested answers

The receiver has to read a screen rather than listen to someone; the message may be more carefully constructed in written form, allowing less chance of misunderstanding; the message may not be restricted to the communicators, as it can be stored in a computer's memory, rather than being transitory and short-lived like speech.

Listening

1 Before students go through the questionnaire, elicit the meaning of *day-dreaming*, *misinterpreting*, *butting in* and *fidgeting*.

Students then work through the questionnaire on their own and discuss their answers in pairs. Ask them to think briefly about the qualities a good listener has, eg patience and courtesy. This will lead into 2, where students check their understanding of relevant nouns and adjectives.

2 Elicit the missing words and extend the list with any adjectives or nouns which came up in the earlier discussion.

▶ Answers

alert
attentiveness / attention
restrained
respect

Students quickly complete the sentences in pairs to check their understanding.

▶ Answers

1	alert	4	attention
2	respect	5	attentive
3	restrained	6	restraint

Explain that one of the main challenges at CAE level is for students to extend their vocabulary range substantially. Ask them to turn to the Vocabulary Resource on page 194 and find list 6.1: Adjectives to describe character. They should scan the list for the adjectives they have just been using. Where opposites are given, elicit example sentences from students.

3 Explain that students are going to hear a monologue about speech and listen for the topics listed, so that they can complete the ordering task. Check that they understand *whisper*, *nod*, *chatter* before they listen.

▶ Answers

1 Tone 2 Volume 3 Speed 4 Pausing
5 Quantity

Tapescript

N = Narrator

N The human voice has a remarkable musical range. There are wide differences in the tonal qualities of individual voices, for a person's voice is unique, just as fingerprints are. Even during ordinary conversation, people constantly alter the pitch of their voice, using high and low notes.

In addition to varying the musical pitch of the voice, a person can amplify or soften their voice, producing anything from the loudest shout to the quietest whisper. Actors, teachers and others whose work requires them to address large audiences without a microphone, often use a loud form of speech which is more effective than shouting. This is known as 'diaphragm speech'.

Some people are naturally fast talkers, others slow, but nearly everybody tends to speak faster when excited, and the meaning is easily lost. A fast speaker who is listening to a slower one is often tempted to finish off the other person's sentences. Slow talkers find this irritating but seldom have the chance to say so! Many people find reading aloud a problem. At meetings, for example, they tend to read too quickly. The listeners may be too polite to point this out, and bad communication results.

Breaks in conversation are also a feature of some individual styles of speech. These tend to occur most frequently when someone is thinking aloud, particularly about his feelings. In face-to-face communication, a gap is usually acknowledged by the listener with a nod or an 'mm' noise, to show that he is still paying attention. But when such gaps occur over the telephone, the listener often wonders whether the speaker is still there. Some telephone speakers can achieve better communication by nodding less over the phone and using more 'mms' and 'uh-huhs'. These noises (known as 'pause fillers') serve a very useful purpose in conversation. Not only do they show the speaker that he or she is still being listened to and that his or her words therefore have some value; they also imply that the speaker himself is valued within the relationship. Timing is very important here. Most of us have probably at some time or other listened with only half an ear, simply saying 'yes' or 'no' in the right places, and then startled the other conversationalist by saying the wrong one at the wrong time.

How much we say is another important factor. Almost all of us feel that we talk either too much or too little when we are with other people. The origin of this self-judgement can often be traced back to the parental discipline imposed in childhood. Chattering is part of the natural development of speech in childhood, and good parents listen carefully and patiently. Children who are told too often to 'shut up' and not talk nonsense can very easily feel restricted in conversation in later life; they become reticent and are easily hurt.

Ask students whether they agree that children who are too frequently silenced become *reticent* in later life. Write the words *reticent*, *reserved* and *taciturn* on the board. These words are very close in meaning. Can students specify any differences?

reticent – reluctant to tell people things

reserved – unemotional, keeping feelings hidden

taciturn – quiet and uncommunicative, possibly appearing unfriendly

4 Explain that students are now going to hear four short snippets. Ask them to evaluate each speaker according to the four descriptions given, a–d. Before they listen, check that students understand the words and phrases used in the descriptions.

Point out that they will have a matching task in the CAE listening test, where in addition to answering questions about content, they will often have to listen out for attitude and manner.

After students have completed the matching task, ask them to speculate on what each speaker does for a living, giving reasons for their answers.

NB Students should focus on the male voice in the first extract, the interviewee in the second extract, and the female voice in the fourth extract.

▶ Answers

Speaker 1b (Customer relations person or Manager)

Speaker 2c (Politician)

Speaker 3a (Tour guide)

Speaker 4d (Housing officer / Social worker)

Tapescripts

Extract 1
(A = Customer; B = Customer relations person / Manager)
A … I would like someone to come back and check it, as soon as possible.
B It's not working properly?
A No …
B Have you read the booklet that came with it? It's worth doing that first.
A But if the installation was wrong …
B Er, I'm sure it was properly installed. Our personnel are highly trained you know. I suppose we could come back and have another look at it, but the fitters are booked up this week and next.
A It is rather urgent. I mean, it could be dangerous.
B No, no … you needn't worry on that score. Everything we supply meets approved safety standards. I would suggest that you read the instructions carefully and try again. There's probably a simple explanation. *(pause)* Can I leave it with you? …

Extract 2
A = BBC Interviewer; B = Politician
A … So, what *are* the prospects for employment now and in the immediate future?
B Well, we have done much to protect jobs in the last three years, with business tax cuts and other financial incentives. And I might add, our track record in the creation of new jobs has been consistently better than the previous government's performance. If you consid…
A But my question was …
B Just let me … let me … I hope you'll have the courtesy to let me finish. If you contrast the desperate situation as regards unemployment under the previous government … if you take that and compare it with what we have done, it all becomes crystal clear.
A With respect, you still haven't answered my qu…
B I can only underline again how much we have done as a party to keep as many people in work as possible. But you know, in these times of world recession, there are many tough decisions to be made and we haven't shied away from those decisions, however hard they are. And another thing, when people talk about …

Extract 3

A = Tour guide

A Well, I'll make a start. I hope you had a pleasant flight. My name is Mandy and I'll be with you for the next five days. During the journey to the hotel I'll be pointing out some of the sights of the city. The traffic's bad today so it may take us quite a while to get there. It's diabolical in fact, the traffic, the worst it's ever been. But I'll, as I said, be talking to you, er about the sights, er of the city. Right. We're going through the suburbs at the moment so there's not much to see but I'll try …

Extract 4

A = Counsellor / Housing officer; B = Client

A Okay David. Thank you for coming in. I understand you have a problem you need to discuss. Would you like to tell me in your own words what's wrong?

B It's the flat. It's miserable. It's not fit to be lived in.

A Right. David, I am going to need a bit more information. What is the actual problem?

B It's not fair, it's affecting the health of our baby. The doctor said so.

A I see … but you're going to have to be a little more specific. What exactly is affecting her health?

B It's the rooms, they're so damp. We asked to be re-housed last autumn, you know.

A I didn't know that. Believe me, I understand your problem. But equally, you must understand that we've got a real shortage of accommodation at present. Let's try to sort something out in the short term, okay? Now, could you just give me a few details for this form?

B We did all this last time. You must have this information in a file somewhere.

A I'm sorry, I have checked and there doesn't seem to be anything. Look this won't take long …

Speaking Student's Book p 10

Refer students to the Exam tip. This section focuses on Part 1 of the speaking test and additionally encourages students to be aware of the importance of turn-taking in the paired format.

1 Students think what they would say about these topics before asking their partner. They then work in pairs and take notes, which can be referred to when they introduce each other to the second pair. Try to monitor the whole class, so that you can assess the students' use of linkers in their introductions.

2 Point out to the whole class how important it is to link what you say, and ask students to use some of the given conversation linkers in their revised introductions.

3 Students decide on their roles. Give them a few minutes to look at the cartoon strip and prepare to talk about it.

Ask students to keep talking for the full minute; the other student in each pair should attempt to use

pause fillers where possible. Circulate in order to assess each pair.

4 Tell students that the strategies listed will be essential for Parts 3 and 4 of the test. They should look at the advice for speakers and listeners. Explain why these strategies are necessary for balanced conversations, eg introducing deliberate pauses allows the listener to react to what you have said. Ask students to add to the two lists, perhaps by recalling some of the content of the previous listening tasks.

5 Divide the class into groups of three and ask them to choose their roles. The 'observer' could time the conversation and assess each participant's turn-taking skills. When the groups of three are all ready, ask them to turn to page 197 and discuss the cartoon, answering the two questions.

Reading
Between the Lines ▼

Introduction Student's Book p 12

> **Optional lead-in**
>
> Ask students to form pairs. One student pretends to follow the movement of a lizard across the classroom wall, from left to right. The other student studies the person's face carefully and describes the eye movement, which will probably be a series of small jerks. This eye movement is used in reading.

1 Ask students to read the text and to time themselves. An average reading time on a text of this length would be three minutes (100 wpm). By speed reading in the way the text suggests, the wpm could be increased to 200 or even 300, that is, as little as one minute's reading time.

▶ **Answer**

An efficient reader would process written material as groups of words rather than as single words, widening the eye span.

2 Discuss the statements quickly as a class.

▶ **Answers**

1 disagree   2 agree   3 agree

3 Students do the activity in pairs and compare results. A slow reader looks at each word individually. An average reader reads pairs of words (eg *reading speed*), while a more efficient reader sees at least three to four words at a time (eg *your reading speed significantly*). Encourage students to think about this as they read the next text.

Reading

1 Ask students to discuss the phrases in pairs.

▶ **Answers**
1 failure
2 not leather
3 fake diamonds
4 poor people

They are examples of *doublespeak*, ie language that is unclear and has been made more complex, possibly to hide the truth and make it more palatable.

Ask students if similar terms exist in their own language.

2 Ask students to predict the sorts of people who might use *doublespeak* before they read the article. Remind them to time their reading. Check that students understand the following vocabulary:
blanket term – a general word that covers everything (like a blanket)
tolerable – acceptable

Note
The article is written by William Lutz, an American who teaches at Rutgers University and is Chair of the 'Committee on Public Doublespeak' for the National Council of Teachers of English in the USA. He is also editor of the Quarterly Review of Doublespeak.

▶ **Answer**
The following professions are mentioned: government officials, the bosses of a company, any specialists such as lawyers, accountants, scientists.

When students have finished reading, ask them to work out their reading speeds. Then ask students whether they think the article accurately describes how certain people use language today.

3 Students discuss the terms in groups of three, each student writing a brief definition for one, and then check their definitions with the article.

▶ **Answers**
the euphemism – a word or phrase meant to avoid causing offence or make a truth less hurtful

jargon – the special language used by members of a profession, trade, etc.

inflated language – elaborate terms used, for example, to describe ordinary jobs

Spend a little more time on the three paragraphs concerned, checking understanding of the vocabulary below:
harsh – hard, severe
distasteful – unpleasant, unpalatable
pretentious – appearing important but not so (used to show the writer's disapproval)
esoteric – understood by only a small number of people
laying off – firing, making redundant

4 Ask students to match the adjectives in pairs, taking turns to do each one.

▶ **Answers**

1 e	3 a	5 f	7 h
2 c	4 g	6 b	8 d

Optional activity

When students have completed the exercise, ask them to look up the compound adjectives in their dictionaries and find suitable collocating nouns, eg *labour-saving* devices, *far-reaching* consequences, etc.

Writing
Writing it Right ▼

Introduction   Student's Book p 14

Ask students to focus on the idea of the target reader, as they will need to write for a specified reader in CAE Paper 2. To be successful, their writing needs to have a positive effect on the reader, that is, it needs to convey the right message clearly and in a suitable register.

Students discuss in pairs letters they have sent or received where the tone may have been rude or tactless, describing the effect on the reader or on them in each case. If they are reluctant to do this, tell them about your own experience – or invent an extreme example to illustrate the point!

Writing

1 Refer students to the Exam tip on the different types of writing required for CAE and remind them that they can look at the Exam Factfile for further information. The Writing Resource on pages 184–192 gives examples of Paper 2 tasks.

Spend a few minutes considering the aspects given and explain the WRITE mnemonic, which covers the main requirements of any CAE writing task.

2 Students look at the extracts in pairs and for each one decide the source, target reader and reason why they might have been written.

▶ Answers

Source	Target reader	Reason
A Introduction to a book review on children's fiction	parents students other writers, especially of children's fiction	to stimulate interest
B Leaflet or guide book on historic buildings	tourists art / architecture lovers	to stimulate interest
C Letter of complaint to a tour company	manager of Customer Relations department / owner of company if small	to demand action
D Internal business report or memo accompanying a report	director / manager of a company – who is the writer's superior	to give information
E Note, postcard or letter	a close friend	to give information
F Student publication or notice	fellow students	to advise students how they can save money

3 Students answer the questions on their own, making notes as they look at each extract, before comparing their findings with another student.

▶ Answers

	register	tone	facts or opinions?	descriptive?	action?
A	neutral	impersonal	opinions	yes	no
B	neutral	impersonal	both	yes	no
C	formal	personal	facts	no	yes
D	formal	impersonal	facts	no	yes
E	informal	personal	opinions	yes	no
F	informal	personal	both	no	no

4 Students do this exercise in pairs or as homework.

▶ Answers

1 E All the words are appropriate and can be used informally.
2 C *deceived* could also be used in this formal context; the other two words are too informal.
3 D *assess* and *judge* could also be used in a formal report; the phrasal verb *size up* is inappropriate, as it is informal.
4 E *odd* and *bizarre* could be substituted; *abnormal* is too formal and inappropriate for the context.
5 F *boring* and *dreary* could be used; *monotonous* is unlikely to be used by students in this context and is fairly formal.
6 B *splendid* and *superb* fit in with the descriptive style; *great* would be inappropriate, as it would sound too informal.
7 D All the words would be typically used in a formal report.
8 A *emotional* and *nostalgic* could be used; *corny* is too informal.

5 Refer students back to the two phrasal verbs given in **4** (1: *bowled over* and 3: *size up*), which are only appropriate in informal contexts. Students then complete the sentences in pairs.

▶ Answers

1	increased	5	wait	9	visiting
2	turn in	6	polished off	10	told off
3	find out	7	specify	11	let you down
4	arrange	8	put off	12	avoid

6 Encourage students to use a few phrasal verbs in their writing, which could be set as homework. Refer them to the Vocabulary Resource on page 193.

▶ Suggested answer

Model postcard:

I'm really sorry, but I'm going to have to put off lunch on Thursday. My boss wants me to go to a conference and I just can't get out of it. What about fixing up another lunch for the following week? How about Tuesday? Hope to see you then.

Love

Editing   Student's Book p 17

1 Students skim the text and decide on the target reader.

▶ Answer

would-be writers of teenage fiction

2 Refer students to the Exam tip on one kind of proofreading task in Paper 3. Then look at the three

example answers given and explain that they must
write the word(s) and necessary punctuation in the
spaces provided. Suggest that students proofread
the text individually and then compare their
answers in pairs.

▶ Answers

1	character's / characters'	10	√
2	write in	11	Third,
3	inside the	12	narrative is
4	√	13	√
5	pitfalls	14	Wheatley
6	can't	15	'What
7	√	16	it's
8	clumsy).	17	writes. I
9	characters		

3 Ask students to discuss the questions in small
groups or as a class and encourage them to give
specific examples of books they have read, either
in English or in their own language.

Structure
What do you Mean? ▼

Student's Book p18

Try not to dwell on in-depth grammatical explanations
at this stage as the grammar points which appear in
this section will be dealt with during the course.

Ask students to discuss sections **A–K** in groups of three
or four. Alternatively this could be done as a test, or for
homework to be reviewed in the following lesson.

A
▶ Answers

1 *might* = this is a possibility
2 *could* = the department is capable of doing this
3 *would* = is willing to do this under certain conditions
4 *should* = this is what the department ought to do /
   there is an obligation on the part of the department
   to do this

B
▶ Answers

1 b   2 c   3 a

C
▶ Answers

1 'We'll try to work harder.'
2 'We're trying to work harder.'
3 'We've tried / We tried to work harder.'

D
▶ Answers

1 b   2 a

E
▶ Answers

1 b   2 a

F
▶ Answers

1 c   2 b   3 a

G
▶ Answers

1 Martin is always telling lies.
2 Martin is very rude.
3 Martin has (just) moved in next door / moved in next
   door some time ago.

H
▶ Answers

1 a You saw the whole performance.
  b You saw only part of what was actually
     happening.
2 b *to set* happened after Paul remembered. First he
     remembered, then he did it.
  a *setting* happened before Paul remembered. He did
     it and remembered it later.
3 a The speaker didn't manage to talk to his boss.
  b The speaker talked to his boss but it didn't do
     much good.

I
▶ Answers

1	b + d	4	f
2	b	5	a
3	e	6	c

J
▶ Answers

1 b   2 c   3 a

K
▶ Answers

1 b   2 c   3 a

2 Fighting Fit

The unit deals with different aspects of sport and health, with an emphasis on looking after your own body.

Listening and Speaking
Alternative Therapies

Optional lead-in

> **Optional lead-in**
>
> Ask students to explain the meaning of *alternative* in the title and elicit other possible collocations, eg *alternative technology*. They could then suggest words with an opposite meaning, eg *conventional*, *traditional*.

Introduction   Student's Book p 20

1 Ask students if they have personal experience of alternative therapies. They should read the four descriptions quickly and match them to the photographs.

▶ **Answers**

A 2   B 3   C 1   D 4

2

▶ **Suggested answers**

Alternative therapies do not use drugs or medicines; a doctor is not involved; the treatment takes place in a non-medical setting. In the case of iridology, the treatment is preventative rather than curative.

In most cases drugs or medicine are prescribed after a medical condition has been diagnosed.

3 Give students two to three minutes to list their own reasons, before beginning the paired discussion.

▶ **Suggested answers**

General reasons might include wanting to feel more healthy or wanting to try something different.

Specific reasons for one type of alternative treatment might be to find out your actual state of health and be in a position to improve it; for relaxation; as an alternative to drugs and medicines; because it has been in use in China for centuries and must therefore be effective.

Listening   Student's Book p 21

As this is the first focus on the listening paper, tell students that there are four sections to the paper and that all recordings apart from Part 2 are heard twice. In the Part 1 activity covered here, students have to complete sentences by filling in the gaps with suitable words or phrases. Refer students to the Exam tip and point out that there may need to be some reformulating of the information heard, in order to make it fit grammatically into the given sentence. The exercises in this section will increase students' awareness of this feature.

1 Ask students to read the sentences quickly before listening to the tape. Students do not need to write down the differences in wording. You may prefer to ask them to cover exercise **2** while they look at **1** as the next exercise shows some parts of the tapescript.

Tapescript

> **A = Acupuncturist**
>
> **A** As an acupuncturist I think it's important to understand the philosophy of Chinese medicine, which includes the belief in *chi* – the body's energy flow. If you have an even flow of *chi* you are in good health. What acupuncture offers is an ability to tap into the *chi*. It's then possible to readjust a person's flow of energy if it has become unbalanced.
>
> Before I treat anybody I take some time to study a patient's medical history. I also read the body's pulses. We can take the pulse at 12 different places and each place relates to a different organ.
>
> From this information I can decide if there are any blockages in the flow of energy or indeed any surges of energy. It's at this point that I decide where I'm going to insert the needles. These needles increase or reduce the flow of energy when they're inserted and twisted at the appropriate meridian points. Don't worry – it doesn't hurt and you won't bleed!
>
> Now, I believe that acupuncture can benefit most people suffering from disease or who are in pain. In China it's used as an anaesthetic. I myself used it on my wife when she was having our last child. It certainly seemed to reduce her need for pain-killers.
>
> I run two practices. There is great interest and I have a long waiting list. I think the reason for this is partly because conventional medicine has become increasingly impersonal. Ordinary doctors are over-worked and don't have enough time to spend on each patient. It's often easier and, and … quicker for them to hand out pills than to give proper personal attention.
>
> What acupuncture does is encourage the body to heal

itself which is, after all, er, a natural tendency. There is nothing drastic about the treatment, and I think people feel more in control of their bodies, than when they're subjected to all that high-tech equipment in a modern hospital.

2 Ask students to look at the tapescript extracts for 1–6 in pairs and compare them word for word with the answers.

▶ **Answers**

There are differences in wording for 3, 5 and 6.

	Tapescript	Answer
3	*the flow of energy having become unbalanced*	*more balanced*
5	*the body's pulses*	*(the patient's) pulse*
6	*blockages in the flow of energy or indeed any surges of energy*	*blockages or surges (of energy)*

In 1, 2 and 4 the sentences as a whole are worded differently, but the wording of the answers is the same.

Now ask students to look again at sentences 7–10.

▶ **Answers**

The relevant extracts are

7 *These needles increase or reduce ...*
8 *In China it is used as ...*
9 *...than to give proper personal attention.*
10 *...people feel more in control ...*

Play the tape right through again.

3 Students now do a similar Part 1 task on their own. Before they begin, elicit the meaning of *migraine* and ask students to predict what they may hear about the topic.

4 When students are ready, play the tape. Give them two or three minutes to write their answers and then play the tape a second time for them to check what they have written.

▶ **Answers**

1 live in cities
2 sleep enough / have enough sleep / get enough sleep
3 conventional
4 homeopathic remedies
5 the application of
6 six treatment sessions
7 understand
8 disappear

Tapescript

P = **Presenter**
P A great many people have headaches. To many, they're merely a nuisance that can easily be cured by taking a couple of aspirin. For some however, bad headaches become a nightmare. Headaches of such severity are

nearly always due to migraine. Cases of migraine are on the increase, largely due to stressful city living, where noise and pollution are contributing factors. In addition, it is recognized that particular foods and wine can bring on a migraine, as well as inadequate sleep.

Conventionally, treatment is with painkillers, which are usually ineffective, especially if the patient suffers from nausea. A more successful approach is to use alternative therapy. Mild bouts of migraine can be relieved by homeopathic remedies, usually in the form of tablets which dissolve under the tongue and do not irritate the stomach.

Acupuncture produces excellent results in cases of severe migraine. Four needles applied to points of the face give rapid relief, and freedom from attacks can be achieved after as few as six treatment sessions.

Hypnosis is another technique which can be used. Many people misunderstand hypnosis. An hypnotic state is simply one of deep relaxation. You are still in complete control and cannot be made to do anything against your will. Hypnosis is an effective cure for migraine as it induces a trance in the patient. Because of this intense relaxation the migraine attack eventually disappears.

English in Use Student's Book p 22

Tell students that there are six questions testing different aspects of grammar and vocabulary in the English in Use paper. Refer them to the Exam Factfile for further details. The focus here is on Part 1, the vocabulary cloze, which will be a familiar format to any students who have already taken PET and the revised FCE.

Note
Maureen Lipman is a well-known actress in Britain. She has appeared in films and on television, as well as in the theatre.

1 Ask students to read the extract, focusing in particular on the underlined words.

▶ **Answer**

The underlined words are all adjectives.

Elicit examples of other parts of speech, eg adverb, pronoun, etc.

2 Students take it in turns to say why the three other words in each set do not fit the gaps. Encourage them to look again at the surrounding context for content or language clues.

▶ **Answers**

1 A *innovative* cannot be used of a person.
   B *first* is inappropriate given that there are many other people who have a similar problem.
   C *foremost* does not fit the context given.

2 A The previous sentence implies that she works hard, so she cannot be *apathetic*.

C   *gruelling* cannot be used of a person.

D   *spent* is also inappropriate for a person.

3   B   *severe* does not collocate with *rest*.

C   *acceptable* does not convey the idea of 'amount'.

D   If *minimal* were used in the gap, it would mean no rest at all.

4   A   *compatible* is followed by the preposition *with* not *to* and the meaning would be altered.

B   *alike* does not fit, because of *to*.

D   *proportional* would not make sense.

3   Students read the rest of the article and give reasons for their choice of answers in pairs. This could also be set for homework; students check in pairs in the following lesson.

▶ Answers

5   B   The other words cannot be used after *on*.

6   C   *damages* and *ruins* cannot be used for people in this context. Someone can be a *wreck* but the plural form is not possible.

7   B   *complain of* or *about*; *experience* does not collocate with *from;* you can have a head<u>ache</u>, but you cannot 'ache' from *migraine*.

8   D   *foreseen* and *maintained* are not appropriate in the context and *regarded* does not collocate with *to*.

9   A   *experimented* needs *with*; *searched* needs *for*; *proved* may be a 'false friend' with *tried*.

10   D   *assists* needs in + *ing*; *improves* and *restores* do not fit grammatically.

Vocabulary   Student's Book p 23

Confusable words are focused on regularly during this course. Try to make students more aware of them so that they use the right vocabulary in their writing and speaking.

1

▶ Answers

A *stimulant* is something that makes your body speed up in some way, for example coffee.

A *stimulus* encourages action of some kind, for example pictures are often used at the start of a unit as a stimulus to discussion.

The article contained the word *stimulant*.

1 d   2 b   3 a   4 e   5 c

2

▶ Answers

A doctor *treats* or *cures* a patient, whereas *heal* is used to refer to a part of someone's body, eg *a bruised arm heals*. If a patient has been *cured*, they have got better or

recovered. However, to *treat* someone does not mean they will necessarily recover.

1	cured	5	heal
2	treated	6	healed
3	heal	7	treated
4	cured, treated	8	cured

Speaking   Student's Book p 24

This activity is early preparation for Parts 3 and 4 of Paper 5, where students discuss a given topic in pairs and summarize their views. It is not necessary for them to reach a consensus, provided they 'agree to disagree'.

1   Students look at the pictures and speculate about the type of holiday before reading the extract from the brochure to see if their predictions were correct.

Notes

facilitators – people who help or facilitate others to achieve something, can also be used of organizationas.

revitalising – making healthy or active again.

oneness – feeling at one with; see also 'in tune with' in the previous paragraph.

▶ Answer

The holiday is an alternative type where the focus is on health and general well-being.

2   Students discuss the reviews briefly in pairs. Ask them what they understand by the expression *ragbag of riches*. (A *ragbag* is a varied collection of things. Originally, the term referred to a bag that was used to store odd pieces of material.)

3   Check that students understand the meaning of the adjectives in the two lists. Ask them to suggest useful phrases for agreeing and disagreeing with opinions (see the list below) and refer them to the relevant section of the Vocabulary Resource on page 194. They then discuss the advantages and disadvantages of going on an Atsitsa holiday in pairs for five minutes. Summarize the class's views on the board.

agreeing with an opinion: disagreeing with an opinion:
You're right there.   *I don't think so.*
You've got a point there.   *I don't agree (with you).*
I think you're right.
So do I, etc.

agreeing partly:
Well, I agree up to a point.
All right, but …

agreeing strongly: disagreeing strongly:
You're absolutely right.   *I totally disagree.*
I couldn't agree more.   *I don't agree at all.*

4 Encourage students to relate some of their views to health and fitness in addition to any other reasons they give for wanting to go, or not, on a holiday like this.

Optional activity

The discussion in **3** and **4** could be extended into a short piece of written homework (120 words), where students argue the advantages / disadvantages of going on such a holiday.

Writing
Sport for All ▼

Introduction   Student's Book p 25

Optional lead-in

If individual members of the class have experience of long-distance running, or indeed of any other individual sport, other students can ask them for details of their experience and report back to the whole class.

---

1 Ask students to discuss the pictures in pairs.

▶ **Suggested answer**

The pictures illustrate opportunities in sport for the disabled and disadvantaged; the issues of sponsorship and high budget professional sport; the status of the amateur; team games versus solo activities, such as a marathon race.

2

▶ **Answer**

The people mentioned are inexperienced runners and do not appear to be taking the event too seriously, eg Andrew Arduini should not be drinking wine and the runners from Paris should not be eating a heavy meat-based meal the night before a marathon. Also, they do not appear to have followed a rigorous training programme.

3 Students discuss the questions in pairs.

▶ **Suggested answer**

Physical skills required: stamina, good muscular condition, low to average blood pressure.

Mental skills required: courage, self-belief, determination.

Writing   Student's Book p 26

This is the first look at a Part 1 question and students should focus on the material that they have to read for this part of the exam. Refer students to the Exam tip and draw their attention to the fact that although they have to extract information from a given text, they must reproduce it in their own words and in a style and register appropriate to the task.

Thorough reading of the question and an awareness of what exactly is required are clearly essential. This sensitization process is fundamental to successful performance in CAE Paper 2.

Understanding the task

1 Ask students to read the task rubric only and check that they have fully understood what is required. Elicit an explanation of the term *Fun Run* – a shorter distance run, often to raise money for charity, where the emphasis is more on enjoyment than a fast finishing time.

Then ask students to read the input material, which consists of some information on facilities and a note from the club committee. Clarify any unfamiliar vocabulary, for example *refurbished*.

Selecting ideas

2 Students do not have to cover all four gyms. They should decide on one or two places that seem to offer the right kind of facilities and make some notes on these, expanding the information given where appropriate, and deciding how the facilities would benefit the club members.

Focusing on the reader

3 Ask students to reread the exam rubric, ie task description and the club note. They can discuss the likely age range of the club members and write their answer with this in mind.

▶ **Answer**

The register should be informal. Clues in the note include the friendly opening from the committee, reference to *info*, and the emphasis on 'Fun'.

Planning your answer

4 Stress that students should spend time planning their writing in order to organize their ideas properly. Some suggestions of useful language are given below.

▶ **Suggested answers**
  • Introduction
  As you know, ...
  ... thought some tips on how to train / get ourselves in shape might be useful

• Training
Diet, relaxation
... thought it would be fun to train together ...
... we can spur each other on ...
... the park is ideal for jogging ...
... we could pamper ourselves ...

• Supper party
How about an alternative night out ...

• Ending
Together we stand – disunited we fall!

Writing

5 Students should keep to the word limit specified, which will allow them to include a reasonable introduction, to give some detailed information about the training sessions and a separate paragraph on the supper party. The ending can be brief, but should be suitably friendly and encouraging.

Remind students to check their work for grammar, spelling and punctuation. They should also look out for any inconsistencies in register, such as language that is too formal or rather unfriendly in tone.

Checking

6 This checklist will be extremely useful for students to refer back to every time they do a writing task. Students can look at the Writing Resource on page 169 for another example of a Part 1 task.

Reading
Bad Habits ▼

Introduction   Student's Book p 28

1 This introductory discussion could be done in pairs, with each student reporting the other's views to the class, as in Part 4 of the Speaking test.

2 Encourage students to elaborate on their reasons for considering the activities to be anti-social or not.

Reading

Refer students to the Exam tip. As the time allowed for Paper 1 is 1 hour (plus 15 minutes to transfer answers to the answer sheet), students will need to have efficient reading skills to complete all the tasks effectively.

1 This activity leads in to the main text and demonstrates when skimming a text is sufficient to extract the information required.

▶ Answer

The main theme is passive smoking at work and how to introduce limitations on smoking in the workplace. The leaflet is aimed at employers and employees.

2 Students should read the recommended procedure for matching headings to paragraphs carefully. Give students between 10 and 15 minutes to complete the matching task. Ask them to review their answers in pairs and discuss the words and phrases that helped them to decide.

NB As this is the first time that students are trying this type of multiple matching task, they have been given eight headings to match the same number of paragraphs. In the exam, there will be more headings than paragraphs.

▶ Answers

1 G
2 A (This is called 'passive smoking'.)
3 E (a complete ban)
4 H (well-recognized safety hazards / health hazards to individuals who smoke)
5 B (beyond doubt that smoking is a major cause of disease / health problems)
6 F (scientific studies / results of this research)
7 C (those who already have a respiratory disorder / more distress to this group)
8 D (improve employee morale / reduce arguments / reduce time lost / diminish cleaning bills / reduce fire risk)

3 Ask students to quickly note down their own opinions about whether or not smoking should be banned from public places. Students then discuss their reasons in pairs or groups of three.

Style   Student's Book p 30

This section looks at how prefacing structures relate to formal texts. They will be of use to students, particularly in Paper 2. Ask students to look for similar examples from newspapers and non-fiction books.

1

▶ Answers

1 It is a fact that
2 It is fully understood that
3 It seems to be the case that / It is a fact that

2 After students have first thought of possible adjectives, refer them to the relevant section of the Vocabulary Resource on page 193.

Answer

Other adjectives commonly used in this way include *likely, certain, possible, probable.*

3

▶ Suggested answers

It has recently been suggested that banning smoking in restaurants is threatening the businesses concerned.

It cannot be denied that passive smoking is a threat to health.

It is now agreed that smoking is the most common cause of lung cancer.

4 Ask students to produce sentences of their own using some of the reporting verbs they find in the Vocabulary Resource on page 195.

Structure
Healthy Eating ▼

Introduction   Student's Book p 31

Ask students to discuss the different adverts briefly in pairs or groups of three.

English in Use

A Ask students to read the extract and answer the question.

▶ Suggested answer

Diets have no long-term effects and we should try to accept the way we look.

B Tell students that for Part 2 Paper 3, the grammar cloze test, there are no multiple-choice options as there are in Part 1, the vocabulary cloze. Give students 15 minutes to do the cloze on their own and then compare their answers in pairs.

▶ Answers

1	to	6	to	11	to
2	more	7	as	12	whose
3	have	8	in	13	with
4	that	9	it	14	a
5	their	10	are	15	than

Optional activity

Students focus on the gapped items and make a list of the kinds of words that are gapped in this grammar cloze, eg comparative forms, prepositions, pronouns, auxiliaries. This will help them to identify more quickly the words needed to complete the spaces in other grammar clozes.

Modals and meaning   Student's Book p 32

A

▶ Answers

Modals are not tested as there are too many possible variations. Auxiliaries, however, often fit into a discernible grammatical construction and are more easily identifiable and less ambiguous, usually expressing differences of time and number, and forming passives, questions and negatives.

Students find the eight modals on their own.

(You) would (be better off)
(You) must (be supremely confident)
... (she) should (be on a diet)
... (we) would (be getting thinner)
... (dieters) needn't have (bothered)
... (they) should (have been more strong-minded)
... dieting may (be bad for you)
... (who really) must (lose weight)

Ask students to discuss the meaning of the modals in pairs.

▶ Answers

1	should (be)	5	would be better off
2	must (be)	6	would (be)
3	needn't have (bothered)	7	may
4	should have (been)	8	must

B

▶ Answers

1	would	5	May
2	needn't be	6	needn't
3	should	7	may, may
4	must	8	must

Number 5 has a different meaning from the options given in **A** as, here, *may* is used to ask for permission or politely offer to do something.

Language activation

Students' Snack Bar

Your language school is planning to open a (new) snack bar. In small groups, students use the modals they found in **A** and used in **B** to discuss what kind of food might / could / will / should / shouldn't be served. Put the following on the board:

microwave meals

sandwiches

salad

national dishes

Two groups then compare their ideas.

Modals and the perfect infinitive

A   Students discuss the questions in pairs. Encourage them to use the weak form of *have* when saying the possible combinations.

▶ **Answers**

need and *can* are not used in the positive.
can't /couldn't have done are opposites of *must have done*.
will / might / should have done can refer to the future when used in the future perfect with *by* , eg *by next Thursday*.

B

▶ **Answers**

1 c   2 a   3 e   4 b   5 a   6 d

C

▶ **Answers**

1   shouldn't / oughtn't to
2   wouldn't
3   needn't
4   might / may
5   couldn't / can't
6   needn't
7   shouldn't
8   can't / couldn't
9   may / might, may / might
10   would / 'd
11   shouldn't / needn't
12   should

Need   Student's Book p 33

Students discuss A–C in pairs or groups of three.

A

▶ **Answers**

In 1, *needn't* followed by the perfect infinitive without *to* means that she did go on a diet; in 2, the verb *need* with the auxiliary *didn't*, means that she did not.

B

▶ **Answer**

2 is correct.

C

▶ **Answer**

1 would be rarely heard.

Must, can't, mustn't, needn't

A   Students discuss the questions in pairs or groups of three.

▶ **Answers**

1   This is a logical assumption to make. / He is the manager. (deduction)
2   It is essential that you do this. (obligation)
Opposites:
1   He can't be the new manager. (He doesn't look the part.)
2a   You shouldn't / ought not to keep your feelings to yourself.
  b   You mustn't keep your feelings to yourself. (It's harmful.)
  c   You needn't keep your feelings to yourself. (Share them with us if you want to.)

The past of *must* in 2 is *had to*.

B

▶ **Answers**

1   must be waiting
2   can't be waiting
3   must find
4   can't have gone
5   needn't panic
6   needn't bother

Practice

Students can complete this task in class or for homework.

▶ **Suggested answers**

1   needn't / shouldn't have
2   should have checked the time
3   must look for it
4   can't / couldn't have (done) ... must be mad
5   must be joking / can't be serious
6   wouldn't / mightn't have made that mistake ✗
7   may / might phone later
8   had to / needed to
9   mustn't / shouldn't eat anything / be given anything to eat
10   must not / should not go in

Language activation

Modals in action

With a partner or in a small group, students comment or speculate on the following situations using modals from this section. Different students read out one situation each to the rest of the class or the teacher photocopies examples for each group.

1 There's a terrible noise coming from next door.

2 Your best friend's just been fired.

3 You've done the shopping but realize you are going out to dinner.

4 You've spilt cooking oil on your new trousers.

5 You've invited some friends to your house for dinner at 8 o'clock but it's after nine and there is no sign of them.

6 You are having a meal in an expensive restaurant and decide that the food you are eating tastes very strange indeed.

7 You thought your next-door neighbours were hard up but recently you've noticed they've bought a new car and are wearing expensive clothes and going out a lot.

8 You see a large furniture van outside your neighbour's house.

▶ Suggested answers

1 The neighbours must be knocking down a wall.
2 She must have argued with her boss once too often.
3 I needn't have bought all that fresh food.
4 I should have changed into my old clothes.
5 They might've forgotten.
6 It can't have been cooked properly.
7 They might've inherited a lot of money.
8 They must be moving.

Extra activities

There were several phrases with *as* in the article on page 31. Should your students require practice in this area, you may like to give them the following exercises.

A In the article you came across these phrases:
1 *as early as* (line 8)
2 *as many as* (lines 8 and 15)
3 *as they put* (line 16)
4 *as a personal failure* (line 18)
5 *known as* (line 24)
6 *as great a risk ... as* (line 24)
7 *seen as* (line 32)

When do you use *as ... as*?

Are there any variations of *as ... as*? If so, what are they and when do we use them?
What does *as* mean in 3?
What does *as* mean in 4?

B Read through these examples of *as* then decide which words and phrases (listed in a–h below) are the nearest in meaning to *as* in 1–9. More than one answer may be correct.
1 *As* I haven't much time left this afternoon, I'll have to deal with this tomorrow.
2 *Just as* I was about to leave, I remembered the tickets.
3 *... such as ...*
4 *As far as I'm aware ...*
5 *As* a doctor, I would recommend ...
6 *As for me ...*
7 He raised his hand, *as did* everyone else.

8 *As far as* I'm concerned, ...
9 *... as to whether ...*

a concerning the question of
b to the best of my knowledge
c when / while
d in the capacity of
e if you want my opinion
f in the same way that
g for example
h because

C Complete the following sentences with a suitable phrase containing *as*.

1 There's no answer to this problem _____ I'm concerned.
2 _____ Paul, he's a fitness fanatic.
3 We still have no confirmation _____ they have found a cure for the disease or not.
4 Speaking _____ , I would advise you to learn ten new words every day if you want to pass the exam.
5 Modern drugs _____ penicillin are no use against viruses.
6 They announced the flight _____ I sat down with a cup of coffee.
7 He began to protest loudly, _____ most people in the room.
8 _____ applicants seem to have the right kind of medical qualifications, I'm afraid we have no alternative but to re-advertise the post.

▶ Answers

A We use *as ... as* when we want to point out that things are equal in some way.
We often use *so ... as* after a negative form.
as in 3 means *because*.
as in 4 means *like*.

B
1 h   3 g   5 d   7 f   9 a
2 c   4 b   6 e   8 e

C
1 as far as
2 As for
3 as to whether
4 as a / your teacher
5 such as
6 just as
7 as did
8 As none of the

3 Getting to Know You

The unit looks at relationships, as well as personal feelings and emotions.

Reading
Silent Speech ▼

Introduction Student's Book p 34

1 Ask students to think of famous people or film characters whose physical appearance might be described by one of these words. Elicit similar adjectives that could be used in physical description.

▶ **Answers**

1 cowering 2 straight-backed 3 round-shouldered
4 slouched

2 Check that students understand the meaning of the adjectives before they begin speculating.

Optional activity

Ask students to think of adjectives they would use to describe a member of their family, a friend, a colleague and themselves, giving reasons for their choices.

Reading

1 Students say what they think *silent speech* means before reading the introductory text in the box to see if their ideas were right.

2 Students read the article quickly and answer the two questions.

▶ **Answers**

Body language is important because of how it influences communication.

Effective body language can give the user more confidence and the upper hand in communication.

3

▶ **Answers**

1 what happens when our body language doesn't match our words
2 making someone feel 'small' or insignificant
3 strategies or methods of dealing with a situation
4 technique used to gain an advantage
5 imitation of what someone else is doing
6 move away slowly, in a series of small movements
7 get the message
8 intrusion

4 Refer students to the Exam tip. Following a skim read, students will have to read the text in more detail to be able to answer the multiple-choice questions which follow. Emphasize the value of the 'elimination' process in answering multiple-choice questions, particularly when they are unsure of the right answer. Go through the stages carefully with the students.

5 Give students 10 minutes to work out the answers on their own and then compare their answers in pairs.

▶ **Answers**

2 C (*And walking tall increases and creates confidence.* line 39)
3 D (*Perhaps because their parents were undemonstrative ... movement* line 63)
4 B (*edge away slightly* line 81)
5 A (*The more expansive we are, the more powerful ...* line 94)
6 A (*When two people meeting make eye contact ... 'eyebrow flash'.* line 105)

6 Students discuss their views briefly in pairs.

Optional activity

Students could extend this topic by developing a questionnaire on attitudes to body language, self-confidence and social interaction. This could be used with students in other classes, or with friends and contacts outside class.
A broad topic will yield more questions. Questions should have a choice of three distinct options. Encourage students to try out the questionnaire, which will practise their oral skills in a paired situation. They can then report back to the rest of the class with their findings.

Style   Student's Book p 37

Refer students to the features listed and encourage them to use them when writing articles.

▶ **Answers**

The features are important as follows:

Short headings signpost meaning and also help to break up the text of the article, making it easier to read.

First sentences summarize the content of a paragraph and underline the main message.

Examples help to bring the text alive, engaging the reader and making the meaning of the statement obvious.

Quotes from specialists add authority to what is being said.

Writing
The Generation Gap ▼

Introduction   Student's Book p 38

1 Ask students to discuss the picture briefly.

2 Remind students to time themselves as they read the text.

▶ **Answers**

The *shinjinrui* are Japanese teenagers who are challenging authority and the values of the older generation.

They believe that working hard to earn a lot of money is less important than enjoying leisure time and being with family and friends.

If there are Japanese students in your class, you could ask them whether the article is accurate or not.

3 Students could discuss this in small groups of three.

4

▶ **Answers**

Words and expressions to do with:
the young: *youth, teenagers, young people.*
the old: *elders, post-war generation, the older generation, staid, older people.*

1 rebellious
2 staid
3 rebellious
4 staid

Writing

In Paper 2, students may be asked to write a descriptive account of a situation or event, possibly within a letter or a report format.

Sample account

1   a

▶ **Answers**

The letter has been written in order to complain to a new resident about his anti-social behaviour.

As a follow up, you could ask students these questions:

What are your neighbours like? Have you ever had any problems with them? What did you do?

b   Check that students find the inconsistencies, which are outlined below, and decide as a class how the style could be made more appropriate.

▶ **Answers**

Inconsistencies of style in the letter are given in italics below, with suggested formal equivalents.

We've really had just about enough of you.
We have reached the limits of our patience with you.

It's just not on!
This behaviour is unacceptable.

(*You don't have to be so noisy, do you?*)
Either reword: Is it necessary to make so much noise? or omit as the question is another repetition of the complaint.

What's more, your mates left the stairs in a terrible state – they even smashed two windows on their way out!
Furthermore, your friends left the stairs in a terrible condition and two windows were broken.

If you don't and you carry on being a nuisance, we'll kick you out!
If you do not and if you continue being a nuisance, you will be requested to leave.

c   Tell students that letters of complaint are often organized in the way outlined.

Understanding the task

2 Refer students to the Exam tip on writing a descriptive account and stress that a task such as this will ask for more than just a description. Students will lose marks if they do not cover every aspect of the task.

▶ **Answers**

The second paragraph in the task description tells students what they must do, ie write to the company about the problems they had and suggest that more care is taken when matching people in future exchanges.

The writer of the letter would probably hope to get a written apology from the company. Such action would also help future people in the scheme.

The letter should be written in a formal style.

Brainstorming ideas

3 Give students enough time to carry out this stage in pairs and then summarize the main ideas on the board. Ask students to elaborate on these ideas as a class. This will help to provide everyone with sufficient material for their own piece of writing.

Planning your answer

4 Stress that students must paragraph their piece of writing suitably and cover all the elements of the framework. Refer them to the relevant section of the Vocabulary Resource on page 193.

As a guideline, the 250 words could be divided as follows:

Beginning the letter (50 words)

The visitor – what happened (150 words)

Your recommendation to the company (50 words)

Writing

5 Remind students to write in a consistent style throughout and to check their work carefully. Encourage them to build up an idea of what 250 words looks like in their own handwriting. This will take away the need for counting every word.

Listening and Speaking
Big Boys don't Cry ▼

The title of the section is a saying which states that grown men should not show their emotions.

Introduction   Student's Book p 41

Discuss these two questions with the whole class.

Listening

Refer students to the Exam tip on Part 3, which also points up the link between intonation and attitude.

1 Students should spend no longer than half a minute reading through the statements.

▶**Answers**

1 Y
2 N
3 Y
4 Y
5 N
6 Y
7 N

Tapescript

M = Man; W = Woman

M … I mean, do you think there are any real differences left between women's and men's attitudes these days?

W Oh yes. Take illness, for example. It's a well-known fact that all men's illnesses are more serious than women's.

M What on earth do you mean?

W Well, whereas women may feel 'a bit off-colour', have 'just a cold' or 'a slight headache', for men it's much more black or white … they basically recognize only two states of being: men are either fit enough to run the marathon before breakfast and win, or they're too ill to stand up.

M Well, that's not actually true of me. I had a cold last week, but I didn't make a big thing of it, did I?

W True enough … Okay, let's leave you out of it for a moment. What about sports injuries? Just consider the typical performance on a football field. How often have you seen a player rolling around in agony, with the TV commentator predicting broken bones and the end of a brilliant career – and then the very next minute he's back on his feet, running round the pitch, without even a trace of a limp?

M But what's that got to do with your argument?

W It's the same … the same two states … either all or nothing. You men have a code. There's no such thing as a slightly sore leg that aches for a while. Either it's so bad that the man may never walk again, or it's absolutely fine. And it's the same with health in general, as I said – in the peak of condition or else at death's door.

M Well, you have a point about football players, although I think you're taking it a bit too seriously – half the time, they're just pretending after all.

W Which is *just* my point. But what is it that turns them, in less time than it takes to kick a ball, from children in need of someone to kiss them better into fearless men?

M Probably the threat of a goal at the other end of the pitch … I told you, it's an act.

W No, no, no, it's much deeper than that … I think it's all to do with how boys have been brought up. They grow up expecting to be brave … to be stoical. I mean, let's face it, today's New Man may be ready to express his emotions but, when it comes to admitting pain or discomfort, he's as stiff-upper-lipped as he ever was.

M And women?

W Women, when they are unwell and sense they're getting worse, take avoiding action – you know, using medicines, going to bed earlier, or …

M Neither of which is true for you …

W Let me finish … or taking time off work before they reach the stage of collapse. Men on the other hand feel that if they do any of these things it's a sign of weakness. So they end up fighting off an illness until they can hold out no longer. And then, when they collapse with a secondary infection requiring a doctor's prescription and days, if not weeks in bed, they see it as a confirmation – 'Even a man like *me* couldn't shake *this* off.'

M Oh, come on!

W And what's more, when they *are* ill, men revert to playing the role of a child, with their unfortunate partner cast in the role of mother. Not that I would ever mother you, you understand!

M No, no, no. Okay, so what do you think is behind these different attitudes of men and women?

W Well … for one thing, women, unlike men, do take for granted a certain amount of pain and discomfort in life.

M Hmm … I suppose that's true – childbirth, for example?

W Absolutely … and women also feel free to discuss these experiences. Illness is a tricky issue for a man, trapped in a world where he can tell no one but his partner how much he suffers and just where it hurts. It's no wonder you lot behave as you do – and who could blame you for making the most of it while it lasts?

M Well, I still don't think you can include me in your sweeping generalizations.

W Hmm … Of course, there could be another reason why men's attitudes differ from women's. A man knows that when he is too ill to go on, his partner will nurse him. A woman knows she'd better not get that ill!

M I'll remind you of this conversation when you're next bedridden …

2 Ask students to check their answers in pairs and then discuss the woman's views briefly.

Vocabulary   Student's Book p 42

1 Ask students to time themselves as they read the article. Check they understand the following vocabulary before or after they read it.

heralding (line 1) – announcing the approach / arrival of

tug at someone's heartstrings (line 3) – move someone emotionally

vulnerable (line 16) – easily hurt or affected, either physically or emotionally

heart-throb (line 91) – attractive person for whom one has strong feelings

▶ **Answers**

The writer believes that men should be able to cry in public and that those who can do so are happier as a result.

… men who can openly weep are the lucky ones, the emotionally healthy people. (line 19)

Men who can cry easily are the real winners in life, those who are at the same time confident and sensitive. (line 83)

2 Ask students to discuss the views briefly.

3 Students do the exercise first by themselves and then check with the class.

▶ **Answers**

a   tears build up / eyes water and the person starts crying

b   run / person starts crying

Literal

1, 3, 8

Metaphorical

2, 4, 5, 6, 7

NB In number 8, although the actual context is clearly metaphorical, the use of *flowing* to refer to the *rivers* of hair is in itself literal.

4 Ask students to interpret the situations in pairs.

▶ **Suggested answers**

1   applauding audience at the end of a concert / theatre performance / large children's party

2   political rally / demonstration

3   (civil) war, massacre, natural disaster

4   school playground, pupils' demonstration

5   an old, abandoned house

a stream of	tears
	people
	traffic
torrents of	questions
	insults
	laughter
floods of	tears
	ideas
	sunlight

Speaking   Student's Book p 44

1 Students should give reasons for their decisions. As a follow-up, ask what else they could say about the picture including their personal reactions to it.

▶ **Suggested answers**

First: b

Final: a

2 Before students begin the task, ask them to look once more at the picture on page 44 or put another picture on the board. Elicit the prepositional phrases for locating the different parts of the picture, eg *in the bottom right-hand corner*, and then refer students to the Vocabulary Resource on page 194 for a list of other useful prepositional phrases.

Check that students understand what the task involves. They should use the pictures as a springboard for discussion, expanding on the similarities and differences, rather than merely describing what is in each picture. Refer them to the relevant section of the Vocabulary Resource on page 193. Make sure that they spend no more than one minute each on talking about their picture.

Try and listen in on each pair. When they have completed the task, they could place the pictures side by side to see if the other student's picture was how they imagined.

English in Use   Student's Book p 45

This page focuses on the Paper 3 word formation task, introduced by UCLES in December 1999. Students who have already taken the *First Certificate in English* examination will be familiar with the basic format, although the CAE version contains two unrelated texts and 16 items. Refer students to the Exam tip about Paper 3, Part 4.

1 Elicit the four parts of speech represented (adjective, adverb, noun, verb) and then allow students about a minute to sort the words into the four groups.

▶ **Answers**

Adjectives: basic, fundamental, reluctant, sensitive, vulnerable

Adverbs: eventually, significantly

Nouns: amount, capacity, definition, preference, unwillingness

Verbs: abandon, amount, frustrate, tend

(*amount* is both a noun and a verb)

2 Ask students to decide in pairs.

▶ **Answers**

Negative prefixes: de-, dis-, in-, un-, under-

Related words: disallow, rediscover, underestimate/re-estimate, co-exist, displease, destabilize, entrap, disunite/reunite

Compromise.

3 Students should read the first text quickly to find the answer (making compromises in a relationship).

4

▶ **Answers**

The negative prefix in- has been added, and the new ending makes the word a noun.

5 Ask students to work through the text in pairs, taking turns to suggest suitable words for the gaps.

▶ **Answers**

1   undervalue
2   avoidance

3   tendency
4   exploratory
5   unpleasant
6   grievances
7   sympathetically
8   redefined

6 Ask students to complete this second text on their own.

▶ **Answers**

9   disagreeable
10 affection
11 withheld
12 unspoken
13 destabilizing
14 reluctance
15 insecurity
16 unhappiness

Structure
It's Only Love ▼

Introduction   Student's Book p 46

Ask students to discuss the picture briefly in pairs or groups of three.

English in Use

A   Students read the article and decide on an explanation of *a love map* together.

▶ **Suggested answer**

A *love map* is the way in which we gather information about people around us and arrive at a 'map' of our preferences.

B   Ask students to first work on their own and then check the answers as a class.

▶ **Answers**

1	as	9	to
2	an / this	10	you
3	in	11	for
4	if / when	12	have
5	are	13	more
6	of	14	for
7	to	15	is
8	its		

Conditionals in context   Student's Book p 47

Go over this section with the whole class.

▶ Answers

a 2   b 3   c 1
d 3   e 1   f 2

Zero conditional

A   Ask students to check the sentences in pairs.

▶ Answers

Five conditional sentences with similar structures which refer to something which occurs frequently, or is thought to be true:

1 ... *we are not hooked, unless enough of the right bells ring.* (line 11)
2 ... *you may constantly overreact if your adult partner is always criticising your behaviour.* (line 42)
3 ... *if your partner doesn't perform as well as you expect, you may criticise him in the way your parents criticised you.* (line 44)
4 ... *it does give you a challenge – a challenge to work things out, if you really want to grow as a person.* (line 48)
5 ... *even if our love map has clear directions, our destination is not fixed.* (line 53)

The present continuous tense is used in 2 to emphasize the fact that this happens often and is an annoying habit. Note the use of *always* to enforce the idea of annoyance.

B

▶ Answers

The difference in meaning is as follows:

unless means 'if not' and often appears after the main clause.

if means that given a particular set of circumstances, something may well follow as a result.

even if suggests that one set of circumstances would not make any difference to the outcome.

Language activation

Coping with feelings

Students write down a list of four different emotions and feelings. The teacher then puts a 'master' list on the board. Students then choose two of the items from the master list and in small groups ask each other what they do if they're feeling, eg nervous / happy, etc.
eg
What do you do if you're feeling / you feel ...?
Well, if I'm feeling / feel ..., I ...

First conditional

Ask students to work in pairs.

A

▶ Answers

1 ... *even if we don't find a perfect match, our brain circuitry will hunt for the next best thing.* (line 9)
2 ... *if one partner begins to change, the other will automatically respond.* (line 52)

The first example suggests that irrespective of whether something happens or not, the outcome will be the same.

B   **A variation on the first conditional**

▶ Answers

If I've invited someone into my life ... I am giving myself the challenge either ... (line 49)

The present continuous emphazies that this is an ongoing state of affairs.

Language activation

Awkward situations

Ask students to think of one situation they find awkward. Write the situations on the board and then invite students at random to say what they do if this situation has happened to them,
eg *If I've – made a mistake, I try to put it right.*
    – been invited out to dinner by someone I don't like, ...

Second conditional

Ask students to answer the questions in pairs.

▶ Answers

a 2   b 1

Language activation

If I were ...

Write the following situations on the board or dictate them to the students.
– start work for the first time
– leave home to live alone
– take an examination
– hitch-hike round the world
– learn to drive a car
Tell students that different friends of theirs are about to do these things. In small groups, students say what they would do if they were in the same position as their friends.
eg *If I were him / her, I'd ...*

Practice

The two exercises can be set for homework.

A Cause and effect in conditional sentences

▶ Suggested answers

If you're planning to stay here for a while, you might prefer the larger room.
If we had time to study more, we might pass the exam.
If we really loved each other, we would know.
Unless you can agree, you will have to go.
If you've had a row, kiss and make up.
Even if he were to apologize, I wouldn't be able to forgive him.
Even if they begged me, I couldn't do it now.

The conditional sentences beginning with *even if* suggest that it wouldn't make any difference if these things happened.

B Tenses in conditional sentences

Tell students that the word order may need changing.

▶ Answers

1 were, would / 'd take, travel
2 Don't ask, want
3 see, will / 'll tell
4 are thinking, ought to / will have to / must / should find
5 were, would you answer
6 had, would not / wouldn't ask
7 Don't accept, are, have made
8 had, could not / couldn't afford

What if …?

Ask students to decide in groups what course of action they would take if …

- their family didn't approve of their new friend.
- they'd lost their house keys.
- they were offered a job abroad.
- they ran out of money late at night.
- their car broke down on a motorway.

Students then compare their decisions with the other groups.

▶ Suggested answers

If my family doesn't approve of your new friend, I'll meet him / her on the quiet.
If I've lost my house keys, I'll call a locksmith.
If I were offered a job abroad, I'd take it if the conditions were good.
If I ran out of money late at night, I'd go to a cash machine.
If my car broke down on a motorway, I'd call for help on my mobile phone.

Extra activity

There were several prepositions in the article. Should your students require practice in this area, you may like to give them the following exercise.

Prepositions

In each of the following sentences, a necessary preposition has been omitted. Decide which of the following prepositions should be inserted and where.

around   into   with   to   in   for

1 There are certain signs of the zodiac which are more compatible than others, according experts.
2 This leaflet is the perfect guide the solar system.
3 It is not always advisable to marry someone you have fallen madly in love.
4 This is a period reflection on our future hopes and plans.
5 I invited them the kitchen for a cup of coffee.
6 Although we realize that it is virtually unobtainable, we continue our hunt happiness.
7 I am sick and tired of being told off not handing in work on time.
8 Which course have you decided to opt?
9 There are many pitfalls along the way our search for the perfect partner.
10 I feel that some way I have offended you.
11 Suddenly everything clicked place and I remembered where I had met him.
12 I put my arms her and gave her a hug.

▶ Answers

1 (according) to
2 (guide) to
3 (love) with
4 (period) for
5 (them) into
6 (hunt) for
7 (off) for
8 (opt) for
9 (way) in
10 (that) in
11 (clicked) into
12 (arms) around

4 Can You Believe It?

Listening and Speaking
Strange but True

Introduction   Student's Book p 48

1 Discuss the questions as a class.

▶ **Answer**

The picture shows the Marfa Lights in Texas, USA, where bright patches of light appear in the sky for no apparent reason.

2

▶ **Answer**

The account describes 'ball lightning'.

3 Check that students know the meanings of all the words, which are used later in the listening exercises, before asking them to discuss how they would feel after such an experience.

English in Use

Remind students that there are two basic types of proofreading task in Paper 3 Part 3: one deals with spelling and punctuation (as seen in Unit 1) and the other focuses on words which are grammatically incorrect or do not fit in with the sense of the text. This unit looks at the second type.

1 Ask students to read the first part of the task before they begin proofreading. Students explain in pairs why the words are unnecessary.

▶ **Answers**

0   The definite article is not needed in combination with a profession or field of study.
1   Both prepositions would not be used here together and *out* is the unnecessary word, because on its own it would not make sense (*of* would also be needed).
2   Although it is possible to say *lots of*, the word *of* is unnecessary with *Several*.
3   The word *while* does not fit grammatically. Note that students have to read the following line to decide this.

2 Advise students to read the whole text quickly and then return to it for a more careful line-by-line read.

▶ **Answers**

5   the
6   √
7   only
8   out
9   then
10   √
11   must
12   √
13   that
14   √
15   too

Listening   Student's Book p 50

Refer students to the Exam tip on Part 4 of Paper 4. Tell them that in the exam itself no pictures accompany the tasks and that they are used here for classroom use only. Let students know that they will hear a variety of speakers and accents.

1 Give students enough time to decide what the pictures show. Encourage them to tell the class about any personal experience or knowledge of these phenomena that they have.

▶ **Answers**

The pictures show:
a   a UFO
b   the Northern Lights
c   a shooting star
d   a solar eclipse
e   an earthquake
f   an avalanche
g   ball lightning
h   corn circles

2 Students should listen out for content clues in the first listening.

▶ **Answers**

Speaker 1 g *(a bubble of light, It was just larger than a basketball)*
Speaker 2 e *(furniture started moving)*
Speaker 3 a *(peculiar aircraft)*
Speaker 4 b *(cloud of many colours – pinks and greens and blues)*
Speaker 5 d *(it did shine through briefly – and a bit of it was covered.)*

3 Students now listen again and answer the five multiple-choice questions. Stop the tape after each speaker and check students have understood correctly.

▶ Answers

1 B   2 C   3 A   4 C   5 B

Tapescript

Speaker 1
I was on a canoe trip with a group of High School buddies, when we spotted a deserted cabin that could be used as a campsite. My friend and I ended up in the back room of the cabin. The rain was now a downpour, but the cabin was stuffy, so I went and opened the window a crack. Then we saw what looked like a flashlight moving around outside the opened window. To our complete amazement, the 'flashlight' began to squeeze through the open, one-inch crack above the window sill. As we watched, a 'bubble' of light slowly floated into the room. It was a little larger than a basketball.

Speaker 2
It was a very strange experience. I woke up and it seemed very quiet outside. Suddenly the furniture started moving – the bed was swaying from side to side. Pots on the table were rattling and papers sliding about. I felt utterly confused. I couldn't sort out in my head what was happening around me. After a couple of minutes it stopped. It was reported later, on the lunch-time news. There was a lot of structural damage in towns to the north of here. It has really affected me, it was so unexpected. I felt so, so vulnerable.

Speaker 3
This very bright flash was coming from a group of objects far up to the north of Mount Rainier. I saw a chain of peculiar aircraft approaching very rapidly. They seemed to be flying in formation. Looking at them against the sky, and against the snow of Mount Rainier as they approached, I just couldn't make out any tails on them, and I had never seen an aircraft without a tail! They were pretty large, and there were nine of them.

Speaker 4
Perfection! An incredibly moving event! It must have been about two o'clock in the morning, and we'd all just about given up hope. I looked out towards the sea, and at that moment there appeared a sort of swirling cloud of many colours – pinks and greens and blues. The whole thing only lasted for a minute or so. We all stood there, open-mouthed, drinking in the sheer beauty of it all. It was just magical. I still feel shivers up and down my spine when I talk about it.

Speaker 5
I was dragged along by a mate. 'Best thing you'll see in your lifetime,' he said. We got to the park and there were lots of keen people there already, with their cameras all set up, pointed at the sky. But you couldn't see much, there was that much cloud. Finally, it did shine through – briefly – and a bit of it was covered. So what, I thought, it was nothing special. Then the sky clouded over again and that was that. We went back home.

Vocabulary   Student's Book p 51

Tell students that the particles *up* and *out* occur very frequently in phrasal verb combinations. Suggest that they keep two lists of these phrasal verbs (more will be looked at in Unit 7) and write their own sentences to show the meaning.

Before they start, ask students if they know what any of the phrasal verbs with *up* and *out* mean. Ask them to look at the gapped sentences and see if they can guess the meaning of the phrasal verb which will complete each gap, eg in **1**, a phrasal verb will be needed which means 'invented'.

▶ Answers

1   had made up / was making up
2   taken out
3   break out
4   've run out / am running out
5   ran up / had run up
6   make out

Speaking

1 Divide the class into groups of three. This task involves students in turn-taking and trains them in tactful interruption, which will be useful in Part 3 of the speaking test.

2 Refer students to the relevant sections of the Vocabulary Resource on pages 193 and 195.

▶ Answers

Excuse me, but that isn't quite right.
Could I just say something about that?
I don't think I agree with you there …

Reading
Lost and Alone ▼

Introduction   Student's Book p 52

1 In pairs, students should focus on the idea of isolation and discuss the effects of being alone for long periods of time.

► Suggested answers

becoming introverted, experiencing irrational fear, appreciating those around you more.

2 Students group the words and then explain their meanings. Some of these words appear in the reading text which follows.

► Answers

Relating to loneliness and isolation:
solitary
abandoned
remote
exile
deserted
reclusive

Other words:
conceited – excessively proud of oneself
weary – extremely tired
eccentric – odd or capricious in behaviour
intimate – closely acquainted
celebrity – famous person
gregarious – fond of company

Reading

Refer students to the Exam tip. The gapped text question requires scanning skills and an awareness of text cohesion. The task in this unit focuses on both elements and is an introduction to gapped texts (an exam task will be done in Unit 7).

1 Ask students if they have seen the film by Werner Herzog, *The Enigma of Kaspar Hauser*, or read anything about him.

2 Students should concentrate in particular on the reference markers that are highlighted.

► Answer

Paragraph E follows on.

Ask students to pick out the words and phrases to do with vocabulary in this paragraph:

a phrase ...
the word 'horse' ...
referring to both as 'boys'.
His knowledge of words increased ...

3 Ask students to complete the task in 10 minutes.

► Answers

The reasons for this order are given in brackets.
B (*his own story. / For as long as he could remember ...*)
F (B finishes the story *so far* and F continues.)
D (This is a logical progression after the attack.)
A (*... the object of endless interest.* + *It seems that all this attention ...*)
C

4 Students discuss the phrases in pairs.

► Answers

1 a luxurious and comfortable lifestyle
2 believing he had carried out his commitment to Kaspar Hauser
3 a doctor who had been asked to come urgently
4 something that challenged the accuracy of the story
5 public life
6 people had grown tired of the phenomenon, as it was no longer new
7 only seventeen months

5 Ask students to discuss these questions first in pairs and then as a class. As this is an unsolved mystery, there are no definite answers.

Style   Student's Book p 54

1 Tell students that these time references will be useful when writing accounts where narrative skills are called upon.

► Answers

A *Back in Nuremberg ...*
B *When he woke up ...*
C *Then, only a few ...*
D *For the next two years ...*
   Then a solution ...
E *... from day to day*
   ... gradually ...
F *Suddenly ...*
   Then ...
   Later ...

2 Draw students' attention to three of the ways in which the writer involves the reader.

Writing
Predicting the Future

Introduction   Student's Book p 55

Ask students whether they know anything about Nostradamus and his predictions. Then ask if they believe the claim that the events are mentioned in his writings and elicit their views on the two prophesies for the future.

► Answers

1989   The Fall of the Berlin Wall
1990   Nelson Mandela is freed
1992   Florida Hurricane
1995   New hole in the ozone layer

Writing

Refer students to the Exam tip on writing a competition entry.

Sample entries

1 a Discuss the two pieces of writing as a class.

▶ **Answer**

Entry B is the winning entry. It is appropriately organized, engages the reader, is original and fully addresses the task.

b Spend time on this analysis of the two pieces of writing, as the aspects listed are important to successful writing of competition entries.

▶ **Answer**

Requirements of the competition

A does not expand on how the writer would like to spend time with the person.

Title

B only.

Organization

A is rather rambling and badly paragraphed.

Opening sentence

B's grabs the reader's attention while A's is dull and merely factual.

Sentence length

A's sentences are generally much shorter than B's, eg compare the opening sentences.

Questions

A has none; B uses them rhetorically to raise a point of view or new topic. *What, for example, was the secret of his military success?*

Repetition

A has a lot of this.

Relevance

B keeps to the point. In A, there is a lot of irrelevant material relating to the writer and his opinions.

Personal angle

Whereas A includes personal information in an irrelevant way, in B the comparison with the writer's own age and life is well-written and contributes to an original ending.

Conclusion

B's final sentence rounds the piece off strongly while A's finishes with an irrelevant comment about the magazine.

c Students read through some of the features of Entry B. A fuller list of adverbs can be found in the Vocabulary Resource on page 195.

Understanding the task

2 Make sure that students understand in what time period they are writing.

▶ **Answer**

The task contrasts the 22nd century with now, so covers a span of approximately 100 years.

Brainstorming ideas

3 Encourage students to think of other aspects of lifestyle once they have discussed the picture. Refer them to the relevant section of the Vocabulary Resource on page 191.

Focusing on the reader

4 Ask students to work on titles and opening sentences in pairs. They should remember the impact of Entry B's opening sentence and try to engage the reader's attention in a similar way. Then ask students to draft one or two rhetorical questions which are relevant to the task. Students could look at the Vocabulary Resource for other descriptive language. Finally, ask students to discuss in pairs which tenses could be used in this task and then refer them to the structure section in this unit. Remind them that they are to write from the future.

Planning your answer

5 This could either be done in pairs or as part of the homework assignment. Advise students to spend about 10 minutes on this planning stage.

Writing

6 Students could check each other's work and be asked to judge the effectiveness of the piece of writing they have read. Additionally, the class could adjudicate as if this were a real competition, giving reasons for their choice of winning entry.

Structure
Noisy Spirits ▼

Introduction Student's Book p 59

Ask students to discuss the picture and questions briefly in pairs or groups of three.

English in Use

A Students should mention the arguments for and against which appear in the text and can then give their own opinions.

► Answers

Arguments for: Julio's experiences could not be explained away.

Arguments against: there is usually a reason for seemingly inexplicable events, and they may also be the invention of lonely people who want someone to talk to.

B Ask students to complete the task in 10 minutes on their own, and then compare their answers with their partner.

► Answers

1 when / while / if
2 worth
3 from
4 someone / somebody / people / others
5 example / instance
6 that
7 at
8 without
9 as
10 to
11 nothing
12 causing
13 on
14 her / the
15 with

Tenses in accounts and narratives

Student's Book p 60

A Elicit the names of the tenses from the class.

► Answers

1
a past continuous
b the future in the past
c simple past
d past perfect continuous
e past perfect simple

2 a d e
3 simple past
4 the future in the past
5 past perfect simple
6 past continuous and past perfect continuous

B Ask students to complete the sentences on their own and then compare their answers in groups of three.

► Answers

1 was falling, spotted
2 had been working, noticed, moved
3 decided, went, had
4 was working, was doing
5 placed, made, was, went

6 was travelling, occurred
7 said, had never noticed, broke
8 were playing, was having, heard
9 had been running, started
10 was, sounded, changed

Language activation

Chain story

One student begins a spoken story using either one of the sentences 1, 6, 7, 8, 9 from **B** or a sentence of their own. The next student continues the story, and so on round the class. Students can write down each additional sentence so that they have a record of the complete story. They then compare their story with a partner's. Any mistakes can be corrected at this stage.

Past perfect, simple past

Ask students to look at the questions in pairs. Check their answers after each section.

A

► Answers

Barry knew it was wrong to steal. = so he decided not to, or: but he decided he was going to do it anyway!
Barry knew it had been wrong to steal. = he had already done it even though he knew he shouldn't have!

Sally never saw the film. = she didn't see the film at all.
Sally had never seen the film before. = she was seeing it now for the first time.

B

► Answers

1 before the glass broke:
   – it had been 12 inches from the edge of a shelf and it had risen at least two inches to clear the objects in front of it.
2 before the investigator began to look into the strange case of the lamp:
   – a thermal switch had accidentally been incorporated into the circuit and the woman had learned to time requests to coincide with the lamp switching on and off.

C

► Answers

1 past perfect (had finished), simple past (was)
2 simple past or past perfect for both verbs (was / had been), (had proved / proved)
3 simple past (pointed), past perfect (had written), simple past (was)

Practice

Students discuss their answers in pairs or groups of three.

▶ Answers

... one occasion in particular when I (*experienced*) this disturbing phenomenon.

A few years ago I (*was teaching*) a student Physics in an upstairs lecture room where I (*had never taught*) before. I (*had reached*) the part of the lesson where we (*were discussing*) radioactivity when I (*was*) swamped by a feeling of *déjà vu*. I (*knew*) I (*was*) about to refer to a book in my office. I also (*knew*) that on a previous occasion I (*had gone*) to collect it from the office. I (*turned*) to my student and (*asked*) him if we (*had done*) the work already. He (*looked*) puzzled and (*replied*) that we (*had not done*) anything like it before. However, my awareness of the experience (*did not make*) the *déjà-vu* feeling go away, even when I (*tried*) not to repeat the pre-set pattern.

Language activation

Personal experience

Students think of, or invent, an occasion when they had a feeling of *déjà vu* and write a short paragraph about it using as many of the tenses in the Practice exercise as possible. Students can then read out their paragraph to a partner.

Used for, used to, be / get used to, would

Student's Book p 61

A Answer the questions as a class.

▶ Answers

   a   3, 4
   b   1
   c   2

used to fly expresses a past habit. To express the same meaning about the present, we use the simple present tense, *fly*. The present equivalent of *objects would fly* is *objects will fly*.

B

▶ Answers

You could use *would* in 2.

Would can be used instead of *used to* to describe repeated actions in the past but not to describe past states and situations.

C

▶ Answers

   1   He was accustomed to it – it presented no problems for him.
   2   This suggests that he might have found it difficult at

first but eventually he learned how to do it successfully.

   a   in the interrogative:
       Was Julio used to handling ...?
       Did Julio get used to handling ...?
   b   in the negative:
       Julio was not / wasn't used to handling ...
       Julio didn't get used to handling ... would be used when further information is supplied, eg until he had been there for a few months.
       Julio never got used to handling ... (is more common and less awkward)
   c   in the present:
       Julio is used to handling ...
       Julio is getting used to handling ...

Practice

Students complete this on their own in class or for homework.

A

▶ Answers

   1   got used to
   2   used to
   3   get used to
   4   used for
   5   wasn't used to / couldn't get used to
   6   Did ... (your brother) ... use to ...
   7   Did ... (your brother eventually) ... get used to ...
   8   used to / would
   9   used to
   10   getting used to
   11   used to / would
   12   was used for

You could substitute *would* for *used to* in 8 and 11, where it describes a past action, but not in 2, 6 or 9, where it describes past states or situations.

Language activation

Adapting to circumstances

Students think about when they first started a new school or a new job and make a list of two things they:
a used to do.
b got used to doing.
c couldn't get used to doing.
d used in order to help them do their work successfully.
When they have completed their lists, students interview each other in pairs.

B Students choose three of the suggested prompts to write a paragraph either in class or for homework. Alternatively, students can brainstorm their ideas in small groups, make some notes, and finish writing their paragraph for homework.

5 All Walks of Life

Listening and Speaking
Lifestyles

Introduction   Student's Book p 62

1 Students discuss the title and what might be in the article briefly in pairs.

2 Before reading, discuss the photo of the child traveller with the whole class. Students read the article quickly to check their predictions.

Notes
The article is written by a member of a group known as 'New Age Travellers', who were first reported widely in the British media in the mid-1980s. Possibly as a result of finding it more difficult to get a job, together with a growing disillusionment with society, some people have decided that a life 'on the open road' is preferable. Many people find this attitude unacceptable and object to the travellers camping on land which does not belong to them.

They may not all know what happened in 1066 (line 24) a reference to the invasion of Britain by William the Conqueror (of Normandy). This historical fact is commonly taught at school.

▶ **Answer**

  The writer expresses a positive view of the travellers' way of life and gives the following reasons: Children do not need to acquire skills or learn facts at a particular age; the experiences children get if they live as travellers are more practical and enriching; traveller's children are more mature and aware of the needs of others; their experiences prepare them better for a less secure lifestyle.

3 Students reread the text carefully and underline the selected phrases. Encourage them to understand the meaning of the phrases by looking at the surrounding text.

▶ **Suggested answers**

  1 not having the skills or ability to educate
  2 become travellers
  3 they were dissatisfied with society
  4 get a job in preference to other applicants
  5 The children's experiences prepare them better for life.

  6 get on easily with
  7 having the same needs and rights as others
  8 forcing oneself to behave like the majority
  9 struggle against others to succeed

4
▶ **Answers**

  taken to the road; equipped better than most; mix freely; common shared humanity

Optional activity

Ask students to consider why society tends to reject those who do not conform to accepted behaviour. Students make a list of other groups / people who might fall into this category, eg unusual religious sects, political groups, etc. Students then discuss why these groups are rejected.

Listening   Student's Book p 63

Remind students that they will only hear Part 2 once and that it is important to read and listen to the initial instructions as these will tell them what the tape will contain. They should keep the length of their answers to a maximum of three words.

1 Students predict the missing information in pairs.

2 Students listen to the broadcast and complete the gaps. They then compare their answers in pairs. Refer them to the Exam tip on writing notes.

▶ **Answers**

  1 (traditional) festival sites
  2 camping / camping out
  3 sheep chased / have been chased / animals harassed
  4 rubbish (left) / a mess everywhere
  5 no trespassing
  6 causing (an) obstruction / in the way

Tapescript

N = **News reader**; KS = **Kate Simpson**
N As the Summer Solstice draws near, travellers from all over Britain are taking to the roads and heading for their traditional festival sites. Police have already reported a build-up of caravans, lorries and cars in many areas and the M11 at junction 13 is completely blocked.
   In the West, there are reports that at Shepton Mallet travellers have camped out on the recreation ground to the north of the town.

Our reporter, Kate Simpson, is on the phone from Shepton Mallet. Hello, Kate! How are things down there at the moment?

KS Well, I'm here at the campsite at Shepton Mallet and er, I believe things are reasonably peaceful at the moment. I can see from where I'm standing several large lorries which have parked on the side of the road. There are about 20 or 30 people milling around, a couple of dogs and a few children.

N Have there been any complaints?

KS I believe so. Yes. A local resident has just been telling me that she knows of a farmer who has claimed that his sheep have been chased, and that he's had to have several lambs put down. I haven't spoken to him myself, though. Then this afternoon some locals whose gardens back on to the recreation ground reported that their gardens have been trampled and rubbish left lying around.

N So animals have been harassed and there's a general mess everywhere. Have the travellers been defending themselves? Have you been able to speak to any of them?

KS Oh yes. I spoke to the leader of this group here and er, he is at pains to say that as far as he knows there has been *no* trespassing on people's property. He feels that he is within his rights to park his vehicle on the public highway. He says he rejects the claim that they are causing an obstruction. He feels very got at, and is putting most of the complaints down to prejudice by those who don't understand the travelling way of life.

N And have there been any other developments?

KS Yes. I spoke earlier to a police officer. Apparently the local MP has decided that the situation is potentially so serious he is actually …

3 Divide the class into groups of three or four and ask them to focus on ways of handling the dispute effectively, eg who should be in charge, what will the travellers be allowed to do, what can be done to help the residents, etc. Alternatively, divide the class into two groups, one representing the travellers and the other group representing the residents. Give them time to prepare. Encourage each student in the group to think of at least one reason why they should or should not be moved on.

Speaking   Student's Book p 64

1 Tell students that they will not be able to see their partner's picture. Students may need reminding that the use of the present continuous is important in describing actions and activities. Refer them to the relevant section of the Vocabulary Resource on pages 193 and 194.

Optional activity

Ask students to select pictures of people in various social situations from magazines or newspapers. In groups, students could brainstorm appropriate vocabulary to describe what people look like, the clothes they are wearing, etc. This could be a timed competition between groups to see which group knows the most vocabulary.

2 Ask students to discuss the questions in pairs. This will prepare them for a more general discussion in 3.

3 Students discuss lifestyle.

▶ Suggested answers

… how I live my life. | … the way I like to do things. | … what I do that's important to me.

… I give much thought to. | … I feel the need to talk about. | … that matters much to me.

… they generally are referring the pace of life that they lead.

4 Using the adjectives and modifiers given here will help students to practise asking each other questions which can extend the conversation and introduce new angles and approaches.

▶ Suggested answers

Do you have a reasonably relaxed approach to things?

Are you very demanding at work?

Is it true that you were quite energetic when you were at college?

Would you say that you are an extremely organized person?

You're a fairly quiet sort of person, aren't you?

English in Use   Student's Book p 65

1 This activity will help the students recognize differences in style and register between the informal / colloquial language the policewoman uses when speaking and the more formal, written style of a newspaper item. Students are asked to produce the more formal style.

▶ Answers

1 made attempts to
2 had occupied / was occupying / was obstructing

2 Ask students to read the texts again and give them about 10 minutes to complete the report in pairs. Tell them that if they write more than is asked for they will be more likely to lose marks for inaccuracy or incorrect spelling.

▶ Answers
3 approached / neared / moved towards
4 were thrown
5 no one / nobody
6 negotiated / talked
7 leave / move away
8 were closed
9 monitoring / watching
10 over / during

Reading
Family Ties ▼

Introduction   Student's Book p 66

1 Students discuss the quotations about family life in groups of three. Make sure that students understand the underlying irony.

Notes
'Children begin by loving their parents … '
Oscar Wilde: 19th century Irish poet and dramatist.

'Parents are the last people … '
Samuel Butler: 19th century English novelist, essayist and critic.

'Happiness in marriage … '
Jane Austen: 19th century English writer.

'Marriage is the waste-paper basket … '
Sidney Webb: late 19th / early 20th century English socialist economist and distinguished historian.

Reading

1 Refer students to the Exam tip on multiple-choice questions in Paper 1. Students write answers to 1–6 on their own or in pairs. (Note that the wording of question 4 in **1** for the initial skimming task differs from that of question 4 in **2**.)

Note
All that's left is a Band of Gold is taken from the title of a song about the break up of a marriage. *Band of Gold* refers to a wedding ring.

▶ Suggested answers
1 psychological changes
2 try family therapies
3 They are undecided.
4 Some of the problems that children of divorced couples have pre-date the divorce.

5 Some conflict is needed plus an overall positive attitude.
6 Long-term unhappiness and tension can adversely affect your health.

2 Ask students to compare their answers to **1** with their multiple-choice selection. They could also underline the parts of the text that led them to the correct option.

▶ Answers
1 A   2 C   3 C   4 B   5 B   6 D

If there is time, there could be a class discussion or group activity on why the remaining options are incorrect and why they might, at first, be considered possible, ie which parts of the text do they refer to? This could done for homework.

> **Optional activity**
>
> Students select a quotation from the introduction as a heading and write 150–200 words in the form of one of the following:
> • a magazine article.
> • a letter to a newspaper.

Vocabulary   Student's Book p 68

1 Check the students' answer to the first question and then elicit why it could be an 'extended metaphor'.

▶ Answer
The writer uses the image of an earthquake to describe the way dramatic, new psychological theories spread from the USA to Britain. This image can be described as an 'extended metaphor'. The image is developed (the earthquake is followed by a tidal wave) and referred to at several points in the text, eg *movements which first shake that country | The energy of these waves | Britain absorbs the main impact.*

2 Students discuss the expressions in pairs.

▶ Answers
1 reaching Britain
2 to try out
3 adopting the latest theories
4 get back to normal
5 produce an atmosphere

The following are connected to the metaphor in the first paragraph:

coming ashore | following the new tide | to get my feet wet | create a psychological climate.

3 Ask students to discuss the expressions in pairs.

▶ Answers

1 unwell / not 100% fit and healthy
2 making something seem more difficult than it is
3 survive troubled times
4 heard about
5 save money for a future time of need
6 outrage

Exercises **4** and **5** can be done in small groups or as a homework activity.

4 Draw attention to the endings and elicit examples of words using these suffixes. Suggest that students make a note of other suffixes they find in other texts in the coursebook, magazines and newspapers.

▶ Answers

nouns: disagree<u>ment</u>, happi<u>ness</u>, observa<u>tion</u>, relation<u>ship</u>, abil<u>ity</u>

adjectives: harm<u>ful</u>, attrac<u>tive</u>, help<u>less</u>, behaviour<u>al</u>, reli<u>able</u>

verbs: popular<u>ize</u>

5 Students first complete the sentences on their own and then compare their answers in pairs.

▶ Answers

1 demonstrative
2 partnership
3 modernized
4 shyness
5 confrontation
6 eventful
7 hopeless
8 detestable
9 continuity
10 achievement
11 financial

Writing
Socializing ▼

Introduction   Student's Book p 69

1 Students discuss the activities briefly and give reasons.

2 The extracts illustrate the different ways people behave in groups. Ask students to discuss their impressions of the people in the extracts and focus on the implications of belonging to a group. Find out if they belong to any clubs.

Note
Virgin Atlantic: Airline owned by Richard Branson, which offers cut-price tickets to USA.

Writing

One of the writing tasks which may be set in Part 1 or 2 is a report. Tell students that they will be given enough information in the exam for them to decide on the theme, the purpose and the audience.

Sample report

1 a   Students read the report and summarize the aims individually before comparing in pairs.

▶ Answers

Paragraph 1: reason for report
Paragraph 2: 1st problem and reasons for it
Paragraph 3: 2nd problem with two examples, 3rd problem with result
Paragraph 4: 4th problem with reason
Paragraph 5: Conclusion

b   Students underline the following words and phrases:

▶ Answers

Introduce the subject of the report: *I was asked to investigate* and *This report looks at*

Introduce a personal opinion: *many members complained ... and club facilities ... were universally criticized ...*

Link together and order ideas: *After ... | Firstly ... | ... has led to ... which means that ... | Secondly ... | However ... resulting in ... | Consequently ... | The situation has been made worse by ...*

Introduce conclusion: *To sum up ...*

c   Ask students to finish the concluding paragraph in pairs.

▶ Suggested answer

... addresses the issues of bad organization, poor facilities and membership fees. I recommend a new manager is appointed with experience in catering for a younger clientele and ways of reducing membership fees should be investigated.

Understanding the task

2 Give students a few minutes to read through the task and the documents.

▶ Answers

Theme: The rise in vandalism and the lack of social activities in the area plus the council's need to respond to these issues.

Purpose: To summarize the questionnaire responses and the criticisms expressed in the two articles.

Target Reader: Council members.

Selecting ideas

3 Students discuss the questions in pairs.

▶ **Suggested answers**

Significant facts:
– the lack of leisure facilities and the rising number of unemployed youngsters in the town
– the move would result in higher prices and less availability to the less well-off
– more discos for young people, restaurants open late, night-clubs
– Would cost be a significant factor ...?
– I do not earn very much, so most things are too expensive
– There is not much to do in the evening except go to pubs.

Facts supporting each other: not enough facilities / what is available is too expensive / nothing much for young people to do, especially in the evenings

There are no obvious contradictory facts.

Ask students to discuss possible conclusions and recommendations, eg Should the sports hall be sold off? Will extra facilities stop vandalism? What are the disadvantages of late-night venues such as night-clubs?

Planning your answer

4 Draw the students' attention to the suggested plan for the report and encourage them to discuss in pairs what would be relevant and appropriate to include in each of the sections. Refer them to the relevant sections of the Vocabulary Resource on pages 194 and 195.

Writing

5 Remind students to check their work for accuracy and the correct register. Refer them to the Writing Resource on page 191 for another example of a report.

Optional activities

1 Ask students to write a reply to their report in the form of a letter produced by the directors of *Equip Leisure Ltd*.
2 Organize a discussion in which a group supporting *Equip Leisure Ltd* argue their case against a group representing young people in the town. They will need time to prepare their arguments.

Structure
Preconceptions ▼

Introduction   Student's Book p 72

Ask students to discuss the question and pictures briefly in pairs.

Reading

Explain that a *rag-and-bone man* is someone who trades in old clothes, furniture, etc. usually collecting from people's homes with a horse and cart.

A Divide the class into groups of three and encourage them to make their title short.

Note
The original title of this article was *The Flat Season* and came from a series of articles entitled *Urban Myths*.

B Give students about 10 minutes to punctuate the text in pairs. They then compare their version with another pair's.

▶ **Suggested answer**

A friend of mine worked in a council housing department in the north-east. On one occasion, he had to deal with an ageing rag-and-bone man, who had been relocated from his suburban caravan home of fifty years to the top of a high-rise block of flats. The old fellow, reluctant to surrender his mobile abode, settled in grudgingly, and pretty soon complaints found their way to the housing office.

'Well, you see, we hear all these funny grating and grinding noises coming from the flat at all hours. Whenever he uses the lift, it seems like hours before it's free – and there's a strange sort of country-type smell in there – always!'

Aware that prejudice can colour a person's perceptions, the housing officer set out to the block of flats one evening, ready to pacify the neighbours and show them the error of their ways. But when she arrived in the lobby, she found the lift occupied.

'It's that dirty old fellow, love,' whispered a tenant through the crack of a door. 'He goes up and down in the lift all night long. Don't bother waiting. Why don't you use the stairs? It'll be quicker, you'll see!'

The housing officer tackled the staircase to meet the elderly resident on the seventeenth floor. The lift doors opened slowly to reveal the old man and a secret cohabitant – his trusty old bag-of-bones horse, fresh from a run-around outside.

'Good heavens!' stammered the housing officer. 'Are you mad? What d'you think you're doing with that horse in here?'

The old man was furious.

'Eh? What do you mean? The horse can't, well … poor animal – he has to use the lift. In his condition, all those stairs would kill him!'

Comprehension

Ask students to discuss the answers briefly in pairs.

▶ Suggested answers

1 He resented having to move and wanted to stay where he was.
2 They kept hearing strange noises coming from his flat and he seemed to spend an extraordinary amount of time in the lift. There was also an unusual smell in the lift after he had been using it.
3 She thought they might have been prejudiced against the man, who had come from somewhat different surroundings.
4 He seemed to think that it was quite normal to have a horse sharing his flat and that the complaint was about the fact that he had used the lift for the horse instead of taking the animal up the stairs.

Direct and reported speech

A

▶ Answers

Statements:
'Whenever he uses the lift, it seems like hours before it's free – and there's a strange sort of country-type smell in there – always!'

'It's that dirty old fellow, love.' 'He goes up and down in the lift all night long.'

'It'll be quicker, you'll see!'

'The horse can't, well … poor animal – he has to use the lift. In his condition, all those stairs would kill him!'

Advice or instructions:
'Why don't you use the stairs?'
'Don't bother waiting.'

Questions:
'Are you mad? What d'you think you're doing with that horse in here?'
'What do you mean?'

B

▶ Answers

1 Peter said (that) he *was* worried about the test *the following day | next day | day after.*

2 The teacher *told* the children *not to touch the | that* switch.
3 Tom asked his father *if | whether* he had finished the book or not.

Constructions after reporting verbs

Student's Book p 73

A Students do the matching task in pairs.

▶ Answers

1 e, f and g
2 a and b
3 a and b
4 a, b and d
5 c and f
6 a, b and d
7 a, b and d
8 a, b and d
9 g
10 a and b
11 h
12 c and f

B

▶ Suggested answers

1 The neighbours complained that they could hear funny noises coming from the flat at all hours. They also complained that whenever he used the lift, it seemed like hours before it was free – and there was always a strange smell in there.
2 The tenant whispered to the housing officer that it was the old man and he went up and down in the lift all night long.
3 The tenant told / advised the housing officer not to bother waiting. He suggested using the stairs / that she should use / used the stairs, adding that it would be quicker.
4 The housing officer, somewhat taken aback, asked the old fellow if he was mad. He then asked the old man what he thought he was doing with the horse in there.
5 The old man, angered by the housing officer's question, asked him what he meant. The old fellow then said / explained that the horse had to use the lift because in his condition all the stairs would kill him!

C

▶ Answers

It is not necessary to change *would* when reporting direct speech as the modals *would, could,* or *might* do not change whether used after a reporting verb in the past or a reporting verb in the present.

1 It is not necessary to change the verb, when you report what someone often says or something which is a fact or usually true.

2 Because this is reporting what someone says or believes at the moment of speaking.

3 Because this is reporting something you assume somebody will say in the future.

4 See the above reason for modals not changing.

5 The modals *can*, *may* and *will* stay as they are after a reporting verb in the present but usually change to *could*, *would* or *might* after a reporting verb in the past. However you can use *can* and *will* after a reporting verb in the past if you want to stress the fact that something still exists or has not yet happened.

6 *Will* stays as it is after a reporting verb in the present but usually changes to *would* after a reporting verb in the past, eg *He said that if he was going to be delayed, he would phone.*

Language activation

Soap Opera

Students think of a scene from their favourite soap opera or a play they have seen recently, in which an interesting conversation took place. In pairs, students tell their partner who said what to whom. The teacher then chooses one or two students to tell the class about the scene. Students could then write out the reported conversation for homework.

Adverbs

A

▶ Answers

1 a lack of enthusiasm:
grudgingly
reluctantly
hesitantly

2 a loss of self-control:
furiously
angrily
emotionally
aggressively

3 a more positive attitude:
patiently
generously
tactfully
politely
eagerly

B Students complete this exercise on their own and then compare with the rest of the class.

▶ Suggested answers

1 Polly insisted (angrily / aggressively) that she was not a punk – never had been and never would be.
Polly angrily denied that she was a punk – never had been and never would be.

2 The secretary asked Mrs Thompson (politely) if she would care to look through the plans before the meeting.

3 The managing director (tactfully) urged / asked / told Frank not to mention the matter to anyone as it was extremely delicate.

4 The leader of the opposition (aggressively / angrily) accused the Prime Minister of failure and suggested that he / she should admit / admitted that the government had made mistakes.

5 The Ambassador (reluctantly / grudgingly) replied that if pressed, he would probably have to say / admit that he was not in favour of the new anti-terrorist measures.

6 Sally hesitantly explained / replied / admitted / confessed that she had never really given marriage any serious thought.

7 The secretary (angrily) complained / protested (emotionally) that she had had enough and added that she just couldn't take any more.
The secretary furiously announced that she had had enough.

8 The porter (politely) advised the hotel guest to take the lift.
The porter suggested that the hotel guest should take the lift.

Practice

Students should make some notes on the conversation they had before telling their partner. They could write this up for homework.

6 Culture Vultures

The title is a colloquial phrase used of people who are eager to consume culture.

Reading
Time Out

Introduction   Student's Book p 74

Students discuss the pictures of people at an opera and a sporting event in pairs and compare their preferences in entertainment. Then briefly discuss the experience of being in an audience with the whole class.

▶ **Suggested answers**

Aspects to consider include the pros and cons of mass audience events, eg more atmosphere but less comfort / safety; factors in belonging to a small audience, for example friendlier but perhaps a lack of atmosphere if an event is not sold out.

Reading

1 Students skim the text and answer the questions. Ask them to compare any similar publications that exist locally.

▶ **Answer**

It is from a newspaper or magazine and is written for the general public as a guide to local entertainment.

2 Ask students to read all the questions quickly, but tell them not to answer them yet.

3 Refer students to the Exam tip on matching tasks. Explain the matching procedure if necessary, by looking at the questions and list of events A–J. Remind them of the time constraints on Paper 1 and ask them to scan the text for the information required, but not to do the matching task yet.

▶ **Answers**

5 is about *when* an event is taking place.
6 will be in the Cinema section.
7 *free*

4 Students should complete the matching exercise within the specified time of 10 minutes. Tell them

when five minutes have passed to make them more aware of how fast they are working.

▶ **Answers**

1, 2   C and I
3   J
4   H
5   B
6   A
7   F
8, 9   E and I
10, 11   D and G
12   B

5 Ask students to work in pairs, each finding five of the words.

▶ **Answers**

1   radical
2   thaw out
3   spaced-out
4   wreaks
5   sombre
6   boost
7   heart-breaking
8   distinguished
9   jaunty
10   prolific

6 Students do this individually and then compare lists with a partner. Explain that these sets of words will be useful both in writing and speaking (particularly in relation to writing a review in Paper 2, Part 2). Set this for homework if time is short.

▶ **Answers**

Films	Plays	People
double-bill	playwright	playwright
director	theatre	director
film editor	song-and-dance	film editor
cinema	romance	actor
soundtrack	drama	cast
romance	cast	hero
drama	block-buster	villain
cast	special effects	protagonist
block-buster	plot	performer
special effects	tragedy	
screenplay	stage set	
tragedy	premiere	
premiere	performance	
performance	tour	

Optional activity

Students could produce their own guide to local entertainment for the coming week. This could be set as a class project, with students divided into small groups, each responsible for one area (cinema, concerts, dance, art, etc.). Encourage students to use some of the descriptive language from the text and to write in a similarly concise style. The finished guide could then be distributed to other classes.

NB You may prefer to do this activity after the vocabulary section on adjectival order which follows.

Vocabulary   Student's Book p 76

1 Ask students to think about what the first adjectives in each pair convey.

▶ Answer

They are both adjectives that refer to qualities.

2 Students discuss 1–6 in pairs, making the necessary corrections.

▶ Answers

correct: 1, 2, 3, 5
incorrect: 4, 6

3 Ask students to decide on the order in pairs and confirm this on the board.

▶ Answer

Quality, size, shape, age, colour

4 Refer students to the relevant sections of the Vocabulary Resource on page 194. Students write the phrases individually. Encourage them to use their imagination to the full and to write detailed descriptions. In pairs, students then exchange their phrases and check the order of the adjectives used.

▶ Suggested answers

1   a bizarre modern sculpture
2   a precocious young musician
3   a sumptuous 19th century opera house
4   an overweight middle-aged tenor

Speaking   Student's Book p 77

1 Elicit the meaning of *big-budget* and *block-buster* by asking students for some examples of current films of this type. Avoid any discussion of plot or opinion as this comes up in the next section.

Students then read the screenplay summary and evaluate the title, covering aspects such as

punchiness, dramatic quality and enigmatic appeal.

2 Allow at least 10 minutes for this stage. Students work in small groups, discussing the three areas and noting their ideas on each. One member of each group should act as the spokesperson and could write main points on a flip chart, for presentation to the class.

3 Students should assess each group as they present their ideas to the class. At the end, a vote could be taken as to which group has the best ideas.

Writing
In My Opinion ...

Introduction   Student's Book p 78

1 Explain that this section looks at the language of reviews, where both positive and negative opinions are expressed.

In pairs, students divide the adjectives into two lists.

▶ Answers

Positive:	Negative:
under-rated	*unconvincing*
perceptive	*pretentious*
subtle	*trivial*
moving	*phoney*
exquisite	*wooden*
compelling	
intricate	

Play the tape right through.

Note

David Mamet is an American playwright and film director, born in 1947. Of his plays, *Glengarry Glen Ross* (1984) won the Pulitzer prize; *Speed-the-Plow*, written in 1988, is a scathing portrayal of the American film industry. Other films include *House of Games* (1987); *Homicide* (1991). *Things Change* was released in 1988.

▶ Answers

Words from the above lists used in the discussion are:
under-rated
moving
exquisite
phoney
unconvincing
subtle
compelling

Ask the whole class about the reviewers' comments. Students should give reasons for their answers by referring to the adjectives they have ticked or by giving one or two examples they remember from the recording.

Find out whether any students have seen the film *Things Change*. If so, do they agree with the comments made?

▶ **Answers**

Michael Pond: positive

Anna Redditch: mainly negative

(The interviewer's comments are also positive.)

Tapescript

I = Interviewer; MP = Michael Pond; AR = Anna Railton

I For me, any film by writer-director David Mamet is something to savour. His vastly under-rated second film *Things Change*, starring Don Ameche and that archetypal Mamet-man Joe Mantegna, is currently experiencing a revival. It's the story of a lowly New York Italian shoe-repairer, Don Ameche, who, bearing a striking similarity to a member of the New York mob, is approached and asked to become his double and take the rap for murder. His promised reward is the fishing boat of his dreams, once he's served the due time in gaol. Michael Pond, your views on *Things Change*?

MP Well, I must start by saying I share your admiration of Mamet's work. To me, he is a maker of poetic myths and this film is no exception. It's a poignant and moving story, lovingly crafted, with quite magnificent acting by both Ameche and Mantegna.

I Yes, and clearly Mamet also epitomizes that very American duality between hardness and sensitivity – which is a core theme in this film?

MP Yes, very much so. In fact, you could say that he constantly divides his male leads into two types: the pivotal figure who has to take a tough moral decision – in this film the Don Ameche character – and the flash guy who talks big who always attracts the star actor – Al Pacino in *Glengarry Glen Ross* and Joe Mantegna as the vulnerable mobster here in *Things Change*. And I think the reason why the film is so good, so powerful, lies in the dynamics of the relationship between these two protagonists.

I Anna Railton, can I bring you in at this point. A powerful film?

AR I suppose it is – I can't deny that it has a rather unusual intensity. And the two leads certainly have presence. My reservation is that the film is marred by the absence of any significant female characters, which is unfortunate, to say the least.

MP Presumably this is part of the realism? Organized crime is a man's world, where women are viewed as adornments, or as practical providers, as in the exquisite portrayal of the housekeeper-cook in *Chicago*.

I So you'd say that all in all the film is completely authentic in terms of its characterization?

MP Yes, and …

AR Well, I'm afraid I can't accept that. Quite frankly, some of the minor roles were definitely phoney, and in the case of the junior mobsters, the depiction bordered on caricature with a capital C. Absolutely unconvincing at times.

I Mmm, you might have to agree to differ there. But, er going back to Michael's point, although Mamet writes mainly about men, he is not what you would call a macho dramatist, Anna?

AR No, that is true. And I certainly liked the way he brought out the frail ego behind the bravado in the Joe Mantegna part, that was clever, he pulled it off well. But the fact remains that this is a film about men and as such, I couldn't respond to it in a wholly positive way.

I And what of the theme encapsulated in the title itself, *Things Change*?

MP Well actually, that for me is the finishing touch. The film has so many subtle shifts and balances, all of which are very convincing – and indeed compelling. One of the scenes I remember most vividly is the return from that fishing trip, where you have two men from very different walks of life standing on the jetty, trousers rolled up and everything else stripped away. But, of course, as the title says, things change – the big man returns to his house and his role within organized crime, while the little man has to meet his own fate.

I Not entirely as you might expect, perhaps … but we mustn't reveal that final delightful twist in the plot. Anna Railton, Michael Pond, thank you. *Things Change* is back on general release for a limited period – don't miss it.

2 Students look at the tapescript in pairs and decide which phrases would be acceptable in a formal written review, suggesting alternative wording where necessary. Point out to students any of the phrases which could be used in an informal written review, as they will then be able to use these in the writing task which follows.

▶ **Answers**

For me … (acceptable in a fairly informal review. Reword as *In my view / opinion* or *I believe that*)

Well, I must start by saying … (an improvement for a formal review might be to reword the phrase in a more impersonal way, for example *It should first be said that …*)

To me … (reword as *In my view / opinion*)

In fact, you could say that … (acceptable for an informal written review)

And I think the reason why … (reword as *In my opinion the reason why …*)

I can't deny that … (acceptable)

My reservation is that … (acceptable)

all in all (only acceptable in an informal review. Reword as *on balance / all things considered*)

I'm afraid I can't accept that. (a spoken response, so no rewording is possible)

I certainly … (acceptable)

… that for me is the finishing touch (acceptable in a fairly informal review. Reword as *that, in my opinion, …*)

3 Students should have a brief discussion in pairs or small groups.

English in Use   Student's Book p 78

1 This vocabulary cloze could be done for homework if necessary, provided it is covered before the Writing section, as it completes the preparatory work on reviews.

Note

schlock (US slang) – rubbish

▶ **Answer**

The reviewer's attitude is extremely negative, indeed scathing.

2 Remind students of the first training session on Part 1 (Unit 2, pages 22–23), where all four options were considered for each gap. If done in class, students could look at the options in pairs, saying why the alternatives are not possible.

▶ **Answers**

1 D
2 D
3 C
4 D
5 A
6 D
7 A
8 B

3 Students discuss in pairs if they would go to this exhibition. If not, ask them to talk about the kind they would go to. They could also tell their partner about an exhibition they particularly liked and why.

Writing   Student's Book p 79

Sample review

1 a   Students read the review in pairs and underline the positive and negative points.

▶ **Answers**

Positive points:
a powerful first novel
rich and detailed in plot
intricately constructed ... will hold your attention right up to the final page.
book is most moving at times, while at others it is immensely amusing.

vivid references to Ancient Greece to be savoured and enjoyed.
extremely successful in forging the different identities ... as well as introducing some delightful cameo characters
unusually perceptive about New England college life
contrasts ... most skilfully.
I literally could not put it down!
I highly recommend ... a truly magnificent achievement

Negative point:
At over 500 pages, it is just a little too long.

The present tense is used because it is more immediate and brings the plot to life.

b   Students reread the review individually or in pairs to find the adverbs. Refer them to the relevant sections of the Vocabulary Resource on pages 194 and 195.

▶ **Answers**

Intensifying adverbs:
intricately (constructed)
immensely (amusing)
unusually (perceptive)
truly (magnificent)

Adverbs that introduce or specify information:
Predominantly

Refer students to the relevant sections of the Vocabulary Resource on pages 194 and 195.

Understanding the task

2 Students read the task and decide who might read the magazine. Students could include some of the adjectives from the Introduction on page 78.

▶ **Suggested answer**

The magazine would be read by students worldwide, so the register should be fairly informal.

Brainstorming ideas

3 Refer students to the Exam tip and remind them to include all the bulleted points. Students choose different films or plays to review and prepare their notes individually. Suggest that they include at least one negative point if their review is mainly positive and vice versa.

Students then work in pairs and take it in turns to talk through their notes. Their partner should listen and decide whether enough opinion is included and whether the ideas are clearly stated.

Planning your answer

4 Students discuss the question in pairs.

► Answer

Paragraph 1: Introduction and plot

Paragraph 2: Statement of main positive points

Paragraph 3: Focus on additional positive points

Paragraph 4: Negative point and recommendation

Students develop their own paragraph plan from the sample review. If their review is to be mainly negative, they should include a positive point at the end to make it more balanced.

Writing

5 Students write the review in 250 words. Remind them to check their work carefully when they have finished.

There is a further example of a review in the Writing Resource on page 192.

Listening and Speaking
West to East ▼

This section looks at the tension between local culture and global influences, such as satellite broadcasting.

Introduction   Student's Book p 81

1 Students should discuss the statement as a class and decide what it means.

► Suggested answer

The media has the potential to influence people's lives in a negative and harmful way.

2 Students skim the article and discuss the views as a class.

Note
The article appeared in *Asiaweek*, a general interest magazine for adults, distributed in Asia.

► Suggested answers

MTV
- is turning young people into TV addicts.
- promotes the music industry and Asian bands such as *Tang Dynasty*.
- imposes Western culture on the Asian way of life.
- is intensifying the generation gap and threatening local culture.
- is shaping young minds.
- is making stars of MTV veejays.

3 Students discuss the statement in pairs or small groups. Treat the question on satellite broadcasting as a class discussion.

► Suggested answer

People who like MTV think it is *hip* (fashionable and up-to-date) and those who criticize it think it is *hype* (intensive publicity used to sell products).

Listening   Student's Book p 82

1 Refer students to the Exam tip and ask them to look carefully at the table to prepare for the listening task.

► Answer

The missing information consists of titles, times or details about the programme.

2 Students should listen out for the signposts mentioned.

3 Remind students to use no more than four words for any gap. Play the tape once only as this is an example of a Part 2 task.

► Answers

1   Two-part
2   telepathic species
3   7.00
4   *Soccer News*
5   Highlights of
6   Comedy fantasy
7   *Lush Life*
8   jazz session musicians
9   *Racing with the Moon*
10   *Ticket to Paradise*
11   10.30
12   island-hopping

Tapescript

P = Presenter
P   Good evening, and here is our usual round-up of what's on across Sky channels tonight. Starting at eight o'clock, Sky One is screening *September*, a drama set in the Scottish highlands and starring Jacqueline Bisset. This is a two-part mini-series which will be concluded on Wednesday at the same time. Looking ahead to ten o'clock tonight, Sky One has its nightly dose of *Star Trek*. Tonight the Enterprise receives a telepathic species on board, who have the ability to read the crew's minds. I wonder how they'll cope with that!
   If sport is your passion, we have a full programme for you tonight over on Sky Sports. From seven there's international cricket, covering the best of the day's play between England and Australia from Perth. At ten, it's *Soccer News*, with all the latest news and views, as well as the best of the weekend's goals. Following straight on from this at ten-fifteen there's *Tartan Extra*, which has the

highlights of Scottish football, including last night's match from Aberdeen.

For all you movie lovers out there, tonight on Sky we've got some great films for you. First, at eight on Sky Movies you can catch *Toys*, a comedy fantasy starring the zany Robin Williams. Stay tuned to the same channel where, commencing at five past ten, there's a very under-rated film, *Lush Life*. This film, described in *Variety* magazine as 'a moving celebration of friendship and the joy of music-making', has Jeff Goldblum and Forrest Whitaker portraying jazz session musicians. This is a Sky Movies premiere – don't miss it! And still talking of movies, over on Sky Gold at eight there's *Racing with the Moon*. Sean Penn leads this romantic drama, which also stars Elizabeth McGovern and Nicolas Cage.

Finally, to chase away those winter blues, let me give you the best of the programmes on Sky Travel tonight. Showing at six-thirty and nine is *Ticket to Paradise*. This half-hour feature could well be an inspiration for your next dream holiday! At seven-thirty and repeated at half past ten, we really head for the sun with *Caribbean Vacation*, which has information on island-hopping trips and also features some of the various long cruises on offer. So there you have it, just some of the broadcasting on Sky tonight – enjoy!

English in Use   Student's Book p 83

Refer students to the Exam tip on Part 6.

1   Ask students to skim read first for the answer and then to reread the text to analyse the structures.

Note
Derek Walcott received the Nobel Prize for literature in 1992.

▶ **Answers**

He is a poet and playwright from St Lucia in the Caribbean.

a
... and the indigenous ...
... and the folklore ...
... and fluent Trinidadian ...
... and having been brought up ...

The above are all noun phrases (eg *the indigenous Caribbean traditions*)

b
... and his vivid ...
... and the visual images ...

The verbs *informs* and *give* show that these underlined parts are clauses.

2   Students discuss in pairs.

▶ **Answer**

both and *equally*.

The use of *both* here is one of emphasis. Other devices for emphasizing two separate things are:

not only ... but (also)
either ... or
neither ... nor

3

▶ **Answer**

They could not be changed round, as the underlined parts give additional information that depends on the first statements having already been made.

4

▶ **Answer**

The commas signal additional information, given at phrase level.

5   Students skim the text first for general meaning and then look carefully at the options A– J. Give them 10 minutes to complete the task in pairs in class or set this for homework.

▶ **Answers**

1   D
2   B
3   I
4   A
5   C
6   E

Speaking   Student's Book p 84

1   Remind students that there is a list of prepositional phrases in the Vocabulary Resource on page 194. Students do the activity in pairs and should each aim to speak for about one minute.

2   In pairs, students take it in turns to talk about a carnival or festival, each speaking for about one minute. Encourage them to ask one another for more details if anything is not clear, eg *I'm sorry, I didn't quite catch what you said about ...* or *Could you say a bit more about ... ?*

Structure
Virtually Real? ▼

Introduction   Student's Book p 85

Students briefly describe the cartoon in pairs and discuss what they think it means as a whole class. They then briefly discuss the statement below the cartoon.

Reading

Students read the article briefly and answer the two questions.

▶ Answers

> VR can now create the illusion of 'being there' by using goggles to create illusions.
>
> In the future VR will be so sophisticated that we may be able to do all the things that we cannot do in real life.

Will and going to

A Ask students to read the sentences and discuss the differences in meaning of *will* and *going to*.

▶ Answers

> *will* is used to talk about events which are certain to happen, eg *The next Olympic Games will be in ...*, or predictions for the future, eg with *I think ...*
>
> NB *shall* is often used with *I* and *we*. In spoken English *shall* and *will* are frequently abbreviated to *'ll*.
>
> *going to* is used to talk about the strong probability of something happening quite soon, often when there is some visible evidence of what is going to happen, eg *Look at the appalling way that man's driving! He's going to have an accident!*

B

▶ Answer

> In this sentence, *going to* expresses the speaker's *intention* to do something in contrast to its meaning in **A**.

C

▶ Answers

> 1 determination (or for emphasis when a person is angry)
> 2 willingness
> 3 an offer
> 4 an announcement of a decision
> 5 *shall* used with the first person to express the simple future
> 6 a promise

D

▶ Answers

> 1 will / shall send
> 2 'll / will help
> 3 will increase
> 4 shall / will be
> 5 Are you really going to accept
> 6 'll ask
> 7 'll be / 's going to be
> 8 'll / will buy
> 9 are we going to do
> 10 shall / will never do

Language activation

The Great Zoraster

In small groups, students choose one person to be *The Great Zoraster*. The other students think of two questions to ask the fortune teller about the future using *will* and *going to*. The Great Zoraster then answers them!

Present continuous, simple present, future continuous, simple future

Student's Book p 86

A Ask students to discuss the questions in pairs or groups of three.

▶ Answers

> 1 asks what you intend to do, have planned to do or what you think you might do.
> 2 asks if you have made any definite arrangements or plans for the weekend.
> 2 might be followed by an invitation because the speaker has asked a question to find out whether the listener is busy, or free to accept an invitation they might have in mind.
> 1 is a way of asking what someone intends to do but has maybe not yet planned.

Language activation

Future plans and intentions

In pairs, students find out what their partners are doing / going to do
1 this weekend.
2 next month.
3 next year.
Students then take it in turns to tell the rest of the class one thing about their partners.

B Discuss the questions with the whole class.

▶ Answers

> The present continuous and the simple present are both used to talk about definite plans or arrangements for the future.
> The present continuous is used to talk about arrangements for the future, eg *I'm meeting the managing director at 2.30* while the simple present is used to talk about fixed starting times of events, timetables, etc. eg *The coach leaves at 6.30. The new term begins on Monday.*
> The future continuous is used to talk about predictions which you are fairly sure will take place and which may continue for some time in the future.

You have to use the simple future instead of the future continuous when you use a verb which is not normally used in continuous tenses,
eg *This time next week I'll be in Paris.*
It'll seem strange not having to get up early tomorrow.
I'll feel lost without you next weekend.

C   This could be set for homework.

▶ Answers

1   'll / will be working
2   'll / shall / will be
3   will be flying
4   will have
5   'll / shall / will be doing
6   will be
7   'll / shall / will all be living
8   'll / will seem
9   will be telling
10 'll / shall / will be travelling

NB *'ll* can be used in all sentences except 3, 4, 6 and 9.

About to and on the verge of

▶ Answers

are about to be eroded (line 12)
entrepreneurs are on the verge of launching (line 51)

The writer makes the point more dramatic by using these expressions. He is not merely expressing intention or probability. He is also stating that he expects these things to happen very soon.

NB *verge* means an extreme limit beyond which something may happen and could therefore be used in more crucial situations, often when there is still a chance that an impending disaster could be averted. Otherwise, there is little difference in meaning between them.

Extra exercise

Write two sentences about the future for 1–6 using *about to* and *on the verge of*. You will have to make some changes and / or additions to the information in order to be able to use both expressions.
1   scientists / cure for Aids
2   company / bankruptcy
3   Sally / look / tears
4   shop / close
5   appear / Minister / resign
6   rail staff / strike

▶ Suggested answers

1   Scientists are about to find / are on the verge of finding a cure for Aids.
2   The company is about to go bankrupt / is on the verge of bankruptcy / going bankrupt.
3   Sally looks as if she's about to burst into tears / is on the verge of tears.
4   The shop is about to close / is on the verge of closing.
5   It appears that the Minister is about to resign / is on the verge of resigning.
6   Rail staff are about to strike / are on the verge of going on strike / striking.

Practice

Divide the class into groups of three or four. Ask them to select the points they wish to talk about if time is short.

7 Welcome to the Real World

Listening and Speaking
Starting Out ▼

Introduction   Student's Book p 87

1   In pairs, students look at the quotes, pictures and captions, matching as many as they can. Note that two (1C / 2F) could be seen as interchangeable; the actual quotes are as below.

Elicit the meaning of *legendary* in the first caption (widely-known). This word is used again in the listening section.

▶ Answers

   A   4   (*being in front of a camera*)
   B   5   (*films and music*; *clubbing*)
   C   1   (*make (things) happen*)
   D   3   (*very sports-oriented*)
   E   6   (*becoming an actress*; *go on the stage*)
   F   2   (*millionaire*)

2   Students scan the quotes on their own to find the relevant words and phrases.

▶ Answers

   1   quashed
   2   resources
   3   fall into place
   4   potential
   5   predict

3   Encourage students to discuss the statement from both sides and to relate it to their own experience.

4   Ask students to tell the class about any careers advice they have had. If students are still at school and if their school provides this service, ask them to evaluate the advice they are currently getting.

Speaking   Student's Book p 88

1   Ask students if there are similar magazines to *The Big Issue* on sale in their city or town and whether they feel this is a good way for homeless people to earn money.

Students then read the text and discuss it in pairs in relation to their own feelings about school.

Notes
GCSEs – General Certificate of Secondary Education, school examinations taken at the age of 16+
the dole – weekly payments by the state to unemployed people
swots – hard-working students

2   Refer students to the Vocabulary Resource on page 194 for a reminder of how to identify different parts of a picture. Each student spends about one minute describing their picture and then the pair decide on similarities and differences, before looking at both pictures.

3   Students discuss the questions as a class.

▶ Suggested answers

Examples of parental pressure could be encouraging successful school performance, and setting good examples in the family, especially if they're the eldest. Pressure from friends could be staying out late, dressing in a certain way, etc.

Listening   Student's Book p 89

1   Ask students whether they have seen Mariah Carey perform or have any of her records.

2   Students look at the gaps and predict the information in pairs.

▶ Answers

They should be listening for details about:

   1   her brother and sister
   2 / 3 her mother
   4   something that happened a lot
   5   something she started doing at 13
   6   people
   7   jobs
   8   work
   9   how she feels about promoting herself
   10   something to do with recording
   11   an achievement
   12   someone or something she is devoted to

3   Students should write down their answers as they listen.

▶ Answers

   1   (much) older than
   2   a singer (an opera singer)
   3   (musically-talented) friends

4 moved (home / house)
5 to write songs
6 two room-mates
7 waitress
8 studio work
9 reluctant to
10 demo tape / cassette
11 Best New Artist
12 her career

4 Students compare their answers in pairs before listening again.

Tapescript

Part 1
N = Narrator
N How many young women can you think of who reached international stardom by the time they turned 20? Such youthful success stories are few and far between. But Mariah Carey would definitely be at the very top of that list, by anybody's standards. In 1990, when she blasted non-stop up the charts with her self-titled debut album, she was catapulted into instant celebrity. How does such a thing happen?

Born in New York City to parents who separated when she was just three, Mariah grew up with her mother, Patricia, and her much older brother and sister. Mariah's brother is nine years older than her; her sister is 10 years older. Music was a way of life around the house because Patricia was a singer in the New York City Opera. She also taught voice lessons and had lots of musically talented friends who frequently dropped by. All of this had its influence on the girl. By the time she was only four, it was as if Mariah had already seen the future: she knew even then that she was destined to be a famous singer when she grew up. The tough part was a disrupted home life. Mariah and her mum moved at least 13 times, as Patricia sought work as a voice coach. Finally, they settled in Huntingdon, Long Island, in the mid-80s.

Mariah began writing songs at 13. She says she was influenced a lot by MTV, which she remembers as being 'on' throughout her whole teen life. School and study became a problem during her teens, but while her school grades suffered, her skills as a singer and songwriter steadily improved. And her dream never wavered. The minute she graduated from high school, Mariah made the big move to Manhattan, where she roughed it with two room-mates and had a string of jobs that would pay the rent. These included working as a waitress and a hat checker. At the same time, she worked into the wee hours of the night on a demo tape. Finally, good fortune took over and she was given some studio work and gigs singing back-up for other vocalists.

If you consider yourself introverted, it's not the easiest thing to go out and make people aware of you. And shy Mariah's always been a reluctant self-promoter. But she got the classic lucky break when she agreed (also reluctantly) to go to a music industry party. There she met Tommy Mottola, a head executive at CBS records, who took her demo tape without a whole lot of enthusiasm. The story is now legendary. On his way home from the party, Tommy popped Mariah's cassette in the tape deck

and could not believe what he was hearing. He returned to the party to find her, but she had gone. A few days later, like Prince Charming in search of Cinderella, he'd tracked her down and offered her the world – in the form of a recording contract.

In 1990, Mariah realized every artist's dream by winning two Grammy Awards, for Best New Artist and Best Pop Female Vocalist. Her first album sold an unbelievable seven million copies. With that, the Cinderella story was complete. Once Mariah got the gold disc – and several platinums – for her first album, she could have relaxed for a while. But it was right back to the studio to work on album number two, *Emotions*, which sold over a million copies too.

Her lifestyle is about total devotion to her career. Preferring to work at night, Mariah goes into the studio when most people are calling it quits. She usually works till dawn and then sleeps till mid-afternoon. Though she loves to travel, she wouldn't tour at all if she didn't have to. The schedule is a grind, and she doesn't sleep well on the road, and all that affects her voice. And of course, given her shyness, getting up in front of a crowd is not her idea of a good time.

5 Play the tape and ask students to note down key phrases. Write the points on the board and discuss them as a class.

▶ **Answers**

Look inside yourself.
Find your inner strength.
Be proud of yourself.
Be yourself.

Tapescript

Part 2
N = Narrator
N Mariah Carey's got a gift that has given her freedom, fame and the rare opportunity to spend her life doing exactly what she loves. Her advice for success? – to look inside yourself and find your own inner strength, to say 'I'm proud of what I am and who I am, and I'm just going to be myself'. It has certainly paid off in her case.

English in Use   Student's Book p 90

1 Students discuss the cartoon in pairs and work out what letter is missing.

▶ **Answer**

g (aspiring)

Refer students to the Exam tip and remind them that one type of Part 3 task concentrates on spelling and punctuation.

2 Ask students to read the text as a whole before finding the spelling errors. Give them 10 minutes to complete the task.

Answers

1 their
2 √
3 authorities
4 route
5 probationary
6 √
7 offering
8 generally
9 exceptions
10 √
11 √
12 application
13 Institute
14 information

3 Elicit the students' knowledge of double consonant rules and write these on the board.

Answers

1 One vowel and one consonant at the end of a monosyllabic word, eg *cut – cutting*.
2 In words with two syllables or more, one vowel and one consonant when the stress is on the final syllable, eg *upset – upsetting*. However when the stress is on the first syllable, the consonant is not doubled, eg *offer – offering*.
3 One vowel and *l* at the end of a word, eg *travel – travelling*, even if the stress is not at end. (British English only)

4 Ask students to find mistakes in the paragraph which may have been made through mother-tongue interference, eg *Institut* and *informations*. They should then think of other words in their own language which are close enough to English to lead to similar mistakes.

5 Students do the exercise in pairs and explain the meaning of each word or give an example. When they have finished the task, ask them to think of other homophones they know.

Answers

2 wait
3 pole
4 stake
5 heal
6 bear
7 cell
8 grate
9 quay
10 storey
11 draught

Reading
The World of Work ▼

Introduction   Student's Book p 91

1 Elicit the names of the different jobs in the picture and check that students understand and can pronounce all the adjectives. Students then discuss the jobs in pairs and write down some benefits and drawbacks using the words provided.

Answers

(from left to right) doorman, zoo keeper / attendant, manicurist, diver, parachutist, lighthouse keeper, shop assistant, dish washer, mountaineer.

2 Treat this as a class discussion. If students don't know anyone, describe an unusual job to them and ask them to say what they think it is, eg a stunt man or a rat-catcher.

Reading

Refer students to the Exam tip on understanding how a gapped text is organized.

1 Students skim the article and note down the jobs in pairs.

Answers

Job 1 – temporary secretary
Job 2 – arts development officer for a borough council
Job 3 – administrator at the ISM

2 Students skim the missing paragraphs for references to the three jobs, in preparation for **3**.

Answers

A   Job 3
B   Job 2
C   Job 1
D   Job 3
E   Job 2
F   Job 3
G   Job 2

The extra paragraph is F as it is about his outside interests, which are not mentioned in any other paragraph.

3 Students should underline the relevant words and phrases that link the paragraphs.

▶ Answers

1st paragraph: *temporary secretary – typing speed* (C)

2nd paragraph: *very first festival – festival* (G)

3rd paragraph: *the first stage* (B)

4th paragraph: *the next stage – finally* (E)

5th paragraph: *other parts of the job ... quite different* (tasks mentioned in D)

6th paragraph: *also have a more general role – drawbacks – on the plus side* (A)

They then complete the task in 10 minutes.

▶ Answers

1　C
2　G
3　B
4　E
5　D
6　A

4 Students look again at the missing paragraphs and explain the meaning of the phrasal verbs. They should add these phrasal verbs to their lists of *up* and *out* which they began in Unit 4.

▶ Answers

1　ends / finishes / stops
2　finished / closed down
3　developing / planning
4　came / arrived
5　dealt with / decided on
6　mailing / posting

5 Students discuss what they think about Dominic's job in pairs.

▶ Suggested phrases:

On the one hand ... / On the other hand ...

Talking positively ... / On the negative side ...

The advantage is ... / The disadvantage is ...

Optional activity

For working students, a brief written task could be set, where they evaluate the good and bad points of their own jobs using the phrases and vocabulary from this section. Students who are not yet working could do the above task for a job they would like to have.

Writing
Taking Time Out ▼

Introduction　　Student's Book p 94

1 Students discuss working abroad briefly as a class.

2 Ask whether any students have had a year out between school and university or are planning to. They then read the questions and take notes while they are listening.

▶ Answer

She took a year out to take the pressure off taking exams.

The year was not entirely a success as the job abroad didn't work out, but she didn't regret having a break in her education.

Tapescript

N = Narrator

N I left school last summer. I was au-pairing abroad for four months but it didn't work out and now I'm working in a café in London.

　　I'd always planned to take a year out. A lot of my friends ended up doing the same thing because of the grades – loads of them were forced into doing it, to re-take their exams.

　　I wanted to take a year out anyway, because it really took the pressure off the exams – you know, I thought, well, if I did muck everything up I could always do them again within that year. But then there's the big thing of what are you going to do if you *do* take a year out – you can't just stay at home.

　　So I went abroad, and even though I didn't stay there it was fun, apart from the age-old thing of au-pairing and being taken for granted. I was looking after this 14-month-old baby from about half past eight in the morning until half seven or eight at night – very long hours, constantly looking after him. And even though it wasn't in the contract, I used to do things for the mother – like going shopping for her – and she would then start suggesting I did other things, cleaning, ironing, and it became a bit much. It didn't work out as planned. If I'd been able to do something else out there, I would have stayed. I had friends I could have moved in with, but there was no employment so I had to leave.

　　I came back in November. I got a temporary job at the Royal Academy over the Christmas period, then I looked around and at the beginning of January this job came up. I'm really doing it because I need the money for next year.

　　I know when I get to university I'll hear of all these exotic things that people have been doing during their year out – like going trekking – and they'll ask me what did *you* do? – Oh, I worked in a café – big deal!

　　But I'd do the same again. Otherwise, you get locked in, swept along by it all. You've got to do exams, think about university, then you're there. It's good being able to slow down after exams and have a look at what you've done

---

and achieved. I think you need to sort out what you're doing. You've got to have some kind of plan.

Now it's difficult to get back into the cycle of studying. I can't concentrate like I used to, but it won't take long to get back into it ...

Writing

Understanding the task

1 a Students look at the three adverts on pages 94–95 and discuss them in pairs.

▶ **Answer**

New Future provides people with addresses of foreign firms looking for different kinds of employees, *Au pair in America* is for people aged 18–25 looking for a 12-month au-pair programme in the USA and the third advert is for a job guide to working on cruise ships.

Other information you would need is pay and conditions, timing and availability.

b Students read the whole task, including the friends' letter.

Selecting ideas

2 The content of letter **a** will depend on the advert they have chosen. Students should refer to the advert and the friends' advice, including the contractual conditions.

▶ **Answers**

New Future – further details about the jobs involved, as well as likely pay and conditions and what role this company has in providing a job.

Au pair in America – request an application form and ask for more information about length of stay, other exciting benefits, etc.

Cruise ships – request the free guide and ask for more information about pay, conditions and timing.

Letter b should include greetings and comments on the action taken, as well as giving the friends personal news.

Focusing on the reader

3 a Students suggest completions in relation to the advert they have chosen. Refer them to the Vocabulary Resource on page 195 for more ways of requesting information.

▶ **Answers**
- Introduction
  ... your advertisement in ...
  about jobs in ...
- Request for information
  ... further details as soon as possible.
  ... further details about your organization.

- Additional question
  ... how many hours work is involved each week.
  ... is required for the job.
  ... how this guide will help me to get a job.
- Ending
  ... you could reply as soon as possible.
  ... your help.

b Students list any informal expressions they can use.

▶ **Answers**

phrasal verbs: *cut down, come up with, slave away,* (noun: *burnout*)

contractions: *we're, we've, can't, We'd, you're*

ellipsis: *can't wait*

imperatives: *make sure, get, Keep us posted.*

informal punctuation: use of dashes and exclamation marks

abbreviated forms: *ads*

Planning your answer

4 Students use the plan given for letter a and develop a plan for letter b in pairs. Letter b should have at least three paragraphs.

▶ **Suggested answers**

Paragraph 1: Greetings and thanks

Paragraph 2: Which job and action taken

Paragraph 3: Personal news

Ending

5 Remind students to use the appropriate styles in each letter and to check the length of the two letters when they have finished.

Structure
The Rat Race ▼

Note

Rat race – a fiercely competitive struggle for power, especially to keep your position in work or life.

Introduction   Student's Book p 96

Ask students first to discuss the question in pairs before they prioritize the activities. They then compare their order with another pair, giving reasons for their decisions.

English in Use

A Discuss the title with the whole class.

▶ Suggested answer

The professional who quit the rat race / came back to life.

B Students complete the article on their own in 10 minutes.

▶ Answers

1 unless
2 been
3 to
4 of
5 until
6 had
7 than
8 them
9 from
10 There
11 what
12 too
13 all
14 that
15 out

Vocabulary

Students find the words or phrases in pairs.

▶ Answers

1 prestigious
2 menial
3 redundancy
4 throwing in the towel
5 quit
6 solicitor
7 resigning
8 drafting
9 resuming
10 the fast lane

Wishes and regrets   Student's Book p 97

Go through **A–C** with the whole class.

A

▶ Answers

1 (She) *wished she could have more contact with people.*
2 *Gillian doesn't regret resigning from the law firm.*
3 or (regret) *having less money.*
4 *'If only I'd done it* (resigned) *sooner'.*
5 *But I don't miss that* (drafting legal documents) *at all.*
6 *... she wishes she had had time to read* (all those books) *before.*

B

▶ Answers

1 d
2 b
3 a
4 c

C

▶ Answers

1 b and c
2 b and c
3 b and c
4 d
5 a and b

Miss

Ask students to work in pairs.

▶ Answers

1 the dry climate at home
2 having your own car / your family car
3 my friends and family
4 work or school or college during the holidays
5 home comforts, work, etc.
6 the mountains in your own country
7 the comfort of your own room and bed

Regret

A

▶ Suggested answers

1 You left your job then regretted it. The *-ing* form refers to something which happened before you began to have doubts about it. Often we use *having (done)* to express this meaning.
2 You are very sorry about having to tell someone this particular fact but you know how you feel before you say it. The infinitive refers to what you say *after* your expression of regret. This construction is only used with a few verbs which give information, eg *regret to say, to inform, to tell you* ... and is used in more formal contexts.

Rephrased sentences:
1 I regret (the fact) that I left my last job.
2 I regret (the fact) that (I have to tell you) she has left the firm.

B

▶ Answers

1 Peter regrets not putting / having put more effort into the work.
   ... (the fact) that he didn't put ...

2   I regret telling / having told her.
3   We regret to inform you that we are not able to deal
    with your enquiry.
    ... that we are not ...
4   Sally regrets making / having made that mistake.
    ... (the fact) that she made ...
5   I regret not showing / having shown more enthusiasm
    about your idea.
    ... (the fact) that I didn't show ...
6   I regret to say (that) we are unable to enter into any
    correspondence regarding the situation.
    ... that we are unable ...

Language activation

Biggest regrets

Students make a list of about 20 historical figures or famous
people, eg Cleopatra, Lenin, Elvis Presley, Napoleon. The
teacher puts a master list on the board. Students choose one
of the names each and imagine what that person's biggest
regret would be.

Wish

Elicit what is happening in the cartoon.

A   Students should read 1, 2 and 3 before matching
    a–e with them.

▶   Answers
    1   b and c
    2   d
    3   a and e

B

▶   Answers

    now – the simple past / past continuous / could

    the past – past perfect / past perfect continuous / could
    have (done)

    the future – would when we are talking about someone
    else

NB We do not say I / We wish I / we would; we use
could, or the simple past, eg spoke, didn't speak.

C   Students rephrase the sentences on their own and
    then compare their answers in pairs.

▶   Answers
    1   I wish I had had time ...
    2   I wish you wouldn't ask / you'd stop asking ...
    3   I wish I spoke / could speak better French.
        or I wish my spoken French were better.
    4   He wishes he were a million miles ...
    5   I wish John / John wishes he could find ...
    6   I wish I had been able to ...
    7   I wish you didn't have to ...
    8   I wish you 'd / would turn the volume down.

Language activation

Wishes

The teacher outlines the following situations to students
either by dictating them or by writing them on the board.
– live in a very small house
– go bankrupt
– put on weight
– buy an old car
– find it difficult to learn phrasal verbs
– feel very bad-tempered
In pairs, students imagine they are in these situations, add
two situations of their own, then express wishes about now
and the past for each one.

If only ...   Student's Book p 98

▶   Answers
    1   ... he had!
    2   ... she didn't / wouldn't!
    3   ... they would!
    4   ... I hadn't!
    5   ... I could!
    6   ... we were!

Language activation

Irritating habits

Students suggest one irritating habit they can't stand and the
teacher puts a master list on the board, eg untidiness,
cracking your knuckles, leaving the top off the toothpaste.
Students then comment on the irritating habit of someone
they know well, (preferably not a fellow-student!), making a
sentence with If only ... , eg If only Giovanni would tidy up
his room.

Practice

Students make sentences in pairs or for homework.

▶   Suggested answers
    1   I wish I'd gone on that holiday after all!
    2   If only I'd replaced the spare tyre months ago!
    3   He wishes he'd packed fewer things for the weekend.
    4   He wishes he could win the lottery.
    5   She misses her family.
    6   The man wishes he'd known how big the dog would
        grow.
    7   If only we'd arrived earlier!
    8   I wish he'd turn it off!

Going Places

8

Listening and Speaking
Travelling Hopefully ▼

Introduction   Student's Book p 99

1 Ask students to look at the four pictures and then play the tape once only.

▶ **Answers**

Speaker 1 = b   Speaker 3 = a
Speaker 2 = d   Speaker 4 = c

▶ **Suggested answers**

Speaker 1 feels enthusiastic.
Speaker 2 feels bored.
Speaker 3 feels annoyed.
Speaker 4 feels enthusiastic.

Tapescript

Speaker 1
One time when I went to China, my friend Evelyn was with me, and she was a bicycle enthusiast. We wanted to get to the outskirts of Beijing and explore the narrow winding streets. Evelyn rented a tandem, I sat behind, put my walking cane in my rucksack, and we went around Beijing like that.

We rode down quiet alleys, where we saw people mending shoes, selling fruit, talking to their neighbours. Once, we stopped to admire an old man's cane – it was beautifully carved and I showed him mine. We smiled and our eyes met – one of the rare moments in travel where differences melt in an instant.

Speaker 2
The standard, if boring, antidote is to wear loose clothes, remove shoes (take a shoe-horn – as your feet may swell), cat-nap during the journey, eat sparingly, and drink lots of water or fruit juice. Without doubt, this regime will get you to your journey's end in good shape. The trouble is that the sensations induced by hurtling along in a capsule six miles up in the air – euphoria, fear, boredom, excitement, gloom – are not really an incentive for going temporarily on the wagon. Pragmatically, the best advice in this area is to take it easy – bad jet lag is part hangover.

Speaker 3
Buses now sport little stickers asking other road users to let the bus go first. But bus drivers seem to think this is a God-given right and that if you crash into them, it's because you didn't do as their sticker demanded.

Moscow used to have special lanes for the rich and famous; here it's the poor and the old who are driven

around at top speed in traffic-free lanes. I have to sit for hours in a traffic jam at Hammersmith roundabout, while buses tear past, spewing diesel fumes. And who's on them? Well, during the rush hour, there is my wife, for one, but in office hours, they appear to be completely empty. They are not, of course; it is just that the driver's vigorous starts mean that everyone is on the floor.

Speaker 4
As Clive now had to leave for a few days on business, all real necessities were packed in my one backpack. The double load felt lighter than my previous single. My imagination, maybe. On the other hand, maybe I was getting in better shape. I was not however, going to weigh the pack as I had done at the beginning when a scale had made my shoulders droop even more by announcing the load to weigh 75 pounds!

I was constantly delayed by hills, by hospitable villagers who insisted I stop for a cup of tea and a chat; by friendly horses across hedges, who apparently decided we shared an affinity because of my burden, and often came right from the other end of their fields to observe me.

2 Students discuss the questions in pairs or small groups.

English in Use   Student's Book p 99

1 Discuss the four things which may have a negative effect on the environment taking care not to use the words *vandalism*, *accidental* and *indirect* which are necessary to complete the gaps in the text.

1   removing bits of coral reef
2   feet wearing away the Great Wall of China
3   too many tourists in the Ufizzi Gallery
4   infrastructure built to support tourism in Spain and Thailand

2 If your students need extra guidance with finding the correct form of the word, ask them to decide what part of speech is likely to be in each gap. They could do this task in pairs.

▶ **Answers**

(1) tourism   (2) vandalism   (3) accidental
(4) unpleasant   (5) indirect   (6) beauty
(7) environmental   (8) minimise

Listening   Student's Book p 100

1 Divide the class into pairs or groups of three and ask students to decide what might be said about each area.

▶ **Suggested answers**

cost: This was higher than originally predicted.

accidents: There is a possibility of fire which could be more difficult to deal with in a tunnel.

environment: The approach roads and railways will harm the local environment.

ferry services: These will be badly affected or put out of business.

rabies: This could be introduced into Britain by wild animals getting through the tunnel.

2 Refer students to the Exam tip on how to approach multiple-choice questions in the listening paper. Tell them that they will hear two people, a Mrs Jamieson and a Mr Ashton, being interviewed. Make sure that they read the questions only and not options A–D before they listen for the first time and emphasize the need to make a preliminary selection after the first listening.

3 Play the tape again and give the students a short time to make their final selection before asking them to compare their answers in pairs. If there is time, discuss why the alternative answers are not correct.

▶ **Answers**

1 D   2 D   3 C   4 C   5 B

Tapescript

> **I = Interviewer   J = Mrs Jamieson   A = Mr Ashton**
>
> I Hello and welcome once again to *Head to Head*. With me in the studio today are two people who have very different opinions of the Channel Tunnel. They are Mr Frank Ashton, who lives in London and works in Paris and who is a regular tunnel user, and er … Mrs Vanessa Jamieson, who comes from Cheriton, which I believe is the village where the tunnel actually begins, is that right?
>
> J Yes, that's right.
>
> I … and who has been a leading activist in the campaign against the tunnel. Mrs Jamieson, if I could start with you. The tunnel is already being used. You've lost the war. Why continue to fight?
>
> J The reason we haven't given up fighting is because we haven't lost the war. We started fighting when they were building the tunnel because it was disrupting our lives. We are fighting now because the tunnel is unsafe. It's unsafe –
>
> A Oh, that's rubbish!
>
> J … It's unsafe for the people who use it and it's unsafe for the people who live near it.
>
> I Hmm. Mr Ashton, doesn't Mrs Jamieson have a point? I mean, you're a regular user of the tunnel. Aren't you alarmed by all these rumours of safety problems?
>
> A Well, let me first say that I'm very sorry that some people were inconvenienced by the construction work. It was obviously –
>
> J Inconvenienced!
>
> A … It was a very difficult task to choose a route for the tunnel link because of course the whole of the south-east is so densely populated. Mrs Jamieson was one of the unlucky ones. But to say that the tunnel is unsafe simply isn't true. And what's more …
>
> J Of course it's unsafe! The truth of the matter is, and I'm sure Mr Ashton knows it, is that the operators were losing money because of all the delays during construction, so they missed out all the standard safety checks and opened the tunnel anyway. That's why there are still problems!
>
> A Mrs Jamieson really shouldn't believe everything she reads in the newspapers. The only …
>
> J I find your attitude very patronizing!
>
> A If I could finish …
>
> J It's *not* what I read in the newspapers!
>
> A If I could finish … The only problems have been very minor ones, small technical hitches, that sort of thing.
>
> I But what about all the newspaper reports, er … reports of changes in air pressure affecting people's ears, er … reports of leaks … there's a report here about how if there was a serious fire in one of the carriages, that … that the firemen wouldn't actually have enough room to deal with it. Can you really dismiss these as minor technical problems?
>
> A Well, I'm not an engineer. But let me say that as a passenger I feel perfectly safe.
>
> J Well, as someone who lives at the mouth of the tunnel on the English side I don't feel safe! It's a tunnel of death. There's nothing to stop a fox or a dog with rabies from getting into this country and causing an epidemic!
>
> A I'm sorry, but that's just silly! There's no rabies north of the River Seine in France, and even if some rabid superfox did manage to cross the Seine and travel one hundred miles to reach the tunnel, it would find a perimeter fence designed to stop burrowing animals such as foxes. It would also find poison, security cameras, security guards, electrified rails. And each tunnel – because there are three – is about thirty miles long. So, it really would have to be a superfox wouldn't it?
>
> J I'm sorry that Mr Ashton finds the idea of rabies entering this country so amusing. A fox could of course come into the country on a train.
>
> A Or on a ferry for that matter. But that's hardly a reason to close the tunnel!
>
> I I'm sorry, but that's all we have time for. I'd like to thank my guests, Frank Ashton and Vanessa Jamieson for going head to head! Next week, on *Head to Head* we'll be hearing from two people who just can't agree about …

Speaking   Student's Book p 101

Refer students to the Exam tip on Part 3.

> **Optional lead-in**
>
> Take a variety of travel brochures into the class and ask students to discuss the effectiveness of the selected pictures in encouraging people to choose the holidays.

1 Students select three pictures for the safari holiday before comparing their choice with another pair's. Encourage them to use some of the given words and phrases and refer them to the Vocabulary Resource on page 193 for ways of comparing and contrasting.

2 In the exam, there may be a ranking activity in which students are asked to select and order a group of objects, etc. for a particular purpose. Tell students that as there is no right answer, it is the way they justify their choices that is important. Check that students understand all the vocabulary before they begin. Give them no more than four minutes to complete this activity.

> **Optional activity**
>
> Students prepare a list of 10 things they would take on a different type of holiday such as a cruise or a cycling holiday. In pairs, students compare their lists and justify to each other why they would take their chosen items. They then decide on an agreed list of five items.

Reading
The Spirit of Adventure ▼

Introduction   Student's Book p 102

Students discuss the different activity holidays in pairs.

Reading

NB
In the examination, the multiple matching tasks will be based on the text as a whole and not on two distinct parts as in this case. The aim here is to break the task up into two manageable sections as this is the first time that students have come across a text with more than one multiple matching task.

1 Students read through the text quickly, underlining the different kinds of holidays.

▶ **Answers**

expeditions / excavating / nature conservation / teaching English / sailing and mountaineering / exchanges and homestays / learning Esperanto

Write the following words and phrases from the text on the board and check their meanings:

washing kit – soap, toothbrush, etc.

vaccination requirements – necessary injections

anti-malarial treatments – eg quinine

board and lodging – accommodation

swimming gear – costume, trunks

backpackers – travellers with rucksacks

2 Before attempting the matching task, students reread each numbered paragraph and summarize in their own words what each one is about. Give them about five minutes to complete the task. Ask the students to explain why the options which have not been selected are not feasible, eg *Minor ailments* would not be a suitable heading for paragraph 5 because *malaria* is also mentioned.

▶ **Answers**

1 H   2 D   3 C   4 E   5 B

3 Students work in pairs and spend about five minutes on this task.

▶ **Answers**

1 C   2 E   3 C   4 F   5 C   6 A   7 D

Style   Student's Book p 104

Either set this section for homework or ask your students to identify the information and do the matching activity in pairs.

▶ **Answers**

(3) *such a venture* refers back to the types of holiday mentioned in the preceding paragraph.

(7) The first phrase relates to the preceding paragraph: *Not for those of you who don't like exercise.*

(8) The statement refers back to the preceding two paragraphs on excavating and nature conservation holidays.

(11) The reference *another* is to the non profit-making Central Bureau in paragraph 8.

▶ **Answers**

2 b   4 d   9 a   10 c

Vocabulary Student's Book p 104

Ask students to work through 1–3 in pairs.

1

▶ Answers

take up (a) sport / a skill
develop self-confidence / photos
gain self-confidence / experience
make plans
take a holiday / photos
go on a holiday / an outing
go for a swim
do sport
take in surroundings

The following verbs can be used with more than one of the given nouns:
take up / develop / gain / take / go on

The following collocations are in the text:

take up a sport
develop self-confidence
gain experience
take photographs
take in your surroundings

2

▶ Answers

1   has gone for / has been going for
2   take
3   take / go on
4   gain / develop
5   take up (go in for is also possible)
6   went on
7   making
8   gained

Optional activity

Ask students to write their own sentences for the collocations in this vocabulary section for homework.

---

3   Listen to the pairs and make sure that they include some of the collocations in their discussion.

Writing
Travelogue ▼

Introduction Student's Book p 105

1   Ask students to refer to specific details in the pictures as they discuss the questions in small groups or as a class.

2   Students should give reasons for their choices.

Vocabulary

Students read the whole text before choosing the correct option. Discuss why the other options are not possible, eg in 2, the answer is *historical* because the monuments are connected to history; *historic* means significant in history, eg *an historic event.*

▶ Answers

1	foreigners	6	fewer
2	historical	7	trip
3	beaches	8	hire
4	Many	9	spend
5	friendly		

Writing Student's Book p 106

Refer students to the Exam tip on writing a tourist guidebook entry.

Sample descriptions

1   a   Ask students to look at the three descriptions quickly and decide on the source, purpose and target reader in pairs.

▶ Answers

A This is a personal account which could be from a short story or an account of someone's travel experiences. Its purpose is to entertain and it is aimed at the general reader.

B This is an extract from a guidebook and therefore its aim is to give information and make recommendations to tourists.

C This is part of an entry from an encyclopaedia. Its purpose is to give information and it is aimed at the general reader.

b   Ask students to focus on the main stylistic differences in the passages.

► **Answers**

A This passage is written in an informal style and is mainly the opinion of the writer. It uses narrative tenses and contains descriptive adjectives and phrasal verbs.

B This passage is more formal than passage **A**. It contains a mixture of opinion and fact with some recommendations. It uses conditional and present verb tenses as well as modals and contains descriptive adjectives.

C This passage is the most formal and factual. It uses present and past tenses and contains 'factual' adjectives.

Understanding the task

2 Students explain why the extract they chose is in the most appropriate style.

► **Answer**

Extract B

Optional activity

Ask students to find examples of texts in guidebooks and brochures and to compare them with the extract. In particular they should look at the content and vocabulary. This task could be set for homework.

Brainstorming ideas

3 Before they choose a town, draw the spider diagram on the board and ask the students to give some of the characteristics of the town where they are at the moment. Students can talk about the town they have chosen to their partner once they have brainstormed ideas. The students' task should take about 10 minutes in class or alternatively it can be set for homework.

Planning your answer

4 Refer students to the Vocabulary Resource on pages 194 and 195. Encourage students to use the framework as given. Ask them to complete the suggested phrases, for example:

• *Introduction*:
... why not take a trip to Bury St Edmunds, a bustling market town, a few miles east of Cambridge?
... Edinburgh, capital city of Scotland and an archaeological delight.
(Situated on the coast), at the mouth of the river Mersey, Liverpool is famous for its citizens rather than its buildings.

• *Paragraph three*:
... the Roman Fort situated on the outskirts of the town, close to the cathedral?
... punting down the river if the weather is good.
... the bustling shopping arcades in the city centre will give you ample opportunity to buy those last minute souvenirs.

• *Conclusion*:
... try the open-topped buses which tour the town and the surrounding countryside.
... take a guided tour of the city's ancient and fascinating sewers!

Writing

5 Refer the students to page 188 of the Writing Reference for another example of a guidebook entry.

Structure
Travellers' Tales ▼

Introduction   Student's Book p 108

Ask students to swap stories in pairs. If they prefer, they can talk about something that happened to someone they know.

Reading

Ask students to compare answers in pairs.

► **Answers**

1   A cargo ship.
2   He did not have enough money to travel to London so he decided to work his way there on a ship.
3   He had no desire to enter the freighting business (although he was once attracted by a scheme to buy up old freighters from bankrupt stock and turn them into pleasure palaces!)

Relative clauses   Student's Book p 109

Ask students to discuss the questions in **A** and **B** in pairs.

A

► **Answers**

Relative clauses describe nouns, or refer back, using a relative pronoun, to information already mentioned in the sentence.

1 is defining.
2 is non-defining.

1 means *only* the passengers who checked in early had a long wait; the others did not. The information is therefore needed to understand the full meaning of the main clause.

2 means that *all* the passengers checked in early and they

all had a long wait at the airport. The information is additional and is not needed to understand the full meaning of the main clause.

B

1

▶ Answers

a ... *stories which will bring you fame and fortune as a writer yourself.* (line 6)

b ... *people who join the crew.* (line 22)

c ... *Portugal, which was not on our route!* (line 48)

d ... *a dynamic Dane, who owned those ships in which tourists travel along the shores of Barbados.* (line 53)

2

▶ Answers

a and b are defining.

c and d are non-defining.

Meaning:

a answers the question: *Which stories?* ie only the type of stories which will bring you fame, etc; not all stories will do that.

b answers the question: *Which people?* ie only those who join the crew; not all people will do that.

c This is additional information about Portugal. It is not needed to define Portugal as nobody will ask *Which Portugal?*

d This gives additional information about the Dane, but it is not absolutely necessary to enable us to understand the sentence.

3

▶ Answers

You cannot use the relative pronoun *that* in non-defining clauses or after a preposition, eg *in which*.

4

▶ Answers

who is used for people.

which is used for things.

whose means 'belonging to whom' or 'of which'.

C Students first write their own sentences and then compare them with their partner's.

▶ Suggested answers

1 The fifty people who came on the trip thoroughly enjoyed it. (defining)
2 The Captain, whose name was Worthington / who was called Worthington, was a charming man. (non-defining)
   or The Captain, who was a very charming man, was called Worthington.

3 The sea-crossing, which took several weeks, was rough. (non-defining)
   or The sea-crossing, which was rough, took several weeks.
4 The students who had a young person's railcard paid considerably less for their tickets. (defining)
   or The students who paid considerably less for their tickets had a young person's railcard. (although this answer is less likely)
5 Mr and Mrs Evans, who had made an unscheduled overnight stop in Cairo, boarded the boat there / in Egypt. (non-defining)
   or Mr and Mrs Evans, who boarded the boat in Cairo, had made an unscheduled overnight stop there.

You could substitute *that* in defining clauses but not in non-defining clauses, eg in 1, The fifty people *that* came .... and in 4, The students *that* had ... / paid ...

You could not omit the relative pronoun in these sentences as it is the subject of the verb which follows. The relative pronoun is however quite commonly omitted when it is the object of the verb which follows, eg *The man (who / whom / that) I spoke to on the telephone was very angry.*

Language activation

Being explicit about likes and dislikes
Students think of two things they really like and dislike, eg going to restaurants, dancing, reading, standing in queues. They then in small groups ask each other to be more specific,
eg *Yes, but what sort / kind of restaurants, dancing, queues, etc. do you like / not like?*
Students should reply giving extra information,
eg *The kind of restaurants / dancing that / which ... serve good food / helps me relax / keep you waiting for hours.*

Noun clauses   Student's Book p 109

Ask students to do **A–C** in pairs or groups of three.

A

▶ Answers

Noun clauses:

... *think that ... your fellow travellers will confide stories* (noun clause object of the verb *think*)

 ... *that a cabin on a cargo ship is more expensive than one on the QE2, and (that) your voyage could last a couple of months or more.*

(2 noun clause objects of the verb *is*)

 What you soon discover ... is (noun clause subject of the verb *is*)

B

▶ Answers

Other examples of noun clauses:

1 ... *that everybody should have dinner on board the first evening of entering port, rather than go ashore.* (line 19)
2 ... *that he would never carry cargo, nor sell the ships for scrap.* (line 58)
3 ... *that he would redesign the super-structure, do them up and anchor them ... all around the Gulf of Mexico as floating fun palaces!* (line 60)

These noun clauses are the objects of the main verb.

C

▶ Suggested answers

1 What you said made sense. (subject of *made*)
2 What you did wasn't very sensible. (subject of *wasn't*)
3 He suggested that I became / should become an associate member of the company. (object of *suggested*)
4 I agreed with what she said. (object of *agreed*) / What she said I agreed with. (subject of *agreed*)
5 He explained that he wanted to take me on a world cruise. (object of *explained*)
6 What we discovered was (that) they had tried to deceive us! (subject of *was*)
   or We discovered that they had tried to deceive us. (object of *discovered*)

Adverb clauses

Ask students to do **A–C** in pairs or groups of three.

A

▶ Answers

Adverb clauses make a piece of writing more interesting because they tell us under what circumstances, when, why, or how something happens.

B

▶ Answers

1 b 2 c 3 d 4 a 5 e 6 h 7 f 8 g

Other examples of adverb clauses from the text:

b time:
When I was a teenager,
... *while* incoming waves threatened to deliver the cans of stew straight into the sea below.
before we sailed,
after I'd spent a day with a dynamic Dane,

e reason:
and partly *because* we made an unscheduled stop in a Brazilian port
as our numbers were made up by two stowaways wanting to go and work in Portugal ...

f concession:
although I was tempted
Though the project intrigued me ...

C

▶ Suggested answers

1e *Despite the fact that James is very rich and successful, he isn't happy.* (concession)
2g *Tony went abroad so that he could find a job.* (purpose)
3f *The homework is so difficult that I can't do it.* (result)
4b *I bought the dictionary because I needed it.* (reason)
5d *When I get home, I will phone you.* (time)
6a *If I have time, I'll do the homework.* (condition)
7c *John was walking strangely as if he'd hurt his leg.* (manner)
8i *While I was going home, I met Martha.* (time)
9h *They set up the tent where the ground looked flat.* (place)

Language activation

Tell me more!
Students write nine sentences giving more information about a job or task they have or had to do using each type of adverbial clause, then compare their sentences with a partner's.

Practice Student's Book p 110

Ask students to write the mini-article in groups of three.

▶ Suggested answers

1 What you discover is that it's more expensive than a plane ticket!
2 What you'll find out next is that your fellow travellers are not your type.
3 Some of them are so frightened that they seem to be ready to jump out of the basket!
4 Although the 90-minute trip was interesting, I prefer to have my feet firmly on the ground.
5 After we arrived back safely, the passengers, whose names I can't mention, were so relieved that they all disappeared for a drink in the club house.

Rites and Rituals

Reading
Rooting for Tradition ▼

Optional lead-in

Ask the students what they understand by the expression *Rooting for Tradition*. It means supporting traditional beliefs and behaviour and also refers to one's roots, ie family ties. Encourage them to look up the different meanings of *root* in a dictionary.

Introduction   Student's Book p 111

1 Ask the students to read the poem and in pairs discuss what it is about and whether they feel sympathetic towards the poet's point of view.

▶ **Suggested answer**

The poem expresses the feelings of a refugee or immigrant who has no roots.

Students say which lines in particular show that the writer is an immigrant or refugee, eg *As nowhere do we belong / Who shall we fight for? / Will we ever be free / To belong?*

Elicit the meaning of … *carrying / Our ancestors' coffins in a bag* (They have no place which feels like their own territory to bury them.) Finally, ask students how the poem relates to the title of the section.

2 Encourage the students to be specific about what they would miss and why, eg if they mention food, they should elaborate by saying what dishes they would miss.

Reading

1 Ask students to time themselves as they read the article and compare the difficulties they found in pairs.

Notes

Gujarati – a language spoken in the West of India, North of Bombay.

plastic – the speaker means she felt her life was not worth much.

the 80s, the decade of conservative values – a period when the Conservative party was in power and advocated a return to traditional values.

▶ **Suggested answers**

– differing expectations between their own and the host culture

– feeling ashamed of their background

– different customs

– feeling rejected by the host community

– not feeling comfortable with the host community or their own culture

2 Refer students to the Exam tip on matching sections to topics. Ask them to complete the task in about 10 minutes in pairs and then compare their answers with another pair's.

▶ **Answers**

    1   D
    2   G
    3   H (any order)
    4   F
    5   H
    6   A
    7   B
    8   C (any order)
    9   B
    10 E (any order)

3 Ask students to discuss these questions in groups of three and then to compare their views with the rest of the class.

▶ **Answers**

Views and attitudes to western life:

– It is superficial (*I felt such a plastic person*)

– Asians had to accept the host culture's values and reject their own in order to be accepted. (*To be part of the brave new modern world you had to cast off these people who were 'backward' and 'uncivilised'.*)

– Relationships are more like a game. (*English friends who want to be liked by boys are prisoners of love games.*)

– It is more important to be romantically in love than to respect your partner. (*With romance, you start at the top and come down. We have to work up to love. You then treat it with some respect.*)

– Getting old means losing the respect of the community as you no longer earn or produce anything. (*to get old is to gain respect – not to lose it as in this utilitarian society*)

– It has no respect for other cultures and their customs. (*his culture is denigrated*)

Vocabulary   Student's Book p 112

1 Students find 1–6 in the article before checking their answers in a dictionary.

▶ **Answers**

The forceful language helps to convince the reader of the views held and the strength of the arguments.

1 bitterly
2 destroyed (emotionally)
3 strongly devoted
4 made worse
5 criticized / put down
6 misshapen

2 Ask students to do the matching task in pairs.

▶ **Answers**

1 e   2 c   3 b   4 a   5 f   6 d

3

▶ **Answers**

1 indifferent	5 devastated
2 amicably	6 exacerbated
3 passionate	7 distorted
4 acclaimed	8 delighted

Style

Ask the students to find the features mentioned in pairs.

▶ **Answers**

Paragraph B:
– further details of Naima's shopping trip
– the writer's view that Naima's experience is evidence of a change in Asians' attitude to their identity.

Paragraph C:
– the writer's view on Asians rethinking their identity
– an example from the writer's experience to stress this.

Paragraph D:
– Amina's views on love and marriage
– Her views are quoted.

Paragraph E:
– Kamla Jalota's view of family life is quoted
– an example of her own family to illustrate this
– the writer's view on the development of attitudes to family life amongst Asians.

Paragraph F:
– the writer's view on the reasons for this change
– Jafar Kareem's views on the advantages and disadvantages of this change are quoted.

Paragraph G:
– Kareem's views on the effect of a hostile community on Asian children are quoted.

Paragraph H:
– Arvind Sharma's views on Asian children's experiences at school are quoted.

The article is typical of a journalistic style in which description and example is followed by the writer's views and then supported by further examples or the views of others.

Optional activity

Discuss with the class what would be the most constructive way for them to feel at home in a foreign country. Students write a short paragraph in which they summarize their views and explain how they would retain the best of their traditions while continuing to assimilate into their new surroundings.

Listening and Speaking
Manners Maketh Man? ▼

The title of this section is an old-fashioned saying which means that politeness is a true indication of a person's character.

Introduction   Student's Book p 114

1 Ask students to read the story quickly.

Notes

canvassing – getting political support for
'votes is votes' – a phrase which implies that any vote is worth having.
a cuppa – a cup of tea (slang)
mutt – dog (slang)

2 Discuss the questions with the class. Elicit the difference in meaning between *politeness* (correct forms of behaviour) and *courtesy* (making other people feel comfortable) and give examples of both.

▶ **Suggested answer**

The tale is a cautionary one as it suggests that misunderstandings can happen when you are trying to be (excessively) polite. Encourage students to relate the story to their own experiences.

Speaking   Student's Book p 115

1 Students discuss the questions in pairs and then compare their answers with the rest of the class. Make a list of the different kinds of behaviour on the board and then discuss the effect they have on other people.

2 Tell students that the situations are adapted from a series of books which are aimed at travellers who want to limit the number of social 'gaffes' or mistakes they make when interacting with the local population.

There are no absolutely correct answers for the different situations. Refer them to the two suggested stages for effective interaction in Part 3 of the speaking test.

3 Refer students to the key on page 196 and then discuss the follow-up questions as a class.

> **Optional activity**
>
> Students think of their own situations with three possible ways of behaving. They then swap their situations with others in the class.

Vocabulary   Student's Book p 116

1 Ask students to write example sentences to show how the pairs of words differ in meaning.

▶ **Answers**

gentle – not rough, eg *He is a very gentle dog so I don't mind the children playing with him.*

polite – well-mannered, eg *Tom is a polite young man and always asks how I am.*

customs – traditions, eg *One of the customs in England is to have a roast dinner on Sundays.*

habits – frequent repetition of the same act, eg *My mother has this habit of asking me to lunch when she knows I have another arrangement.*

ashamed – disgraced, humiliated, eg *My son is ashamed of our old car. He wants a Porsche!*

embarrassed – self-conscious / uncomfortable, eg *Edward was embarrassed when he realized he was the only man wearing a suit to the party.*

birthday – the day on which a person was born, eg *My birthday is on the 10th June.*

anniversary – any event commemorated annually, eg *1995 was the tenth anniversary of the Live Aid concert.*

nervous – agitated, eg *I get very nervous before an exam.*

irritable – easily annoyed, eg *Jane was feeling irritable and snapped at the children when they asked to go out to play.*

dependent – (adj) needing support from, eg *No allowance was made for Alex's dependent relatives in assessing his financial needs.*

dependant (noun) – a person who depends on another for support, eg *Alex and all his dependants were allowed to settle in Australia.*

discussion – formal conversation, eg *During the meal there was a heated discussion about who would win the women's final at Wimbledon.*

quarrel – argument, eg *The two friends had a quarrel a year ago and still haven't made it up.*

2

▶ **Answers**

1	polite	5	birthday
2	ashamed	6	discussion
3	dependent	7	nervous
4	customs		

Listening   Student's Book p 117

1 Remind students that it is important to identify the speakers in order to achieve the task. They will hear the recording twice.

▶ **Answers**

1 M   2 B   3 N   4 M   5 M   6 M   7 M
8 M, B   9 B   10 B

2 Students discuss the two questions in groups of three or four before comparing their views with other groups.

Tapescript

> **P = Presenter; M = May Parnell; B = Mr Brownlow**
> **P** Today on *Viewpoints* we're going to be discussing something that affects us all – the manners and behaviour of today's youth. Here with me in the studio is May Parnell, a teacher, from East London. May, you're fresh from the classroom, what are your experiences?
> **M** Hello, John. Well, I happen to believe that most young people are well-behaved and polite, but we do tend to get carried away with what they look like and the language they use.
> **P** You mean they sound rude and look terrible but they're all right really?
> **M** Not exactly – they look different because they have their own fashions and hairstyles, but perhaps more importantly they use different words and expressions.
> **P** Such as?

M My pupils, for example, come out with such things as 'All right, Miss, like what we're doing today?' – which sounds very casual to us but they feel entirely natural saying it and I know they're not being rude …

P Let me bring in Geoffrey Brownlow who is waiting on the line. Mr Brownlow, I believe, er, you were in the army until quite recently, do you have a problem understanding the youth of today?

B No, I think I understand them very well and I think *they* have to understand that we all need to be more sensitive to others. That includes young people talking to us in a way that shows respect for people, and that they acknowledge that older people need to be spoken to in a different way from the way they go on to their friends. Also, why should they think it's acceptable to wear torn, dirty clothes when those around them are doing their best to look clean and tidy, probably with far less money. It's just not on.

P Well, I'm not sure that using your own language code and wearing a particular style of clothes is showing disrespect – what do you think, May?

M No, no, of course not. I believe that generations should respect each other and that includes tolerating differences. I don't expect my children to dress like me or sound like me – nor do they, I'm sure – but this doesn't mean they don't respect me fundamentally. Anyway, I have a sneaking feeling that the sort of way-out clothes some of them wear show how creative they are, even if they haven't much to spend on clothes.

P Yeah, and going back to what you were saying about respect, respect is earned, it's not a right. Adults perhaps need to behave in a manner that makes the young … ?

M You took the words right out of my mouth. Some adults should be ashamed of how they act in front of the younger generation. You know what I mean – getting drunk, swearing and so on.

B … If I can come back in here. It seems to me that society has lost its way. There are so many children today who care more about what they can get out of life rather than what they can put into it.

P You mean, Mr Brownlow, that you think the young are more impressed by what people own than by what kind of person they are? Well, yes, yes, I have some sympathy with that view. How about you, May?

M Well, Mr Brownlow has a point there. And if I can go back to the original point of this discussion, people, not just young people, are less polite than they used to be. It comes of living in a more urban world. There's less need to be courteous to someone you don't know or may never see again.

B Well, if you ask me, too many people and especially youngsters think that they can do what they like, whether it's dressing badly or speaking badly or worse …

M Oh, I think you have a very depressing view of society, Mr Brownlow.

B Well, let's look at what they get up to. All those cigarettes they smoke, all that junk food they eat and dressing in that ridiculous fashion. What a way to carry on …

P Thank you, Mr Brownlow. I'd like to extend the discussion to bring in Jane Webber of Carshalton who has been involved with young people for many years …

Writing
Celebrations ▼

Introduction   Student's Book p 118

> **Optional lead-in**
>
> Ask students on what occasions presents are given or exchanged. Are they always opened in front of the giver?

1 Students listen to the tape and note down the presents that the three people mention and their reactions.

Notes
Chrissie – Christmas (slang)
Post Office Tower – one of the tallest buildings in London
a full Chelsea strip – a replica of the outfit worn by a member of the Chelsea football team.

▶ **Answers**

1 Steve's mother received the same bottle of perfume that she had given to her sister the previous Christmas. His mother pretended she had always wanted it to avoid an argument.

2 Annie's brother gave her a framed postcard of the Post Office Tower, which was also cracked. She thought it was appalling and threw it back at him.

3 James's uncle in Australia gave him a childish board game. He felt insulted.

Tapescript

P = Presenter; S = Steve; A = Annie; J = James
P … Okay, it's 10 am on Saturday the 28th of December and we're going to take calls this morning on Christmas presents. How many of you have just been given some truly awful present? Something you don't need, or the ultimate in bad taste, or something just so mean that you can't believe that it came from someone you know? Phone us now – there are six CDs to be sent out to the best callers on this subject this morning … Yes … who's that?

S Morning, Terry. It's Steve.
P Okay, Steve, what've you got for us?
S Well, it's my aunt. She's got a reputation in our family for being really stingy at Christmas. But this year she excelled herself. She gave my Mum the bottle of perfume that Mum had given her last year – in the same wrapping paper too.
P Can you believe it? And how did the lucky recipient, your Mum, take this, Steve?
S Well it could've sparked off a row – her face went kind of puce, but she didn't want to upset her sister, so she

pretended it was what she'd always wanted, you know the kind of thing.

P Too well, too well. I think you need to give that aunt of yours some of her own medicine. How about sending the perfume back to her again next year, Steve? Then she might get the message. Okay, thanks for your call. We've got Annie on hold – Annie, what particular Chrissie offering do you want to share with us?

A Well, my kid brother handed me this daintily wrapped box on Christmas morning …

P So far, so good. My brother never even bothers to wrap up my present!

A Yes, but wait till you hear what was in the box! I opened it up and it was a framed postcard of the Post Office Tower *and* the glass was cracked! Really appalling – I suppose it was a joke but I was so angry, I just chucked it back at him. I'd made a real effort to get the ideal present for him – a full Chelsea strip – and it wasn't cheap. He completely spoiled the day, I can tell you. And things are still pretty difficult between us.

P Sorry to hear that, Annie. I'm gonna send you your favourite CD to make up for it, okay? And don't be too hard on the kid. Okay, next caller – John, isn't it?

J James, actually.

P My mistake – James, what did Santa bring you then?

J I've got this uncle in Australia who is really out of touch with our family. I mean, he must think I'm still at Primary School or something.

P Sounds ominous on the present front. And what did this uncle send you, James? How old are you, by the way?

J Fifteen. Well, he sent me this horrendous board game called *Chase Bunny*.

P Oh dear. Not your scene, eh?

J Not at all. It's an insult – I feel really sore about it. And when I think what he could've sent me from Australia …

P But he didn't, did he? Well, you get back to chasing bunny round the board, James – and I'll send you a CD to heal your broken heart. Okay? …

2 In groups of three, students discuss the question. Encourage them to say what they think may have been meant by this particular present.

English in Use

1 Check that the students know the meaning of the following words and phrases before they read the article:

fraught – full

digs – rented accommodation, usually a bedroom and sitting room combined ('bed-sit')

▶ Answer

The writer feels that giving or finding presents can be very difficult but that it is possible if you are careful and you feel some affection for the recipient.

2 Ask the students to reread the article more carefully and complete the task in 10 minutes.

▶ Answers

1 G   2 E   3 I   4 D   5 B   6 H

Ask the students whether they agree with the views expressed in the article. If there is time, discuss with the students why the remaining phrases do not fit.

Vocabulary   Student's Book p 119

Ask if students know the meaning of any of the phrasal verbs before they complete 1–8.

spark off – cause or begin (an argument, etc.)

put down – make someone feel inferior

pass off – pretend to be (someone)

go off – ignite / leave

break off – end something

put off – postpone

pass down – leave something as a gift (to the next generation) after one's death

go down (well) – be (greatly) appreciated

break down – collapse (emotionally) / have a mechanical failure

▶ Answers

1	put off	5	to break off
2	to break down	6	went off
3	putting (people) down	7	has been passed down
4	passing (himself) off	8	went down

> **Optional activity**
>
> Divide the class into small groups. Give one of the verbs above (put / break / pass / go) to each group and ask them to make as many *phrasal* verbs as possible. Write these on the board. Each group then chooses six of the phrasal verbs and produces a valid sentence to show they understand the meaning. This can be done as a quiz with groups competing against each other in 10 to 15 minutes.

Writing   Student's book p 119

Sample article

1 a   Students discuss the titles in pairs.

▶ Answer

Differences in the weddings of two countries

b   Students discuss the organization of the article.

▶ Answer

The article is paragraphed unevenly and broken up at inappropriate places.

Paragraph 1: Personal view + Greek weddings described
Paragraph 2: Description of the ceremony continued
Paragraph 3: Description continued + additional
             information
Paragraph 4: Description of a British wedding
Paragraph 5: Description continued + personal view

Suggested improvements:
Join the first three 'paragraphs' as they are all about Greek weddings. End the new first paragraph after *it's all very relaxed and informal*.
Join 'paragraphs' 4 and 5 apart from the last two sentences.
The new third and final paragraph begins *So there you have it*.

Understanding the task

2 Ask students to read the writing task carefully and discuss the style and register.

▶ **Answer**
Chatty and informal.

Encourage students to give reasons for selecting this register, eg the youthful audience, the personal nature of the topic, the informal description of the task.

Brainstorming ideas

3 a   Students tell each other about two of their birthdays.
b   When they have finished comparing, ask them to tell the rest of the class about some of the differences they found.

Planning your answer

4 Students look for the phrases in pairs. Elicit other useful phrases from the class and write them on the board.

▶ **Answers**

• introduce the topic
It has to be said that our wedding ceremonies ...
If you have ever ... you will know that the giving and receiving ...

• give examples
For instance
For example

• introducing contrasting information
On the other hand
although
however
But ...

• introduce a conclusion
So there you have it (informal)

▶ **Suggested plan**
Paragraph 1: Introduction
Paragraphs 2, 3: Description of the celebrations with examples
Paragraph 4: Conclusion + final sentence to explain why their birthday is more or less special than their friend's.

Writing

5 Students should spend about 45 minutes writing the article and then check their work thoroughly.

Structure
No Excuses ▼

Introduction   Student's Book p 121

Students discuss the options in groups of three before answering the follow-up question.

A Students time themselves as they read and think of an appropriate title.

Note
The original title was *On the infinite variety of lateness*.

B Students choose any three of the list.

▶ **Answers**
1   glancing at their watches
2   leaping in and out of taxis
3   throwing notes for the fare
4   dodging people on the street
5   jumping in puddles
6   weaving through the traffic
7   bursting into restaurants
8   hovering nervously in lobbies and entrance halls
9   creeping along rows in cinemas and theatres

Present perfect vs simple past

Student's Book p 122

Discuss the differences between the two tenses with the class as a whole.

▶ **Answers**
The simple past is used to refer to a single action, now finished, which happened at a definite time in the past. Although it is not always necessary to mention the time, the reference in the mind of the speaker is clear, ie he knows when he was born!

The present perfect is used to refer to something which started in the past, and is still continuing now.

Language activation

Experiences

In small groups, students talk about different experiences, asking each other initial questions in the present perfect and follow-up questions in the simple past,

eg *Have you ever ... ?*
No, never! / Yes, I have.
When, where, why did you ... ?

Suggested topic areas:
– food
– entertainment
– travel
– work
– awkward moments
– accidents
– sporting activities

Language activation

Great Inventions

The teacher writes the following information on the board but leaves out the dates. Students have to discuss when these things were invented.

Inventions

Artificial satellite (1957)
A printing press with movable type (1438)
The Atomic Bomb (1945)
The airship (1852)
The ballpoint pen or biro (1940)
The telephone (1876)
Morse Code (1832)
Artificial limbs (1560)

When students have decided on the dates, they then discuss which invention has been the most and the least useful.

Present perfect simple vs continuous

Ask students to discuss the questions in **A** and **B** in pairs.

A

▶ Answer

2 sounds more natural, as it emphasizes the length of time the action has been going on, and the fact that the speaker is probably still trying to fix it but with no success!

B

▶ Answers

a 8
b 1, 2, 3, 4, 5, 10, 11
c 9, 10, 11
d 8, 9, 10, 12
e 7, 8, 9
f 1

For and since

A

▶ Answers

for is used to emphasize how long something lasts, eg *for a year*, *for months on end* and is followed by a reference to a period of time.

since is used to indicate when the action began and suggests that it is still going on, eg *I've been here since 1992*, *since 2 o'clock* (and I'm still here). It is followed by a reference to a single point in time.

for is not used in expressions of time using *all*, eg *all day*, *all night*.

B Students expand the notes on their own.

▶ Suggested answers

1 I've been standing in this queue for 20 minutes.
2 Mark has been working in this office since 1989.
3 We've been studying English for 3 years.
4 We've been discussing this matter since the meeting began.
5 I've been writing addresses on these envelopes since six o'clock.
6 We've been waiting to see the new house for a very long time.

C Students complete 1–12 in pairs. This exercise can also be set for homework.

▶ Answers

1 haven't seen / *for*
2 is **or** has been / *since*
3 has been / –
4 has been / *for*
5 has not been getting / *since*
6 has been applying / *(ever)* since
7 have you been doing / *since*
8 have been threatening / *for*
9 has been working / –
10 have been screaming / *(ever) since*
11 has been spending / it *ever since*
12 have been wondering / *for* / has become

In 11 you have to use *ever since* because it comes at the end of the sentence.

Language activation

Lottery Winner

Ask students to imagine that a friend of theirs has won a huge sum of money on the national lottery and to think of four things their friend has done / been doing since the big win. They then compare their ideas with a partner's.

Long

▶ **Answers**

We could insert *long* in 1 and 2. It could not be used in 3 as it is only used in modern English in the negative and interrogative. You could use 'for a long time' in 3 instead. In the positive form, it is usually only used in a more formal context, eg *Historians have long realized that ...*

1   I haven't been here *long*.
2   Have you been here *long*?
3   I have been here *for a long time*.

Yet and still   Student's Book p 123

A

▶ **Answer**

He still hasn't finished!

B

▶ **Answers**

1
My husband still hasn't booked a table for dinner on Saturday night.
My husband hasn't booked a table for dinner on Saturday night yet.
My husband has yet to book a table for dinner on Saturday.
NB The third construction can also be used in 2, 3, 5, 7 and 8.

2
The children still haven't told us their plans for the weekend.
The children haven't told us their plans for the weekend yet.

3
The employment agency still hasn't contacted me.
The employment agency hasn't contacted me yet.

4
Has the post still not come?
Hasn't the post come yet?

5
I still haven't told you the best part of the story.
I haven't told you the best part of the story yet.

6
Has your sister still not started her new job at the Central Hospital?
Hasn't your sister started her new job at the Central Hospital yet?

7
The committee still hasn't decided on a possible course of action.
The committee hasn't decided on a possible course of action yet.

8
The police still haven't made the news of the arrest public.
The police haven't made the news of the arrest public yet.

Future perfect simple and continuous

A

▶ **Answers**

In 1, the tense is used to talk about something which will have been completed or finished *by* or *before* a certain time in the future, ie you could call this a 'past in the future'.

In 2, the tense is used to emphasize the length of time the action lasted and to state that the action is still going on and will continue to do so in the future.

In 3, instead of saying 'I'm sure this is something you have done', the writer uses the tense to talk about something which he is fairly certain will have been completed or finished before a certain time in the past, ie you could call this a 'future in the past'.

B   Tell students that they will need to use a passive form in one of the sentences.

▶ **Answers**

1   won't have come (3)
2   will have been working (2)
3   Will the coach have reached (1)
4   won't have organized (3)
5   won't have finished / will (1)
6   will / 'll have been married (1)
7   won't have organized (3)
8   will have finished (1)
9   will have realized (3)
10 will / 'll have been writing (2)

Language activation

Future activities and achievements
Put a list of future times on the board, eg
– by tonight
– by the end of the week
– by the end of next year
– in two years' time
– in five years' time
Students imagine what they will be doing or will have done and make sentences using the future continuous or the future perfect and the times on the list.

Talking about someone else

Ask students to prepare this talk for homework. They can then tell their partner about the person they have chosen in the following lesson.

Who Cares ?

Reading
The Care Label ▼

Introduction   Student's Book p 124

Divide the class into three or six groups, depending on the class size, and give one of the views to each group. After 10 minutes, regroup the students according to the view they discussed. Students then compare their opinions.

Reading

1 Ask students to read the article quickly and then discuss the meaning of *fashion compassion* in pairs.

▶ **Suggested answer**

It is fashionable for celebrities such as super models and rock stars to become involved in charitable causes. Like fashion they are highly visible and possibly superficial.

Notes

Feed the Children – a registered charity
foster children – children cared for by 'substitute' parents
sound bites – short excerpts from a speech, etc. suitable for TV reports

2 Ask students to complete the task on their own in 10 minutes.

▶ **Answers**

   1 B   2 C   3 E   4 A   5 D   6 F

3

▶ **Answers**

   1B *hotel, Bianca Jagger, the UN*
   2C *both these women, Bianca Jagger*
   3E *all these women, they can jet*
   4A *But the women, Sting*
   5D *All this ... , Charities large and small ...*
   6F *By all accounts ...* (gives another example of the negative impact of fashion)

4

▶ **Answer**

Paragraph G will not fit into gaps 1–5 because it introduces an unrelated way in which a charity could raise its profile. It will not fit into gap 6 as it introduces a positive rather than a negative aspect of charity.

5 Students discuss the meanings of the phrases in pairs or groups of three.

▶ **Suggested answers**

   1 were very expensive / hard to get
   2 invented the phrase 'compassion fatigue'
   3 to give the women credit for their work (look up *due*)
   4 and there are huge numbers of them (look up *legion*)
   5 All this may sound like unfair criticism (look up *carping*)
   6 appropriately dressed in fashionable 'army uniforms' (look up *togged up* and *chic*)
   7 walking heavily / with effort down a lane (look up *trudging*)
   8 by such well-known experts (look up *luminaries*)

Style   Student's Book p 126

1 Ask the class to give reasons for their answer.

▶ **Answer**

   a

2 Students discuss the sentences in groups of three.

▶ **Suggested answers**

   1 There is a suggestion that it is inappropriate for a model to visit a disaster site for what could be seen as a 'fashion shoot' for African-style dress.
   2 The suggestion is that Iman's visit is more about how she looks in the setting of Africa and that her soulful expression may just be an act for the camera.
   3 The wealthy women who visit the disaster areas of the world today are compared directly with the *Ladies Bountiful* of former times who also gave to the poor and in a similar way were rewarded for their charitable efforts. They also look good in the photographs which are taken of them in 'caring' poses.

3 Discuss the question with the whole class. Consider the two main conflicting points of view expressed by the writer, ie it is useful to have famous people working for charities as more people will take an interest and donate money, etc.

Famous people get involved because it gives them good publicity and this is not appropriate in the context of human tragedies.

Writing
Cruelty or Conservation? ▼

Introduction Student's Book p 127

1 Ask students for their reactions to the photograph before they complete the questionnaire.

2 Students discuss the pros and cons of abolishing zoos. This activity prepares the students for the writing task that follows.

Writing

Understanding the task

1 Ask students to read the task and the extracts quickly. Explain any vocabulary items they do not know.

▶ Answer
The council, the letter writer

Selecting ideas

2 a Students should underline the negative language and the relative points.

▶ Answers
Friend's letter:
depressing working here as the animals are miserable and the cages are too small.
None of the animals are very healthy
Erol is in a bad way ...
The latest disaster ... the building of the new aquarium

Article:
(The zoo provides) *hours of pleasure*
(Erol is) *still going strong*

Advertisement:
Take a ride on Erol our friendly elephant
Visit the new aquarium

b Students work in pairs and make a list of other points in the article they would like to address. Refer them to the appropriate sections of the Vocabulary Resource on pages 193 and 195.

c Remind them that they will lose marks if they copy whole phrases from the input material.

d Stress that although they are allowed to include some points of their own, they must make sure that they have first addressed the relevant points in the article, etc. Even if they are against the closure of zoos in general, they must support the closure of this zoo.

Focusing on the reader

3 Ask students to think of possible opening phrases.

▶ Suggested answers
Dear Sir
I read an article in your newspaper recently in which you suggest that it would be a shame to close down Barbarham zoo as it has given so much pleasure to people over the years. However, I would like to point out ...
Dear Sir
I am writing with regard to ... / With reference to your recent article

Planning your answer

4 Students discuss points a–c and then study the sample letter in the Writing Reference, selecting any phrases which might be appropriate for the task. Refer them to the relevant section of the Vocabulary Resource on pages 193 and 195.

5 Advise students to spend no more than 45 minutes on this.

His talent for writing led him at the age of fifteen to become a reporter in the House of Commons. It was here that his genius for describing comical characters, and his anger over social injustice were noticed by MPs and the general public. In 1838, he began publishing the *Pickwick Papers* in weekly instalments and by the age of twenty-six, Charles was famous in Britain and the United States. In fact, Dickens went on to write such powerful stories that Parliament passed laws to stop the various scandals he depicted so vividly. For example, some of the cruel boarding schools he described were forced to close down after such bad publicity.

Charles had a wonderful gift for creating larger than life characters, many of whom were based on the people he knew. In particular, the unreliable Mr Micawber in *David Copperfield* was apparently modelled on his own father. When, in 1870, he died from a stroke at the age of fifty-eight, he was mourned all over the world.

Listening and Speaking
Are you a Good Citizen? ▼

Introduction   Student's Book p 130

Students discuss the questions in their groups and then tell the class which two problems they would try to solve.

Listening

1 Ask students to tell you what they know about Charles Dickens. Students then read the gapped sentences quickly and consider the type of words which might fill the gaps.

2 Remind students that they will hear the tape once only.

▶ **Answers**

1	(experiences in) childhood	5	to close down
2	(being in) debt	6	(own) father
3	reporter	7	fifty-eight / 58
4	social injustice		

Tapescript

N = Narrator
N … Now take Charles Dickens. He had a sad and difficult childhood but he used it to give life to the characters and stories he created. His father was a naval clerk who was always getting into debt, which eventually led to his imprisonment. As a result, Charles had to leave school and go to work in a factory, pasting labels on to bottles of shoe polish. This went on for two years and his description of this period of his life in *David Copperfield* showed how deeply it affected him. In 1824, his father finally managed to pay his debts and Dickens was able to return to school.

Vocabulary   Student's Book p 130

1

▶ **Answers**

In the example *go on* means to progress, move on.
1 talk a lot about a subject, especially in a boring or complaining way
2 lasted for / continued
3 an exhortation used to encourage or persuade someone to do something

2 Students discuss the meaning of the verbs in pairs before comparing their answers with another pair's.

▶ **Answers**

1 must do other things
2 getting old
3 become popular
4 understand / learn
5 provided / organized
6 caused
7 agreed to do
8 has employed

English in Use   Student's Book p 131

Refer students to the Exam tip on reading through their completed texts in Part 4.

1 Make sure your students read the complete text before deciding as a fuller understanding of Elizalde's connection with the tribe is given in the last sentence. He did not simply dicover them but also studied them and adopted orphaned children from similar tribes.

2 Your students could do this task in pairs.

3

▶ Answers

1   sympathetic (adj.)
2   doubtful (adj.)
3   undiscovered (adj.)
4   suspicion (noun)
5   notoriety (noun)
6   mischievious (adj.)
7   forgery (noun)
8   minorities (noun)

4

▶ Answers

1   assumption
2   endless
3   comparatively
4   recruitment
5   inflexible
6   additionally
7   confidence
8   shortages

Speaking   Student's Book p 132

1 Ask students to read through the dilemmas and discuss them with a partner. Tell them that there are no right answers but remind them to give each other the opportunity to express opinions and to give reasons for their choices.

2 Students compare their decisions with another pair and choose the most difficult dilemma.

3 Ask groups to make their selection in four to five minutes.

Structure
A Caring Image ▼

Introduction   Student's Book p 134

Students discuss the ideas and decide on the most and least successful in small groups.

Reading

Ask students to read the advertisement and find the information. When they have read it, ask them if they think this is a good way of raising money.

▶ Answers

– People entering the competition can send a donation to help four designated charities.

– a Caribbean cruise for two, a flight on a supersonic aeroplane, or the latest photographic equipment, ten travel alarm clocks or calculators.

– Amateurs (adults *and* children) should send in a black and white or colour photograph of a very special image which succeeds in showing a caring situation. The deadline for entries is the end of next month and the people's name and address must be put clearly on the back of entries.

Gerunds   Student's Book p 135

Ask students to discuss **A** and **B** in pairs.

A

▶ Answers

1   *Raising* – used as the subject of the verb and sentence
2   *persuading* – used after a preposition
3   *collecting* – used as the object of a verb

B

▶ Answers

Examples in the text:

1   as the subject of the verb:
    Entering our exciting competition ...

2   after a preposition:
    ... is on caring.
    ... succeeds in capturing ...
    ... the essence of caring ...
    ... look forward to receiving ...

3   as the object of a verb:
    ... like messing about with cameras ...
    ... enjoy taking impromptu photographs ...

Language activation

Love it – or hate it!

In groups of two or three, students find out two things their partners love or hate doing most. The teacher puts a master list on the board. Students then take it in turns to guess why their fellow-students love or hate doing these things. Fellow-students then tell the rest of the class if the explanation is correct or not.

Present participles

A Tell students that there are eight examples of
present participles to be found.

▶ **Answers**

*the caring world
exciting competition
amazing prizes
deserving charities
caring support
ever-rising costs
a caring situation
it must be eye-catching!*

B

▶ **Answer**

When sending your photograph(s) ...

C Students rewrite the sentences on their own and
then compare their answers with their partner's.

▶ **Answer**

1 While / When living in Africa, he wrote his most
   successful books.
2 If / When trying to start a car engine from cold, you
   may need to pull out the choke.
3 While / When studying at university, he decided that
   he wanted to become a politician.
4 When watching TV, you are advised not to have the
   volume turned up too loud.
5 While staying in Rome, we came across some old
   friends we hadn't seen for ages.

Infinitive or present participle?

A Elicit the difference in meaning from the class.

▶ **Answer**

In 1, you watched him for the whole of his performance
and you may even have arranged to be in a certain place
for that purpose.

In 2, you may have seen him giving a part of his
performance which continued for some time but it was
not necessarily your original intention to see it all.

B Students complete the sentences on their own.

▶ **Answers**

1 sing
2 dancing, singing
3 rehearsing
4 arguing
5 staring
6 give

Verbs followed by a gerund or infinitive with no difference in meaning

Students discuss **A** and **B** in pairs.

A

▶ **Answer**

I would like is followed by an infinitive not a gerund. It
expresses a specific preference rather than a
generalization.

B

▶ **Answer**

to have because the gerund is not used after a verb in a
continuous tense.

Verbs followed only by a gerund or only by an infinitive

Student's Book p 136

Students divide the verbs into two lists.

▶ **Answer**

Gerund	*Infinitive*
deny	afford
keep	seem
practise	agree
dislike	learn
suggest	pretend
avoid	expect
mind	promise
consider	threaten
finish	refuse
miss	wish

Verbs followed by either a gerund or an infinitive depending on their meaning

A Need

▶ **Answers**

You cannot say *you don't need buying expensive equipment* as the negative form of *need* has been used.

1 means that it is necessary for you to do something.
2 means that you think something should be done.
3 using the passive infinitive means that you think someone ought to do this.

Negative:

1 You don't need to / needn't buy special equipment for this type of photography.
2 This camera lens doesn't need cleaning.
3 This camera lens doesn't need to be cleaned.

B Try

▶ **Answers**

In 1, you did write to them but the letter did not achieve the desired effect. In 2, you did not manage to write to them despite your efforts.

The first example could be completed:
... no reply.

The second example could be completed:
... find the right words ... move my wrist.

C Remember

▶ **Answers**

In 1, the infinitive refers to things that happen *after* you remember.
In 2, the gerund refers to things that happen *before* you remember.

Other verbs which follow the same pattern and meaning:

regret, forget, stop, go on

Language activation

Memories

In small groups, students tell each other about their very first, their worst and their best memory, making sentences using, *I remember -ing ...* and explaining why that particular memory sticks in their mind.

D Ask students to complete the sentences on their own.

▶ **Answers**

1 remembers spending
2 regret to say
3 need cleaning
4 don't need to explain / needn't explain
5 tried to remember
6 Try not to make
7 remember to phone
8 regrets not working / not having worked harder
9 tried fiddling
10 needs looking into

Practice

Students should find out as many details as possible from their partners before telling the class something interesting they have discovered.

Today's World

Reading
The Beauty Myth

Introduction   Student's Book p 137

1 Discuss the question with the whole class.

2 Check that the students understand what the statements are saying. Encourage them to give examples to support their views.

▶ **Suggested answers**

– The beauty industry can take advantage of the fact that we want to believe that its products can make us look younger and more attractive.

– Our society only values those who are young and attractive.

– Society does not value those who are older and more experienced.

Reading

1 Students read the article and discuss the question as a whole class.

▶ **Answer**

The writer believes that contemporary society tends to ignore the positive qualities people acquire with age, such as experience and knowledge, particularly if they are female.

2 Ask students to match the underlined sections to the options A, B, C or D and to focus on the differences in wording.

▶ **Answer**

D is the correct option.

3 Students choose the correct options on their own in about 15 minutes before comparing answers as a class.

▶ **Answers**

The parts of the article which relate to the correct option are given in brackets.

2B (*To give skincare scientific credibility, beauty counters have now stolen a veneer of respectability from the hospital clinic ...* line 26)

3 A (*Imedeen works from the inside out, providing the skin with nutritional and biochemical support. ...* line 56)

4 C (*... the medical journal in which the study of Imedeen is published is a 'pay' journal – one in which any studies can be published for a fee ...* line 97)

5 A (*... women will go on investing in pots of worthless goop ...* line 134)

4 Students discuss the writer's views as a class.

Style   Student's Book p 139

▶ **Answers**

Giving an opinion:
Our ability to believe what we want to has, in the past, made life easy for the beauty industry (line 21)
Let's see more mature wrinkled women in attractive, successful, happy roles and let's see men fighting to be with them (line 135)

Speculating:
Is this really just a harmless game, though? (line 40)
But can shrimp shells really do the trick with wrinkles? (line 85)

Reporting what someone said:
she begged to know where she could get the treatments I had mentioned (line 17)

Brian Newman ... explains that the compound has a specific action in the gut ... (line 88)
Undeterred, he insists the most important point to establish is ... (line 107)
According to Pamela Ashurst ... (line 116)

English in Use   Student's Book p 140

In Unit 5, students were asked to produce a formal register. This time they are asked to produce a more informal register.

1 Discuss the questions as a class.

▶ **Answers**

The clinic claims it can improve people's looks through cosmetic surgery and the letter writer seems to believe this.

2 Ask students to compare the register of both texts and to ensure that they make the necessary changes for each gap. They should complete this task in about 10 minutes.

– The letter is informal and therefore uses informal
structures and vocabulary, eg *I've*, *get something done
about*, *Sounds dreadful*, *So how about it?*

– The words *works well* used in the letter are more
common in informal contexts than its more formal
counterpart *benefits from* in the advertisement.

2	of any	8	taking / getting
3	fit / blend in	9	shape
4	show (you)	10	dramatically
5	look like	11	getting
6	rid	12	high / good
7	dieting / on a diet		

3 After students have discussed the questions in
pairs, make a list of the pros and cons of cosmetic
surgery on the board.

Optional activity

Students respond to the letter in writing, saying
whether or not they think that cosmetic surgery is
a good idea and if they think it's necessary for the
writer or themselves to undergo treatment. Write
about 100–150 words.

Listening and Speaking
Alternative Technology ▼

Introduction   Student's Book p 141

1 Ask students to read the paragraphs and say what
they understand by the term *'low-tech' solutions*.
(relatively basic scientific solutions). Draw their
attention to the following collocates in the
paragraphs *combat the problem* / *serious threat* /
posed a threat …

► Answer

A	practical preventative	C	growing high-yield crops
B	biological control of pests	D	alternative energy sources

2

► Suggested answers

Benefits:
A is cheap / easy to use.
B is cheap / not labour intensive.
C needs no fertilizer or irrigation and is therefore cheap to
produce and suitable for areas subject to drought.

D is non-polluting / cheaper than nuclear power / will not
run out.

Drawbacks:
A It may be difficult to find a source of uncontaminated
water / children and parents may need to be
supervised.
B The natural agent may turn out to be more damaging
than the original pest / it is difficult to control once it
has been introduced.
C The specially developed plant may not be acceptable
to the people who need to eat it.
D Some people consider them ugly and noisy / there may
not always be enough wind for the turbines to work.

3 Discuss the question as a class.

► Suggested answers

A	antibiotics	C	chemical fertilizers
B	pesticides	D	nuclear power

Speaking   Student's Book p 142

1 Students discuss the possible disadvantages of
nuclear fuel and alternative energy sources in
pairs. Refer them to pages 193 and 195 of the
Vocabulary Resource for useful ways of presenting
arguments and comparing and contrasting.

2 Students then compare their decisions with
another pair's.

3 Groups discuss all three questions briefly or
alternatively ask them to choose only one of the
questions and to discuss this in more depth.

Vocabulary

Ask students to read the sentences and discuss the
meaning of the missing verbs. Students complete the
sentences in pairs.

► Answers

1	hand over	6	talked over
2	passed over	7	get over
3	hand over	8	take over
4	taken over	9	got over
5	look over	10	take over

Listening   Student's Book p 143

Refer the students to the Exam tip on Part 2.

1 Students quickly read through 1–10 to see what
kind of information is required.

Note
hectare – 10,000 square metres

2 Play the tape once only while students complete the information.

▶ Answers

1 (almost) 240 metres
2 densely forested area / Kamoros
3 (in the) 1980s
4 17 / seventeen
5 73,000
6 (at least) $12 billion
7 electricity
8 Asian Banks
9 (a) Brazilian company
10 25–30 years

The following information was heard more than once: 17 studies, $12 billion, 73,000 hectares

Tapescript

> I = Interviewer; L = Dr Lim
>
> I   Today we are looking at several large aid projects taking place, or about to take place, in Asia. The first is a huge dam almost 240 metres high which will be built in a densely forested area near Kamoros. I have with me in the studio Dr Lim, a representative from a non-governmental group which is opposed to the scheme.
> Dr Lim, perhaps you could explain why you're against building what could be Asia's largest and most prestigious project?
>
> L   Yes, well the project has been controversial from the start. In the 1980s when it was first put forward as a possibility there was a public outcry, not only locally but from all over the world. It was seen then as a potential environmental disaster and 17 studies later there is nothing to change our view.
>
> I   So these 17 studies did not reassure you?
>
> L   Certainly not, especially as none of the findings were ever published. You see what the government has ignored, is the plight of the tribes who inhabit this region. They are aiming to take over and flood an area of 73,000 hectares where three tribes live. This densely wooded area is their home. Moving them to some isolated swamp lands in the south is simply not acceptable. Apart from anything else the cost is phenomenal – at least $12 billion – and then the aim is not to benefit the local inhabitants, but to channel the electricity under the sea to Malaysia. On the way they will lose about a quarter of that through leakage!
>
> I $12 billion does sound a lot of money; will Britain be contributing?
>
> L   No, the UK is contributing £234 million to another dam project in the North. This dam will be funded entirely by Asian banks, while the construction contract has been handed over to a Brazilian company.
>
> I   Well they know all about dam building in Brazil! So, what is the root of your complaint, Dr Lim?
>
> L   What we are objecting to is government lack of concern – they're going to spend billions flooding 73, 000 hectares of forest and they don't really care about those who will be affected by the project. There has been no proper consultation procedure, and for a project whose benefits will only last between 25 and 30 years this is not just short-sighted, but shows a flagrant lack of concern for the environment.

3 Students discuss whether or not the eight statements are true or false in pairs or small groups.

▶ Answers

1 F   2 F   3 T   4 T   5 F   6 F   7 F   8 T

Writing
Improving your Environment ▼

Introduction   Student's Book p 144

Students discuss the pictures in groups of three. If necessary, give them the following vocabulary to help their discussion.

litter (v / n)   graffiti (n)   pollution (n)   vandalism (n)
rubbish (n)   pollutant (n)   vandal (n)
wilfully destroy   polluting (v)
damage (v)

▶ Suggested actions

– form a local group to clean up specific areas

– form a local pressure group to raise public awareness

– write to the local newspaper

Writing

Sample leaflet

1   a   Elicit the meaning of *Green Belt* from the students (an area surrounding a town or city where new buildings or other developments are prohibited). Students read the leaflet and answer the question.

▶ Answer

The leaflet has been produced to inform people of a project which aims to protect and improve the local environment.

b   Ask students to look at the leaflet in greater detail and discuss the four aspects in groups of three.

▶ Answers

• headings break up the text into manageable paragraphs and help the reader focus on the important points.
• bullet points highlight the items in a list.
• a footnote explains any terms which readers may not be familiar with.
• short paragraphs enable readers to get information quickly and also make points easier to remember.

c

▶ **Answer**

The present tense is used as it is more immediate and tells readers that this situation is happening now.
The writer uses imperatives to encourage action, eg *Come on one of our guided walks | Explore and enjoy your local countryside.*

d

▶ **Answer**

The register is semi-formal and the tone is neutral to appeal to a broad audience.

e   Students discuss the questions as a class. Ask them if there is, or has been, a similar project where they live.

Optional activity

Either refer students to the leaflet in the Writing Reference on page 190 or give them other examples of leaflets. Ask them to analyse the leaflet(s) in a similar way (as in 1a–d) or, if the students have easy access, ask them to collect their own from libraries, theatres, cinemas, travel agents etc. In pairs students compare leaflets and decide which they prefer and which are more successful in getting their message across, giving their reasons.

Understanding the task

2   Check that the students understand the following: short-listed, best-kept town.

▶ **Answer**

The purpose of the leaflet is to inform local residents of the award and to encourage their active involvement in improving the look of their town.

Brainstorming ideas

3

a   Students discuss existing problems in small groups. Write a master list of these problems on the board for the whole class to refer to.

b   Students discuss different ways of improving the town, eg if one of the problems is a river polluted with rubbish, a group could be organized to clean it up.

c

▶ **Suggested answer**

At the beginning as an opening paragraph heading, or repeated at the end with a contact name and address.

Focusing on the reader

4

▶ **Answer**

Semi-formal / neutral, but with a friendly tone as it is addressed to local residents.

Planning your answer

5   Ask the students to compare their layouts in pairs or groups of three. Refer them to the relevant sections of the Vocabulary Resource on page 195.

Writing

6   Refer students to the Writing Resource on page 190 if they did not do this in the optional activity above. Ask them to find examples of the features of leaflets which have been highlighted in this unit.

At this stage of the course students should be aiming to complete the writing task in about 45 minutes once they have understood the task and planned their answers.

Structure
'Designer' Babies ▼

Introduction   Student's Book p 146

Discuss the question as a class.

English in Use

Ask students to complete the gaps on their own in 10 minutes.

▶ **Answers**

1   to
2   if
3   been
4   an
5   other
6   be
7   of
8   of
9   with
10   which
11   Like
12   on
13   have
14   its
15   as

The third conditional

Students discuss **A–C** in small groups.

A   Meaning

▶ Answers

Did you live in Darwin's time?

Were you shocked by the publication?

The answer to both questions is clearly 'no'.

Questions:

Did Darwin publish his theories?

Did the Victorians find themselves in a dilemma?

Answers:

Yes, he did.

Yes, they did.

B   Form

▶ Answers

The tenses are:

the past perfect in the conditional part of the sentence.

the past conditional in the main part of the sentence.

In the main part of the sentences, you could use:

may (possibility)

might (less certain)

could (they were capable of feeling this).

C   Variations in form and meaning

▶ Answers

a *Supposing that* reinforces the improbability of the situation and is a little more dramatic and colourful than *if*.

b In literary English, if the verb is *had*, *should*, or *were*, the verb may be put first and *if* can be omitted. There is no difference in meaning but the stylistic device gives more emphasis to what is being said.

c *might* creates uncertainty. It is much less definite than *would*.

Language activation

> **Supposing that ... ?**
>
> Students think of one very important event or occasion in their own lives. In small groups, students ask and answer questions, beginning with *Supposing that ...* about what might have happened if things had been different.

Conditional link words   Student's Book p 147

A   Ask students to match the link words in pairs.

▶ Answers

1   c

2   d

3   c

4   b

5   a

As / so long as and *provided / providing that* have the same meaning.

B   Students complete the conversation in pairs.

▶ Suggested answers

A   supposing (that)   had been   would have been   wouldn't

B   even if   had lived   wouldn't have had

A   wouldn't have been   unless   had had

B   would have been   so / as long as / provided / providing that   had been

A   would have hated   Even if   you had travelled   would not have had

B   so / as long as / provided / providing that   had made   would have had

A   'd / had been   wouldn't have been

Language activation

> **Another place, another time!**
>
> In small groups, students imagine that they had been born in another place at another time and talk about their feelings and reactions to the idea, giving reasons for how they would feel.

Mixed conditionals

Students discuss **A** and **B** as a class.

A   Second and third

▶ Answers

In 1 *Did you buy the car?* – yes
      Are you short of money now? – yes

In 2 *Did you buy the car?* – no
      Are you short of money now? – no

Tell students that in this construction the meaning implies that in reality things are different.

B

▶ Answers

In 1 *Is Tom lazy?* – yes
      Did he help you? – no

In 2 *Does Sonya speak English?* – no
      Did Sonya have to come to English classes? – yes

Practice

Ask students to work on their own and then compare their answers with a partner.

▶ Answers

1 If we hadn't read the book, we wouldn't be so well-informed about the matter.
2 If we'd phoned the rescue service, we wouldn't still be stranded on the motorway.
3 If I liked the countryside, I would have settled down there.
4 If Peter liked foreign films, he would have gone to the cinema.
5 If the children needed help with their homework, they would have asked us for it.
6 If I had (any) children, I would have bought a big house.
7 If I had met the right person, I would be married now.
8 If Philip had good eyesight, he would have become a pilot.

Language activation

If we could turn back the clock!

In small groups, students think of two or three dramatic and topical stories in the news and discuss what could / might have happened if circumstances had been different. Students then compare their ideas with another group.

Extra exercise

Make conditional sentences from the following notes. Complete the sentences in any way you think suitable but try to use different link words and mixed conditionals if appropriate. Any reasonable answer is acceptable.

1 … antibiotics (not discover) …
2 … the USA (not declare independence all those years ago) …
3 … the French Revolution (not take place) …
4 … nuclear weapons (not invent) …
5 … human beings (not evolve) …
6 … there (be no wars) …
7 … we (look after our planet) …
8 … computers (not appear on the scene) …
9 … the children (be tired after their long journey) …
10 … Bob (fail his driving test tomorrow) …
11 … space travellers (find life on other planets) …
12 … Mary (be so selfish) …

Let's get Organized

Reading
The Customer is Always Right ▼

Introduction   Student's Book p 148

1 Students discuss the cartoon strip as a class. Ask them to discuss what being assertive means and to think of advantages and disadvantages of behaving in this way.

▶ **Suggested answer**

The cartoon strip is illustrating the fact that the customer's 'assertive' behaviour is inappropriate.

2 Students discuss the saying in pairs or small groups. Encourage them to think of incidents in their own experience to support their views.

Reading

1 Students read the paragraphs quickly.

▶ **Answer**

Providing good customer service.

2 Ask students to divide up the paragraphs in pairs.

▶ **Answers**

General principles: B   C   D

Specific examples: A   E   G

Students should be able to relate a general principle to a specific example(s) and complete the task in about 15 minutes.

▶ **Answers**

The phrases which link the paragraphs are given in brackets.

1D *... had cost advantages over small ones ... | In the 1990s, small businesses still have lots of advantages ...*

2B *Their staff are trained, positive, approachable ... | and* (the bosses) *exhibit the same attitudes as the staff ...*

3C *... we are going to lose business to competitors who already do so ... to the Americans, the customer is a king, but to the Japanese, the customer is a god.*

4E *Take my mechanic, for example ... / If the car breaks down within a week ...*

5A *Does he charge more? Yes he does ... | They charge top price but ...*

6G *When you go into her surgery ... | When we get there, she gives the kids a sweet ...*

3

▶ **Answer**

Paragraph F does not fit because the first sentence cannot be logically connected to anything in the given text.

> **Optional activity**
>
> In small groups, the students discuss what they would include in a leaflet on customer care. Ask each group to prepare a leaflet of this kind for the employees of a particular organization. Refer them back to the advice on writing leaflets in the previous unit.

Vocabulary   Student's Book p 150

Ask students to discuss the questions in 1–3 in pairs and to practise saying the words using the correct word stress.

1

▶ **Answers**

inexperienced   invaluable
imperfect   immature
irrational   illegible

im- is usually followed by m, p or b
ir- by r
il- by l
in- by v or a vowel

2

▶ **Answers**

unconscious, dishonest, misjudged

Difference in meaning:

un- = not
dis- = lack of
mis- = wrongly / badly

3

▶ **Answers**

subnormal, under / overvalued, overloaded

sub- = below
under- = below, usually negative, too little
over- = too (much) (although overtime = extra time)

4 Students complete the text on their own and then compare their answers with their partner's.

▶ **Answers**

1	underpaid	5	impatient
2	understaffed	6	illegal
3	inefficient	7	uncommunicative
4	substandard	8	disinterested

English in Use   Student's Book p 150

1

▶ **Suggested answer**

He / she is too tense to enjoy any kind of leisure activity.

2 Students complete the task on their own in about 10 minutes.

▶ **Answers**

1	an	9	they
2	at	10	if
3	of	11	the
4	at	12	Nobody / No one
5	off	13	one
6	all	14	on
7	up	15	get / become / be
8	but		

3 Students either work on their own or with another student (ie put two Student As together, two Student Bs together). Check they choose suitable words and follow the advice given. After completing the task, Students A and B complete each other's cloze.

4 Students discuss the questions in pairs.

Optional activity

Write their ideas for relieving stress on the board. Ask students in groups of three or four to put the activities in the order they think is most beneficial. They should reach a decision together and justify the order.

Writing
When Things Go Wrong ... ▼

Introduction   Student's Book p 152

1 Stop the tape after each speaker and discuss the answers as a class.

▶ **Answer**

The four people are talking about a bank.

Speaker 1: a clerk, who thinks the bank is friendly to work in and fairly efficient as there have not been many serious complaints.

Speaker 2: the manager, who believes in a tough management style to produce an efficient operation and is not very sympathetic to his customers or staff.

Speaker 3: a customer, who does not comment on this particular bank but believes that most similar organizations are inefficient and make mistakes.

Speaker 4: a customer, who is very critical of the bank's inefficiency.

Tapescript

Speaker 1

Well, I've been here for 15 years, and in all that time I've never been called anything except Mr Brown by those above or below me. Yes, it's quite formal. I always wear a suit and tie, but I think that's right because people have to feel they can trust you. After all you're dealing with their most valuable possession! As a place to work it's OK – I mean it's quite friendly and there's some satisfaction in doing what you do well. However I do get bored from time to time – I want to climb over the counter and shout out 'I'm a real person, it's me!' Of course, I don't. The most difficult part of the job is dealing with customer complaints. It's easier on the phone, but it can be so embarrassing when they come in and start ranting on about that standing order they cancelled and we haven't, or the loan they say we promised hasn't come through. You learn to be very diplomatic and luckily we get very few serious complaints.

Speaker 2

Well, as manager of this branch, my main objective is to run a smooth and efficient operation. I expect my staff to achieve certain goals that have been agreed to. As long as everyone knows what these are and tries to achieve them and, more importantly can be seen to be achieving them, then I'm happy. If not, then they are out on their ear. Sounds a bit draconian, but I believe in standards. The customers have a right to believe that we are doing the best to offer them a fast, error-free service. If mistakes do occur, I tend to think in the first instance that the customer has got it wrong. They usually have, believe you me! And some of the stories I have to listen to. You just wouldn't believe! The number of dogs that eat account statements and prevent the owners from knowing they are in the red!

Speaker 3

I'm afraid I'm pretty cynical about most organizations. Their main aim seems to be to outwit you and if you find anything not to your satisfaction, then it's probably because *you* are being unreasonable in expecting a particular service. Catching them out has become a bit of a sport for me these days. It's better than cowering away and accepting whatever they dish out! I was in my branch of *Leeds and Hadley* the other day when this old fellow comes in and complains to the girl behind the counter that he hasn't received a new cheque book and could he have one now, please? Well, you should have heard the excuses. And then to cap it all she

---

said they couldn't give him one there and then as it would have to be printed up specially with his name and so on. Now the old chap got quite ratty at this and the girl scurried off for the manager. So I turned to him and told him to threaten to close his account immediately unless they gave him one. Unfortunately, at least for me who was enjoying the spectacle, the manager came and apologized and offered him a temporary cheque book.

Speaker 4

It wasn't till I moved back to Britain that I had any trouble with my account. Of course in a place like Malaysia the name Greenhalgh is going to stick out like a sore thumb. Back in Britain we Greenhalghes are two a penny, or at least in Kirkbride they are, apparently! Anyway, it wasn't till half way through the year that I spotted some odd goings-on in my account. Instead of the princely sum of £800 going into my account each month I was actually being credited with £8,000. Now what's a nought or two between friends you may ask? But I was worried, and though I toyed with the possibility of becoming a millionaire in a year or two I did query it eventually. It was a sheepish under manager who phoned to tell me that the wrong account had been credited with my salary cheque. There was a sting in the tail though, when he finally asked, somewhat critically I thought, why I hadn't noticed before? 'I trusted you', I replied weakly and allowed him to get away with it!

2 Ask the students to say what is meant by 'efficiency' before discussing their experiences of different organizations in pairs. What differences might there be in the way customers and staff view efficiency?

Vocabulary   Student's Book p 152

1

▶ Answers

1	a	6	i
2	g	7	e
3	j	8	b
4	f	9	d
5	c	10	h

2

▶ Answers

2 faulty workmanship
3 free of charge
4 consequential
5 to attend to
6 In the event that
7 making a claim
8 statutory

Writing

Refer students to the Exam tip on writing letters of complaint. Check that they understand the meaning of *indignation*.

Sample letters

1 a Students compare the letters in pairs or small groups, discussing the aspects given.

▶ Answers

Letter A is more appropriate because:
– the letter clearly states in chronological order what took place.
– the register is formal.
– the complaint is expressed clearly and in appropriate detail.
– the language is straightforward and the writer says what he wants to happen (*I would appreciate it if ...*) and an address is given where the parcel can be collected.
– there is no unnecessary repetition of information.
– there is appropriate paragraphing, a reference to the transaction is given at the top of the letter and the salutations are correct.

Letter B is inappropriate because:
– the information is not given in order and is repeated.
– the register is informal and the writer expresses too much emotion.
– not all the necessary information is given, eg where can the parcel be collected?
– it is not clear what the writer wants to happen; he seems to just be letting off steam.
– there is unnecessary repetition. (*So please let me know what you are going to do about it. | I still don't know what you are going to do about it.*)
– only one paragraph is used, no reference is given and the final salutation is incorrect.

b Students discuss the questions as a class.

▶ Suggested answers

It is better to complain in writing if: there has been no response to an earlier face-to-face complaint, if the supplier / service is far away, if a written record of the complaint is necessary for guarantees, etc. and if the complaint is complex or involves other organizations or people.

Face-to-face complaints are better if you can speak directly to those responsible easily and if the complaint is straightforward.

Understanding the task

2 Students should take care to read the task and accompanying material carefully.

▶ Answer

You would hope that the manufacturer will offer to collect the CD player, repair or replace it free of charge, and return or replace it more quickly than they say in their letter as it is still under guarantee.

Planning your answer

3 Students read points 1–6 and check that they have all the information they need from the material. Refer them to the relevant sections of the Vocabulary Resource on pages 193 and 195.

4 Students should write their note in an informal, friendly style and make sure that they address all the points that Jill mentioned.

Writing

5 Set the writing task for homework and refer students to the Writing Resource on page 184.

Listening and Speaking
A Room with a View ▼

Introduction   Student's Book p 155

1 Check that the students understand the meaning of the words and phrases. Those that they may not know are explained below:

austere – without decoration / formal
functional – practical / basic
open-plan – a large, undivided room
cluttered – full of objects
cramped – lacks space
oppressive – heavy atmosphere
messy – untidy
up-to-the-minute – fashionable

Optional activity

Ask the students to produce five sentences using the words in **1** showing they understand their meanings, eg *I like to keep my office neat and tidy so that I can find things easily. / We are a very untidy family and the house is always cluttered with our belongings.*

2

▶ Suggested answers

1   b
2   c, e
3   d, f
4   a, g
5   b, h

3 Students discuss each of the pictures in pairs. Ask them to choose where they would like to work the most or the least.

Listening

1 Students read through the statements before they listen to the tape for the first time.

▶ Answers

1 Y 2 N 3 N 4 Y 5 N 6 N 7 N 8 N 9 Y 10 Y

2 Students reread the four sentences marked with a *Y*. Ask them to listen to the tape again and say who expressed the views.

▶ Answers

1 c 4 c 9 c 10 b

Tapescript

J = Jane; M = Martin

J My first job was for a shipping company in London – well the main office was in London but it had offices all over the world. It was a good job, I mean the pay wasn't bad, the people were OK and my boss was great …

M So why did you leave?

J I never seemed to feel well while I was there. For the first time in my life I developed some sort of asthma or hay fever or something …

M Really? You mean you were coughing and spluttering all over the place? Was it air-conditioned?

J Yes, I couldn't bear it; not being able to open the windows, breathing in everybody else's germs and so on.

M Sounds as though it might have been a 'sick building'. I worked in one once – air-conditioned like yours, and we all used to go down with colds and flu or bad chests and things like that. At first the managers just said it was our imagination or that we weren't happy in our work, but I really believed it was to do with the building. When I left there I went to work for a firm who were based in an old house – wonderful – I could open the windows and breathe *real* air!

J Do you think there was something in the air then, in your old place?

M I'm sure there was – though we couldn't prove it. Mind you, it can't just be air-conditioning, because the place I work in now is the same, yet I feel fine.

J Yes, me too, but I think it's got more to do with the way the office is laid out. I mean where I am now it's spacious, the chairs are comfortable, I've got a lovely view over the park, and there are only two of us to a room. It makes you feel positive, and relaxed! It's a great environment to work in, especially when you compare it to open plan offices. I *hate* open plan offices – it's so distracting – all those phone calls and people rushing about.

M Funny, that's what I like about where I am now. It's busy, people always jumping up and down and coming in with the latest news. It's really exciting.

J Sounds awful to me, but then I have to concentrate hard and try and be creative!

M Oh, so you don't think working in a newspaper's really creative then? I'll have you know I …

J No, no, sorry, I didn't mean that, but it's a different sort of creative. Perhaps you need people buzzing about to stimulate you?

M Yes, yes I do – there's nothing so stultifying as total silence for me …

J Oh peace, perfect peace – I couldn't ask for anything else.

Speaking

1 Students discuss the picture of a marine biologist at work in pairs, covering the aspects listed. Refer them to the relevant section of the Vocabulary Resource on page 194.

Optional activity

Give students different pictures of jobs to discuss as above. Ask each pair to listen to another pair and make constructive comments on their performance.

---

2 Ask students to read through the list of conditions in an ideal job. Remind them that they do not have to agree with each other but they should be able to justify their decisions. They should take turns to speak and help each other to become involved in the decision making. Before they begin, refer them to the relevant sections of the Vocabulary Resource on pages 193 and 194.

When they have finished their discussion, ask the class to think of other conditions they would like in a job.

Structure
Personal Organizer ▼

Introduction   Student's Book p 157

Ask students to discuss the questions in pairs or small groups. Find out which are the most popular ways of remembering things and write any unusual ideas on the board.

Reading

Students skim read the article and discuss the different headings in small groups.

▶ Suggested answer

Organizing the organizer

The passive

A   Form

1 Students discuss the changes needed as a class.

▶ **Answers**

does becomes *is done.*
can do becomes *can be done.*
could have done becomes *could have been done.*

2 Students put the sentences into the passive form in pairs.

▶ **Answers**

a   Fewer letters are being written by hand nowadays.
b   A new printer has been ordered for the computer.
c   Central heating was being installed when the fire broke out.
d   Fortunately, the office equipment had not been damaged by the fire.
e   The manual was printed in Taiwan.
f   Several hundred new workers might be recruited over the next few months.
g   The report by the committee ought to be finished by next week.
h   The report would have been finished sooner if they hadn't been so busy.

3

▶ **Answers**

a   *were ruled*
b   *are being heralded*
c   *are attracted* | (It is) *Said*
d   *have been designed*
e   *can be ordered*

B   Function
Students do the matching exercise in pairs or small groups.

▶ **Answers**

1   a
2   c
3   a
4   b

Some of the verbs are used in the passive form for the following reasons: the person who did the action is often mentioned at the end of the sentence to give special emphasis, or when additional information is given about the person which would make the sentence top-heavy if it were placed at the beginning.

were ruled – b
are being heralded – c
are attracted – b | (It is) *Said* – b
have been designed – c
can be ordered – c

Practice Student's Book p 158

Students rewrite the sentences on their own, then compare their answers in pairs. Tell them that one of the sentences cannot be changed.

▶ Answers

1 The paper is inserted into the printer with the smoother side facing up. (c)
2 The staff were briefed about company reorganization by the managing director from the head office in Halifax. (b)
3 A very serious error has been made by the new company secretary. (b)
4 All the office equipment is going to be updated early next year. (c)
5 This jewellery is made by the local inhabitants on a remote island in the Pacific. (b)
6 (NB *awarded* has two objects so there are two ways of making this sentence passive.)
  Every student was awarded a certificate by the college authorities on completion of the course.
  or A certificate was awarded to every student by the college authorities on completion of the course. (a)
7 The matter has been attended to. (c)
8 I taught myself how to use a computer. (This cannot be used in the passive as it is a reflexive verb.)
9 The exam papers are marked by (a) computer. (a)
10 (NB There are two ways of making this sentence passive. You can use either the impersonal *It* ... or begin *The company* ...)
  It is said that the company is on the verge of bankruptcy.
  or The company is said to be on the verge of bankruptcy. (c)

Language activation

How was it organized?

Students imagine that they recently attended a one-day course or seminar on language learning. In small groups, students try to remember how the seminar was organized using the passive, eg *We were all told to go to ... / The first talk was given by ... / Lunch was served at ... / in ...*
Suggested topic areas:
– the venue
– the timetable
– the speakers
– the activities
– refreshments and breaks
– round up

Have something done

A

▶ Answers

I installed the new computer. (active – I did it myself)
The new computer was installed yesterday. (passive – someone else did it but I don't really know who, or it's not important who ...)
I had the new computer installed yesterday. (causative use of *have* – I arranged for somebody to install it and (perhaps) I paid them)

The writer uses the causative use of *have* in the sentence about the office because he wants to tell the reader that it is possible to arrange for something or somebody else to do the job for you, ie investing in this personal organizer will release you from having to do the job yourself!

B

▶ Answer

In the first example, the car was serviced and you arranged for this to happen.

In the second example, the car was stolen, and you probably did not arrange for this to happen!

Practice

A Students complete the sentences in pairs or for homework.

▶ Answers

1 ... to have a tooth filled.
2 ... just had it cleaned yesterday.
3 ... to have my hair permed.
4 ... to have it repaired.
5 ... have it cut.
6 ... had my handbag stolen.
7 ... to have it taken up.
8 ... are having it decorated.
9 ... is / are having central heating installed.
10 ... had their house broken into.

B

▶ Answer

get would sound odd in 6 and 10 as it would give the impression that you wanted or arranged for this undesirable thing to happen!

C Students compare their lists in pairs or small groups.

Extra activities

Other uses of passive forms

A The phrases below appeared in the article.

1 *as well as pages <u>marked</u> for planning …*
2 *<u>added</u> extras and <u>sewn</u> vinyl*
3 *the difference being <u>reflected</u> in the prices*

In 1 and 2, the past participle is used as an adjective, but why does it come after the noun in 1 and before the noun in 2?

In 3, why is it impossible to place this information before the noun?

Can you expand the words underlined in the phrases using a tense in a passive form?
For example, *pages marked > pages which are / have been marked*

B Now make short phrases containing passives using the information below.

1 … equipment which has been designed for small offices …
2 … small facilities which have been improved …
3 … shoes which have been made by hand …
4 … plans which have been drawn up by the design department …
5 … a letter which has been sent by registered post …
6 … mail which was posted this morning …
7 … a machine which has been built for a certain purpose …
8 … a car which has been produced for overseas markets …

NB In 3, 5 and 7 there are two ways of rewriting the information.

▶ **Answers**

A
The past participle is used as an adjective and it comes:
– after the noun in 1 because some extra information follows, ie *for planning*. Although, in English, adjectives generally come before nouns, when extra information threatens to make the adjective 'top-heavy' it is placed after the noun.
– before the noun in 2 because no extra information is given. The past participle is simply an adjective describing a noun.
– in 3, it is impossible to place this information before the noun because the phrase replaces what is, in effect, a complete sentence. If you replaced the previous comma with a full stop, you could write a sentence which would stand alone.

1 *as well as pages which have been / are marked for planning*
2 *extras which have been / are added* and *vinyl which has been / is sewn*
3 *the difference is reflected in the prices*

B

1 equipment designed for small offices
2 improved facilities
3 shoes made by hand / hand-made shoes
4 plans drawn up by the design department
5 a letter sent by registered post / a registered letter
6 mail posted this morning
7 a machine built for a certain purpose / a purpose-built machine
8 a car produced for overseas markets

13 Law and Order

Reading
Fine Young Criminals ▼

The title of this section is based on the name of the UK band, *Fine Young Cannibals*.

Introduction   Student's Book p 159

1   Ask students to do the matching task in pairs.

Notes
Houdini – Harry Houdini was an American magician noted for his remarkable escaping acts.
Northumbria – northern county of England
crack down on – stop
shop-lifting spree – a bout of stealing from shops

▶ **Answers**

A – *It's time to Crack Down on Crime Babies*

B – *Houdini Kid does it again*

C – *Little Caesars Blamed for Terrorizing Northumbria*

2   Students discuss the questions in small groups.

Reading

1   Students should read the article carefully and discuss the effectiveness of the title. Encourage them to focus on the aspects of Joey's life which reflect adult experiences.

Notes
I dunno – I don't know (slang)
I gotta – I have got to (slang)
fags – cigarettes (slang)
Home Secretary – the government minister responsible for law and order, and immigration
the Artful Dodger – a child thief in *Oliver Twist* by Charles Dickens
Chief Constables – heads of regional police constabularies
go-cart – a home-made vehicle on wheels

Check that the students understand the following words and phrases:

incarceration – imprisonment
hurled insults – swore at
handling – dealing with stolen goods
behind bars – in prison
truncheon – police baton
stigmatizes – brands (the child) (a criminal)
skiving off school – playing truant / not going to school

2   Students should complete the task in no more than 15 minutes.

▶ **Answers**

1 C   2 A   3 D   4 B   5 A

3   Students discuss the relevant phrases in pairs, first for the correct options and then the incorrect options.

▶ **Answers**

Correct options:

1   C – *he became famous when, in October last year, he was locked away ... where he was three years younger than any other inmate ...* (line 18)

2   A – *Their solution was simple: these children had to be punished; the courts needed more powers to put them behind bars.* (line 51)

3   D – *They remember him skiving off school ...* (line 69)

4   B – *They had tried taking him into care but he had simply walked out of the homes where they put him ... he was sent to a secure unit at East Moor outside Leeds.* (line 96)

5   A – *If you throw a child into the sea, it will drown. If you throw it into an English ghetto, it will grow up like Joey.* (line 141)

The incorrect options are based on the following lines:

1A – line 4	4A – line 92
1B – line 3	4C – line 97
1D – line 26	4D – line 98
2B – lines 36 and 53	5B – line 121
2C – line 53	
2D – line 36	
3A – line 67	
3B – line 68	
3C – line 82	

5C – This is partly true but the writer doesn't mention that Joey has been 'forced' to behave in this way.

5D – Although there are references to the police, D is not stated.

4 Students either find the words and phrases in class or for homework.

▶ **Answers**

1 a weight on her mind
2 inmates
3 incarceration
4 crook
5 locked up / locked away / behind bars
6 rioted
7 petty crimes
8 have given up on

Optional activity

Ask students in small groups to write down as many other words and expressions to do with the law and crime that they know in three minutes. The winning group is the one with the longest list.

Listening and Speaking
Let the Punishment Fit the Crime? ▼

Introduction   Student's Book p 162

Tell students that *Three strikes and you're out* is a baseball term.
Treat the questions as a class discussion.

Listening

1 NB Pictures are used here to help the students focus on who is speaking. In the exam, however, there will be no picture-based question in this section of Paper 5; the options will appear in a list.

Ask students to match the speakers to the pictures as they listen for the first time.

▶ **Answers**

1 e 2 b 3 c 4 a 5 d

2 Students compare their choices in pairs. Encourage them to give reasons for what makes the situation more serious, eg in Britain situations 3, 4 and 5 are against the law.

3 Students listen for the second time and match the speakers to the reactions.

4 Refer students to the key on page 196 and discuss the questions as a class.

▶ **Answers**

1e When she says – '... but for those few minutes I thought I was going to have to sleep on the doorstep!'

2f How he says – 'It was a lesson I learned the hard way, I can tell you.'

3b What she says – 'I was flabbergasted!'

4a How he says – 'A bit strong, I thought, specially as I hadn't been riding it ... '

5d What she says – 'I was heartbroken.'

In most cases it is a combination but in 3, 4 and 5 their emotions are clearly put into words.

Tapescript

Speaker 1
Oh, I can remember coming home late one night and my parents had locked me out. I was nearly 16 at the time and I was supposed to be in by 10 o'clock and this time I'd missed the bus so it was nearly midnight by the time I got home. Of course they let me in after a bit, but for those few minutes I thought I was going to have to sleep on the doorstep!

Speaker 2
It was my first week in a new job and my boss had asked me to send a load of faxes to various company branches. It was nearly time to go home when he gave them to me, so I thought they could wait until morning. Unfortunately they were about a meeting the following day and so nobody turned up. There was all hell to pay and in fact after a few more disasters I was sacked. It was a lesson I learned the hard way, I can tell you.

Speaker 3
I was teaching my son to drive at the time and I thought it would be a good idea to see if he could park the car close to the pavement. He did a splendid job, and as we were in town we popped into a few shops to do a bit of shopping. When we came out the car had gone. We thought it must have been stolen so I spotted a traffic warden and ran over to her. She gave me a funny look and asked if it was a red Saab and when I said yes that it was, she explained, stony-faced, that it had been illegally parked and had therefore been towed away. I was flabbergasted!

Speaker 4
I was coming home from the pub last Friday with a couple of mates and as we'd had a bit to drink I was wheeling my scooter along the pavement. Just then a police van drew up and two policemen jumped out. I thought they thought I'd stolen it so I showed them the keys. Instead they breathalysed me and took me off to the station and charged me for being 'drunk in charge of a motor vehicle'. A bit strong, I thought, specially as I hadn't been riding it and if I'd left the scooter outside the pub, it would probably have got nicked!

Speaker 5
When I came back from abroad I did something really stupid. I brought my cat with me. I knew it wasn't allowed,

---

but you see I just couldn't bear to be parted from him and it didn't seem so awful at the time. However I got reported. I never did find out who it was, and although I got told off and fined, which was all pretty humiliating, the worst thing was they took him away and had him put down. I was heartbroken.

Optional activity

In pairs, students could interview each other about situations when they did something which was considered to be wrong. Ask them to talk about how they felt at the time and whether they were treated fairly.

Vocabulary   Student's Book p 163

Students either do this section in class or for homework.

▶ Answers

got nicked in this sentence means 'been stolen'.

1   got off
2   get over
3   get away with
4   got her own back
5   been getting (Simon) down
6   getting at
7   has / 's got the sack
8   made their getaway

Speaking   Student's Book p 163

Tell students that they may find themselves in a group of three in the exam. Explain that this is unlikely to happen as it only occurs when an odd number of candidates is being interviewed.

1   Refer students to the relevant sections of the Vocabulary Resource on pages 193 and 194. Give them about five minutes to complete the task.

2   Students should use the picture as a starting point for the discussion on punishments. Check that they know the meaning of the punishments before they begin the task.

community service – the offender has to carry out certain tasks which serve the community, eg clearing waste ground, cleaning up vandalized areas.

suspended sentence – the sentence of the court is not carried out unless the offender reoffends within a specified time.

probation – a trial period where an offender must not commit another crime and is put under the care and control of a probation officer.

▶ Answers

The picture shows a group of prisoners working on a railway line.

3   Students discuss the questions in their groups of three. One student from each group then reports back to the class.

Optional activity

In groups, organize a balloon debate in which each student has to represent the views of the people listed below on how to deal with crime. The winner is the one who gets the most votes and survives to fly the balloon.

policeman   judge   thief
victim of crime politician   psychiatrist

Writing
Character Assessment ▼

Introduction   Student's Book p 164

1   Elicit the meaning of *con man* (swindler). Play the tape and discuss Bampfylde Moore Carew's lifestyle as a class.

▶ Suggested answer

He probably wanted an unpredictable life and enjoyed tricking people because he was good at it.

Tapescript

N = Narrator
N   Bampfylde Moore Carew came from an aristocratic and well-to-do family. Yet for 60 years he chose to live as a beggar and confidence trickster. He assumed a variety of inventive disguises, studying each role with the dedicated approach of a great actor. The characters he chose to play were all people who had suffered some terrible misfortune – a shipwrecked sailor, a ruined farmer, even a poverty-stricken mother who had been deserted by her husband. His technique was simple but effective. He would present himself at the door of the local great house and, using his knowledge of how such households were organized, would ensure that he got past servants and was able to pour out his tragic story to the master or mistress. But it was not this flair for deceit that made Carew remarkable – there were many beggars wandering the country who relied upon fraud to soften the hearts of their victims. Carew stands apart from them by his sheer audacity. Most beggars were driven to a life of petty crime by poverty. Carew took it up deliberately because he loved

fooling people. He took quite unnecessary risks, even trying out his skill upon people who knew him and his family. One day he talked his way into the house of a landowner, disguised as a rat-catcher. There he discovered among the guests several old acquaintances. For an hour or more he kept everyone amused with country tales, both true and invented. The ladies and gentlemen were delighted to have found such a 'quaint fellow' to improve their tedious afternoon. At last, Carew could stand their superiority no longer. He revealed his true identity and boasted of the ease with which he had tricked them and several of their neighbours. Fortunately for him, they all took it well. Indeed, Carew became something of a celebrity in polite rural society. Noblemen and gentlemen competed with each other to be tricked by the audacious vagabond, who carried on practising his deceptions until the end of his days. Offers of money and property from wealthy relatives never tempted him to a conventional, settled life. He never lacked for hospitality and his ingenious hoaxes earned him more than enough to live well, when he chose to.

2 Students look at the words in pairs and supply the related parts of speech. Ask them to write sentences of their own to show that they can use the related verbs and adjectives correctly.

▶ **Answers**

invent – inventive
dedicate – dedicated
deceive – deceitful
audacious
boast – boastful
ingenious

English in Use   Student's Book p 164

1 Students read the informal note on their own. Ask them to say what it is about (the unjust sacking of a college lecturer) before they discuss the aspects of his character that are mentioned.

▶ **Answers**

kindness, sensitivity, a good listener, supportive of students, good teacher

2 Refer students to the Exam tip on Part 5. Ask them to discuss suitable words and phrases in pairs and to complete the formal note in 10 minutes.

▶ **Answers**

1	express	7	sympathetic
2	withdraw	8	needed
3	support	9	accused of / charged with
4	long-serving	10	trustworthy
5	kindness	11	proof / evidence
6	reliable	12	is / be reinstated

3 Review the answers quickly as a class.

▶ **Answers**

5 (kindness)
6 (reliable)
7 (sympathetic)
10 (trustworthy)

Vocabulary   Student's Book p 165

Students could do this task in pairs or for homework.

▶ **Answers**

1 sensitive
2 sensitive
3 sensible
4 sensitive
5 sensible   sensitive

Writing   Student's Book p 166

Refer students to the Exam tip on writing character references. Tell them that there is a work-oriented task in Part 2, which they should only do if they have the right experience.

Sample reference

1 **a** Students read the character reference and underline relevant words and phrases.

▶ **Answers**

(brackets show double-edged statements)
single-mindedness and thoroughness
clear view of objectives
a flair for prioritizing
dedication ... putting in extra hours
level-headed approach to problems
never daunted ... remains self-possessed
virtually unflappable under pressure
sensitive to the views of other people
(determination)
outgoing personality ... contributes a great deal
(unique sense of humour)

b Students reread the reference and discuss it in pairs.

▶ **Answers**

The weaknesses appear towards the end, eg *a dominant individual ... strength and a weakness.* They are played down by being juxtaposed with qualities.

c Ask students to analyse the structure in pairs.

▶ Answer

Paragraph 1: The writer's connection with the person and length of time known

Paragraph 2: Main strengths at work

Paragraph 3: Additional strengths

Paragraph 4: Weaknesses and contrasting strengths

Paragraph 5: Extra information – social skills

Paragraph 6: Conclusion and recommendation

Understanding the task

2 Students read the task and discuss the job of a tourist guide in pairs. They list qualities and experience, as well as a weakness, and then compare their notes with another pair's.

Planning your answer

3 Students use the paragraph plan of the sample answer as a model and develop their own plan on their own. They could then comment on each other's plans.

Focusing on the reader

4 **a** Students look at the statements in pairs. The second and fourth statements are irrelevant and the fifth statement needs to be tied to a description of the person's English level to be meaningful.

b Remind students that they should write in a formal register.

5 Refer students to the Writing Resource on page 187 and the relevant sections of the Vocabulary Resource on pages 194 and 195. Students should estimate the number of words used and edit as necessary.

Structure
Watch your Step! ▼

Introduction   Student's Book p 168

Students discuss the items in pairs or small groups.

A Ask students to discuss the question in pairs.

▶ Answer

The alarm is a footstep detector, which is designed to react to human footsteps *before* intruders enter the house.

B Students complete the task on their own.

▶ Answers

1   from
2   known
3   something
4   other
5   before
6   to
7   like
8   also
9   are
10   as
11   of
12   between
13   despite
14   if
15   same

Inversions

A

▶ Answers

1   *Never has life been more difficult for a would-be intruder!*
2   *Only when a burglar is busy breaking in do present-day alarms indicate …*
3   *No longer will you need …*
4   *Only by carefully programming Footfall to recognize patterns … can we now reliably distinguish …*

Words which begin the sentences:
Never
Only when
No longer
Only by

The construction changes as the normal word order, ie subject + verb, is inverted to verb (or auxiliary verb) + subject.

These initial words are negative or restrictive in some way, eg *only when* suggests 'at no other time', *only by* suggests 'in no other way'.

You can make sentences more emphatic by putting these rather negative words, and certain other expressions of place, eg *In the middle of the wood stood a small cottage*, at the beginning of a clause or sentence. This device is used particularly in writing, or formal speeches or conversation when the writers or speakers are making a particular point they want to emphasize.

B Tell students to think carefully about which subject and verb they need to invert in 3, 4 and 8 as they contain subordinate clauses.

1   *Not only* was Peter a well-known detective but he became a successful writer as well.

2   *Never before* had Parliament made such dramatic changes to the legal system.

3   *Only when* the intruders had forced their way into the house did they come across the huge Alsatian dog.

4   *Only by* mounting a full-scale investigation did the police discover who the murderer was.

5   *No longer* should organizations expect people to work unsociable hours without being paid overtime.

6   *Seldom* do Heads of State seem to learn any lessons from history.

7   *In no way* was James responsible for the theft of the painting.

8   *Not until* the bank employees opened the night safe did they discover the robbery.

9   *No longer* can the emergency services cope with the huge amount of calls they receive.

10 *Rarely* do we hear about what happens to prisoners after they are released into the outside world.

Language activation

Speaking with emphasis

The teacher provides some dramatic newspaper headlines about topical events. (Students could find these themselves if enough newspapers are available.) Students have to change the headlines into a personal comment made by an eye witness or a participant, eg

MAN JUMPS OFF BRIDGE

'*Never have I seen such a terrifying sight!*'

NO TO SUBSIDIES

'*No longer should the government subsidize …*'

Concessions   Student's Book p 169

A   Students discuss the questions in pairs.

▶ Answers

The writer combines these pieces of information by saying:

Only by carefully programming Footfall to recognize patterns of data can we now reliably distinguish between footsteps and other movements. But despite this, we can't differentiate between the footsteps of intruders and those of family members or neighbours. Although, if people always walked in the same way, at the same speed, in the same shoes, we would even be able to do that!

Despite and *although* introduce the information which seems contradictory.

B   Tell students that they may have to make changes to the options when combining the information.

▶ Suggested answers

1k

Although / Even though the snow was heavy, /
Despite / In spite of the fact that the snow was heavy, /
Despite / In spite of the heavy snow,
we managed to make it home safely.

2i

a   The hotel was extremely expensive – not that we had any intention of staying there.

b   Although / Even though / Despite / In spite of the fact that the hotel was extremely expensive, we decided to book in.

3l, h

a   Many modern alarm systems are highly effective – not that this makes any difference to some would-be intruders.

b   Although / Even though / Despite / In spite of the fact that many modern alarm systems are highly effective, /
Despite / In spite of the effectiveness of many modern alarm systems, they fail to deter intruders.

4l

Although / Even though / Despite / In spite of the fact that a nationwide search was mounted by the police, /
Despite / In spite of the nationwide search mounted by the police, the escaped prisoner was not found.

5c

Although / Even though / Despite / In spite of the fact that fewer prisons are being built,
Despite / In spite of fewer prisons being built,
it appears that the number of inmates is increasing.

6j, d

a   Although / Even though / Despite / In spite of the fact that this is a no-parking zone,
Despite / In spite of this being a no-parking zone,
you are allowed to load and unload vehicles.

b   This is a no-parking zone – not that you would think so looking at the number of vehicles parked here.

7a

Although / Even though / Despite / In spite of the fact that we are making every effort to despatch your order as soon as possible,
Despite / In spite of making every effort … ,
we are having problems with our suppliers.
or the concessional clause could be the second, eg Despite problems with our suppliers, etc.

8b, f

a   More motorways are being built – not that this solves the traffic problems.

b   Although / Even though / Despite / In spite of the fact that more motorways are being built,
Despite / In spite of the building of more motorways,
this doesn't solve the traffic problems / the roads are always congested.

Sentence completion

A Inversions

▶ **Suggested answers**

1 have / had I seen
2 could / did I find
3 can / do
4 did he realize
5 can the children be blamed
6 have I come across

B Concessions

▶ **Suggested answers**

1 Although (the car was expensive), I couldn't resist buying it.
2 Despite (his fear of driving / the fact that he hated driving), he succeeded in (passing his driving test first time).
3 Big cities are often dangerous places to be in alone – not that (it stops people from wanting to live there).
4 Even though (I am terrified of flying / it is expensive), I have decided (to fly to Spain rather than take the train).
5 In spite of (the lack of support), the committee managed to (raise enough money for the new sports centre).
6 The government (brought in the new taxes), despite the fact that (they knew they would be extremely unpopular).

Language activation

It didn't stop us!

The teacher writes a list of negative situations on the board, eg
– no money
– no time
– no friends
– no car
– nothing to wear
– nowhere to go
– nothing to say
– nowhere to eat
– no furniture

In small groups, students make sentences saying what they were able to do, in these situations using an adverb clause of concession. Encourage them to use several different types of concessional clause, eg *Although the boys had no money, they ...*

Extra exercise

Combine the words and phrases in 1–5 with the information in a–d. Which combinations can then be used as part of a longer sentence without moving the comma? There may be more than one possibility for each, eg

Despite our burglar alarm, (we still had our house broken into!)
Even though we had a burglar alarm, (we still had our house broken into!)

1	in spite of	a	we had a burglar alarm,
2	although	b	our burglar alarm,
3	despite	c	the fact that we had a burglar alarm,
4	not that	d	installing a burglar alarm,
5	even though		

Which combinations could be used to introduce contrasting information before or after a clause such as *the office was still broken into*?

Which combination could be used after a clause like *the office was broken into* as an aside?

▶ **Answers**

1 b, c, d
2 a
3 b, c, d
4 a
5 a

In other words, 1 and 3 are followed by a noun or gerund and 2, 4 and 5 are followed by a clause.

1, 2, 3 and 5 could be used before or after a clause such as *the office was still broken into* and suggest a contradiction in terms.

4 could be used after a clause like *the office was broken into* as an aside.

14 Tomorrow's World Today

This unit looks at the information revolution and the growth of new technology.

Listening and Speaking
Robotics

Introduction   Student's Book p 170

1 Students look at the pictures in pairs and speculate on how the robots are used. Encourage them to use modal verbs of speculation in their discussion.

▶ Answers

1 *Robocop*
2 Robbie the Robot from *The Forbidden Planet*
3 R2D2 and C3PO from *Star Wars*
4 *The Terminator*

2 Ask students if they have had any personal experience with robots, eg in the workplace. Discuss the statements quickly as a class or in pairs. Students then compare their decisions with the key on page 196.

Listening

1 Students look through the summary quickly.

2 When you have played the tape, allow students time to compare their answers.

▶ Answers

1 two years
2 25
3 maze
4 miniature version
5 races
6 sensors
7 floating
8 weight categories
9 table tennis
10 menial
11 room-cleaning
12 can-collection

Tapescript

P = Presenter

P In university laboratories, high-tech electronic centres, prestige research institutes, school classrooms and even garden sheds around the world, tomorrow's generation of sci-fi athletic stars are getting into shape for the most amazing event yet on the world sporting stage.

After Barcelona, Seoul, Lake Placid and Los Angeles, the new arena of competitive excellence is to be Glasgow – host city to the first ever World Robot Championships. This supports the city's initiative in placing itself at the leading edge of high technology. Future events will alternate on a two-year cycle between overseas venues and Glasgow, which is home to these championships in the same way as Athens is to the Olympic Games.

Over 500 robots, varying from a thumbnail to almost two tons in weight, will be assembled from around twenty-five countries to participate in the three-day event to be held in the city's prestigious Royal Concert Hall. As Dr Peter Mowforth, Research Director of the city's acclaimed Turing Institute observed, 'However wacky it may sound, this is an event of tremendous significance to the international robotics community. It is what we have all dreamed about for years.'

Each competition in the Championships will be judged, and gold, silver and bronze medals awarded for the best three robots. Here is a preview of just some of the many events planned.

One of the best established robot competitions is the IEE Micro-Mouse. This involves small, fully autonomous wheeled vehicles having to find their way through a maze, first by exploring it and then by planning a route to the centre and racing against the clock. There is also a miniature version, called Nano-Mouse.

Of course, any event of this kind must include athletics contests. There will be two-legged and multi-legged races, where robots race in a straight line against each other. Hurdling is also featured, where robots must use their sensors to detect and then jump a series of hurdles placed in their path. The high jump requires robots to spring into the air and land on a platform.

Other sports include archery and javelin, where robots will throw arrows, darts or javelin and attempt to hit a target. Floating and submersible robots will demonstrate their skill in the swimming pool. There'll be Sumo wrestling with various weight categories. And Robat is table tennis for robots, an event that has been well-established since 1985.

One of the more common uses of robots in the world at large is for menial clearing up. Did you know for instance that robots are used to clean up the Paris Metro? There'll be opportunities at the Championships for robots to show off their skills in this area, with room-cleaning competitions against the clock for robot vacuum cleaners and can-collection, where robots must collect cans and deposit them in a specified area.

These are but a few of the many events you ll be able to enjoy at the World Robot Championships in Glasgow. There'll also be a series of seminars and an extensive trade exhibition. Don't miss it!

English in Use Student's Book p 171

1 The text continues the same theme as the listening in the previous section. Remind students to read the text twice – once for general meaning and then more carefully line by line. They should complete the task in 10 minutes.

▶ **Answers**

1 the
2 √
3 also
4 industrialist
5 for
6 √
7 similar
8 √
9 which
10 √
11 last
12 √
13 to

2 Students discuss the topic in pairs briefly, giving reasons for their views.

Speaking Student's Book p 172

Students do the complete speaking test in pairs, timing themselves for each part. You may wish to use video or audio equipment to record students for later analysis.

Part 1
Suggest students look back at Unit 1, pages 10–11, for a reminder of this introductory part of the speaking test.

Part 2
Refer students to the relevant sections of the Vocabulary Resource on pages 193 and 194.

Part 3
Refer students to the relevant section of the Vocabulary Resource on page 194.

Part 4
Students should discuss the two questions fully, giving reasons for their views.

Reading
Where is the Workplace? ▼

Introduction Student's Book p 173

1 Elicit useful vocabulary for describing the pictures, eg the word 'gridlock' could be used to describe the traffic situation in the picture of Los Angeles. Revise words and phrases for each lifestyle on the board, eg
Los Angeles – *commuting, rat race, burnout*
Scottish isle – *tranquillity, isolation, stress-free*
Students then discuss their preferences in pairs.

2 Students read the extract and discuss the answers in pairs.

▶ **Answers**

John Ruscoe works for a computer company from his home on Orkney, a group of islands off the north-east coast of Scotland.

Elicit the meaning of *broom cupboard* by asking students to describe his workspace. Explain that John Ruscoe is a good example of a 'telecommuter' and refer them to the end of the extract for a description of 'telecommuting' (… *using advanced technology to re-create cottage industry hundreds of miles from commercial centres*.)

3 Play the tape and discuss the questions as a class.

▶ **Suggested answers**

Telecommuting has become slightly more important in Los Angeles since the earthquake in 1994. It was difficult to drive to work for a period of time and the telephone companies promoted the concept to local companies, gaining 4,000 new line installations. However, the majority of Los Angeles' commuters preferred to stick to their old ways.

Tapescript

N = Narrator
N The earthquake that hit Los Angeles in January 1994 devastated key sections of the city's freeways, at least doubling the journey time to work for many commuters. Given this situation, what could be more logical than to let the phone take the strain instead, and telecommute? Pacific Bell and GTE, the two big phone companies in the region, set up hotlines to advise companies that wanted to exploit telecommuting while the freeways were being repaired.
   Howard Rheingold, who has written books about the new technology and changing work patterns, was tempted at the time of the quake to make a forecast. One week after the event, he predicted that there would be an

immediate rise in telecommuting in the area. Early in March 94, a call to Pacific Bell revealed that the hotline had taken 4,600 calls since the quake at the end of January. That may sound a lot, but it's tiny for a city of 5.9 million commuters, of whom about four million travel to work by car. Those calls translated into just 4,000 installations for new lines – 0.1% of the working population. Meanwhile the roads are still blocked in the mornings and nights. Some habits die hard.

4 Keep this discussion brief, but ask students to note down their ideas, as they will be asked to refer back to these in **4** of the next section.

Reading

1 Students skim the report, timing themselves as they read.

▶ **Answers**

The main advantages for employees are that they don't have to waste time and money travelling to work and they can choose where to live. For employers, the advantages are that employees appear to work more productively, the costs are lower and there are more employable people to choose from.

2 Students match the headings to the text individually and compare their answers in pairs. They should take no longer than ten minutes for this task.

Notes

encapsulates (line 5) – expresses (something) briefly
dissemination (line 48) – spreading
trade-off (line 93) – exchange, especially as a compromise

▶ **Answers**

1 D   2 B   3 H   4 I   5 G   6 F

3 Ask students to scan the text for the information required. Five minutes should be sufficient for this task.

▶ **Answers**

a 5   b 2   c 6   d 4   e 5   f 5

4 Students review their ideas in pairs and compare the information on the benefits and problems of teleworking in the text.

5 Students discuss the statements in pairs and then report their ideas to the class.

Style   Student's Book p 176

Remind students that they may have to write a report in Part 1 or 2.

▶ **Answers**

Other examples of prefacing structures in the report are:

The employer can benefit from teleworking in three main ways … (section 5)

A major concern for any employee is … (section 6)

Other adverbs to state a typical situation are:

basically, essentially, normally, typically, usually

Writing
An Electronic Future ▼

Introduction   Student's Book p 176

1 Students discuss the items shown and predict possible replacements, for example cash will probably be replaced by smart cards issued by a bank.

2 Students discuss the pros and cons of the two innovations. Encourage them to talk separately about commerce and travel, both of which will come up in the writing task itself.

Notes

woes – misfortunes
goof-ups – foolish errors (slang)

English in Use

1 Students discuss the illustration in pairs.

▶ **Answer**

It shows an impression of a possible hotel room in the near future.

2 Before students complete the task, refer them to the title and discuss its meaning.

Notes

B&B – Bed and Breakfast accommodation
natty – smart and cleverly designed
globetrotters – worldwide travellers

Students should then complete the task in 10 minutes. Alternatively, this task could be set as homework.

▶ **Answers**

1 H   2 D   3 G   4 A   5 F   6 E

3 Students discuss their ideal hotel room in pairs.

Vocabulary   Student's Book p 178

1   Ask students to explain the meanings in pairs, taking turns.

▶ Answers
   1   add, include
   2   arrive
   3   warm, cook
   4   increase
   5   pay the bill

2   Students discuss the other meanings as a class.

▶ Suggested answers
   throw in (a comment) – add
   throw in (the towel) – give up

   roll up (a piece of paper) – form into a cylinder
   roll up (sleeves) – make shorter
   roll up (of an animal) – curl up
   heat up (of a situation) – become serious

   turn up – arrive
   turn up – be found or noticed, eg a missing object; a new job

   check out – investigate

3   Students complete the sentences quickly on their own.

▶ Answers
   1 checking out   2 throw in   3 heat up   4 turned up
   5 rolled up

Optional activity

The article contains several compound adjectives. Ask students to find these and say why they think the writer has used so many (to reflect the topic by sounding ultra-modern):
in-room
push-button
high-tech
up-to-the-second

Writing   Student's Book p 179

Understanding the task

1   Students read the task in pairs and suggest stylistic features. Then ask them to think of suitable headings for the three elements of work, travel and home. Refer them to the relevant sections of the Vocabulary Resource on pages 193–195.

▶ Answers
Relevant features from the reading section are:
   • *section headings*
   • *adverbs to state the typical situation*, eg *Nowadays,*

travel bookings are generally computerized.
   • *will* and *may* to make future predictions, eg *Within the next few years, it may well be possible to do all shopping from home using interactive TV.*

Other stylistic points to bear in mind are:
   • *giving the report a title*
   • *using impersonal language* (see the revised introduction in 3c for examples)

Brainstorming ideas

2   Students add ideas to the spider diagram, working in pairs or in small groups.

▶ Suggested answers
   interactive TV – no need to go out; shopping on-line.
   travel – computerized bookings; modern fly-by-wire aircraft, where every part of the flight is controlled by computer.
   home – new appliances, such as 'smart' fridges and washing machines, which are fitted with microchips to inform you, in the case of fridges, when certain products are about to be used up.
   work – use of the internet; handheld teleordering sets; fax machines; mobile telephones.

Planning your answer

3   a–b   Students spend five minutes working on their own and then discuss their ideas in pairs.

   c   Ask them to look at the example of a weak introduction and discuss the question.

▶ Answers

Problem:	Suggested improvement:
no title	rework the first sentence as a heading
repetition of 'I'	rework in an impersonal style, eg *This report examines …*
inappropriate mention of winning the scholarship	omit
mixed style in third sentence and inappropriate use of *gadgets*	reword more formally
over-detailed on one aspect	omit the example of computers and fax machines
muddled	state all the aspects of the report clearly together

d   Students then write their own introductions and exchange them.

▶ **Answer**

Model introduction:

This report examines the current and possible future impact of technology in three areas: work, travel and the home. The growth of teleworking is discussed and examples of state-of-the-art office equipment provided. The second section reviews modernization in travel, while the third deals with new household appliances.

Writing

4 Students should check their work carefully when they have finished. There is a further example of a report in the Writing Resource on page 191.

Structure
Technological Trends ▼

Introduction   Student's Book p 180

Treat the questions as a class discussion.

Reading

Students should refer to the following points:

▶ **Answers**

– (Paragraph 1) Instead of making long cuts in the patient's body, the surgeons use an endoscope, an operating telescope, which is passed into the body through a small hole. The image of the operation is shown on a TV screen.

– (Paragraph 3) Benefits: it reduces trauma to the patient; surgeons no longer have to work in crowded conditions and can now work standing upright.

Grammar review   Student's Book p 181

A   Modals

▶ **Answers**

may = possibility
will = certainty
would = conditional / polite form of *will* / past of *will*
could = polite form / past ability
can = ability
needn't = absence of obligation

1   will / 'll
2   may may
3   needn't
4   can
5   could
6   Will / Could / Can
7   May / Can / Could
8   Would

Other modals and what they express:
should   = obligation / conditional
might   = possibility
must   = obligation or logical explanation
ought to = obligation
Also, remember the semi-modals: *need*, *dare*

Modals can:
– form a negative by adding *not* instead of using another auxiliary.
– form an interrogative by inversion.
– be used in short answers.
– be used to form question tags.
– be used as auxiliaries.
– alter the meaning of the verb they are used with.

B   Conditionals

▶ **Answers**

This is the *zero* conditional (*if + present, + present*) and it is used to refer to something which occurs frequently or is thought to be true.

The basic difference between the first, second and third conditionals:

First:
If + present + future – used when there is a possibility or probability of something happening in the future.

Second:
If + simple past, + conditional – used to refer to a set of circumstances which you know do not exist and / or are not likely to, but which could possibly exist.

Third:
If + past perfect, + past conditional – used to speculate about how things might have been different if events had taken another course, but which are now impossible because it is too late to change them.

▶ Suggested answers
(Tell students to be careful in 3 as there is no conditional link in this sentence.)

1   don't find out   will / are going to have
2   shall / will hand in   apologizes / has apologized
3   Had I known   would have prepared
4   had been   would have made
5   had worked   would be
6   had had   would have gone
7   could   would you change
8   had not / hadn't broken   would / 'd be

C Reported speech

▶ Answers

Alf Cuschieri, a leading endoscopic surgeon, says (that) *minimal access surgery* is a real breakthrough. He wishes they had developed it years ago.

He says that it not only reduces the trauma to the patient – it also means that they no longer have to perform major operations by making major incisions.

Changes if the reporting verb were *said*:

Alf Cuschieri, a leading endoscopic surgeon, said (that) *minimal access surgery* was a real breakthrough. He wished they had developed it years ago / before. He said that it not only reduced the trauma to the patient – it also meant that they no longer had to perform major operations by making major incisions.

▶ Suggested answer

Sam asked his mother / mum what she was doing with the tool box.

Maria told Sam not to touch the electric cord.

Sam said he wished his mother / she wouldn't shout at him.

Maria apologized, explaining / and explained that she hadn't wanted Sam to hurt himself.

Sam asked his mother what it / the cord was for.

Maria replied that she was trying to mend the CD player.

Sam wanted to know what had happened to it.

Maria told him that somebody had knocked it off the shelf a couple of days before and it wouldn't work.

Sam insisted (angrily) that he hadn't done it. / Sam immediately pointed out that he hadn't done it.

D Dependent clauses   Student's Book p 182

Tell students that an *active* verb means a 'finite' verb.

1

▶ Answers

a 1 as the subject of a sentence; 2 as the object of a sentence

b 1 defining; 2 non-defining

c eight types of adverb clauses:
1 condition
2 time
3 result
4 manner
5 reason
6 concession
7 purpose
8 place

2

▶ Answers

Examples of noun clauses:

a The development of keyhole surgery means that the surgeon's knife may soon disappear altogether. (line 1)

b Alf Cuschieri wishes they'd developed it years ago. (line 14)

c Minimal access surgery also means that you no longer have to make major incisions to perform major operations. (line 15)

d Keyhole surgeons hope that miniaturisation will make it possible for patients to have their operations performed by robots ... (line 37)

e Telesurgery means that a patient can be operated on by two surgeons who are hundreds of kilometres away from each other ... (line 50)

f Some people believe that such techniques will have been perfected in the next ten years or so. (line 53)

These noun clauses are all the objects of the main verbs in the sentences.

3

▶ Answers

An example of a defining relative clause towards the end of the first paragraph:
– *that will barely leave a scar.*

An example of a non-defining relative clause towards the end of paragraph three:
– *through which light travels.*

It is not possible to omit the relative pronoun in the two examples because in the first, *that* is the subject of the verb *will ... leave* and also refers to a preceding noun (*hole*) which is also the subject of the same verb. In the second, the relative appears in a non-defining clause and after a preposition and cannot therefore be omitted.

4

▶ Answers

Paragraph three of the article:
Examples of adverb clauses of:
– concession
Although in the 1960s flexible scopes were developed ... (line 21)
– reason
As surgeons cannot work in the dark ... (line 32)

▶ Suggested answers

Type of clause:

Sally decided to accept the job:

a because it was exactly what she wanted. (reason)

b so that she could have an opportunity to widen her experience. (purpose)

c although it wasn't exactly what she wanted. (concession)

d   after she had given the matter careful consideration. (time)

e   so quickly that she did not have time to consider the responsibilities it involved. (result)

E   Verb tenses

▶ Answers

1

The present perfect is used in b as no time is mentioned. The writer is only interested in the fact that this has happened, not when it happened, and the result of the borrowing is still in evidence as it is being put to good use. The same tense is used in d because the action has continued right up to the present moment and is probably still happening. In c, however, the simple past is needed because a definite time is mentioned (1960s).

The past perfect is used in a after *I wish* to talk about a wish for things to have been different in the past. Other tenses which can be used after *wish* + a pronoun are *would*, for things to be different in the future, and the simple past to express a wish for things for be different in the present. NB Remember *would* is not used after *I / we wish*; *could* is used instead.

The future perfect tense is used in e to talk about something which will occur and be completed at or before a certain time in the future.

2

a   is / has been tasted
or It was / had been a long time since I tasted / had tasted, etc.
b   have the authors been writing
c   will have completed
d   have been
e   has had
f   had not mentioned
g   had paid   was
h   had had   took

F   Gerunds and infinitives   Student's Book p 183

▶ Answers

Any reasonable answer is acceptable for students' sentences.

1   to regret doing (what you have already done), to regret (to say) – (what you are about to say)
2   to remember to do (after), doing (before)
3   without doing
4   to look forward to doing
5   in order to do
6   to help do / to do (no difference in meaning)
7   to object to doing
8   (I) used to do

G   Passives – the causative use of *have*

▶ Answers

a   active – stating a fact
b   passive – the operations are equally as or more important than *who* or *what* performs them.
c   causative use of *have* – it may be possible to arrange for someone or something to do the job for you.

1   The operating telescope is passed into the body through a small hole.
2   Major incisions are no longer needed / no longer need to be made to perform major operations.
3   The technology was borrowed from other fields by the medical profession. / by the medical profession from other fields.
4   Engine interiors no longer need / have to be taken apart to be checked / for checking.
5   Light is beamed into the area of the body which is being operated on.
6   The surgeons had a TV screen installed in the operating theatre.
7   Ever-smaller miniature and micro-robots are being designed by the Institute of Technology's Artificial Intelligence and Robotics Laboratory.
8   In future patients might be able to have their operations performed by remote control.

H   Inversions

▶ Answers

Inversions are used to emphasize a point.

The word requiring emphasis is placed at the beginning of the sentence and the subject and verb belonging to that part of the sentence need to be inverted.

Negative words, eg *never*, or words which have a rather restrictive meaning, eg *only when*, are used at the beginning of the sentence in this kind of construction.

1   Not only is remote control surgery revolutionary, but it is beneficial as well.
2   Only by investing in further research can we improve our technology.
3   Only when we make / by making technological advances available to everybody, can we truly benefit from them.
4   Not until well into the next century will we be able to take full advantage of the proposed health scheme.
5   No longer do patients have to put up with pain and suffering when they undergo an operation.
6   Never has anything like this been invented before.
    or Never before has anything like this been invented.

Tests

Unit tests and Progress tests

The tests appear in numerical order, the Unit tests first, followed by the Progress tests. Unit tests should be taken on finishing the relevant unit. Progress tests should be taken at the end of Units 5, 10 and 14.

The keys to all Unit tests are on pages 133–135. Those to the Progress tests are on page 136.

There is marking information in the Introduction on pages 9–10 of this book.

The following section contains pages marked 'photocopiable'. The publisher grants permission for those pages to be photocopied in accordance with the following conditions. Individual purchasers may make copies for their own use or for use by the classes they teach. School purchasers may make copies for use by their staff and students, but this permission does not extend to additional schools or branches.

In no circumstances may any part of this book be photocopied for resale.

Unit 1 Test

Vocabulary

Choose the best option A, B, C or D.

1 Look, will you stop _____ in and let me finish my sentence!
   A moving   B pushing
   C butting   D plugging

2 Her young daughters _____ on the sofa, wishing they were out at play.
   A fidgeted   B shifted
   C twisted   D moved

3 I do wish you two boys would be more _____ to the others in the class.
   A dominant   B alert
   C careful   D respectful

4 The man gave a series of _____ answers which told them nothing more.
   A tricky   B uncertain
   C evasive   D elusive

5 It was a totally _____ play that neither of them could follow.
   A obscure   B sombre
   C vague   D shady

6 The announcement about job losses has _____ consequences for the firm.
   A hard-hitting   B far-reaching
   C never-ending   D wide-ranging

7 I'd love to go out with you tonight. The only _____ is that I've got no cash!
   A snag   B pitfall
   C disadvantage   D mistake

8 As the test result was _____, the team of scientists repeated it after ten days.
   A uncanny   B weird
   C abnormal   D unnatural

9 Can you _____ exactly what it is you're complaining about?
   A find out   B turn in
   C work out   D pin down

10 I work in a government department where every document is packed with technical _____.
   A jargon   B euphemism
   C cliché   D phrase

Error correction

Read this text and make the necessary corrections. Tick any lines that are error-free.

11 Peter mark Roget developed the work that still bears
12 his name 'Roget's Thesaurus after almost 50 years.
13 It was published in it's completed form in 1852 and
14 remains to this day one of the most useful reference
15 books to any writer. Roget was actually a doctor a
16 famous medical lecturer and an editor who also
17 worked on a commission that reported on Londons
18 water supply. He also designed a pocket chessboard
19 When he reached the age of 69 and had retired he
20 was able to devote all his time to the thesaurus. He
21 had a fascination with the beauty of words the word
22 thesaurus' is derived from a Greek word meaning
23 treasure house). Rogets main aim in writing the
24 thesaurus was to be able to express himself
25 accurately and, without repetition.

Unit 2 Test

Vocabulary

Choose the best option A, B, C or D.

1 Iridology is essentially _____ in nature.
   A curative   B healing
   C preventative   D treatable

2 Some doctors' _____ to backache is to prescribe pain-killers.
   A technique   B method
   C approach   D process

3 Oriental medicine _____ the mind and body as one inseparable unit.
   A thinks   B believes
   C foresees   D regards

4 A deep wound like this one will take longer to _____.
   A cure   B heal
   C mend   D settle

5 The boy's diet of fried food and chocolate _____ a bad outbreak of spots.
   A developed   B triggered
   C gave   D advanced

6 Living in the actual country should act as a _____ to language improvement.
   A direction   B factor
   C stimulus   D change

7 If you go out of season, the island is a _____ and relaxing place.
   A tranquil   B brutal
   C lively   D composed

8 Katy wanted to _____ everything that had happened at the party.
   A talk   B recount
   C claim   D say

9 It cannot be denied that fireworks are a serious fire _____.
   A accident   B mishap
   C danger   D hazard

10 There is a total _____ on smoking in public places in Los Angeles.
   A ban   B stop
   C restriction   D taboo

Structure

Choose the best option in 11–20.

11 _____ I just add one more point to the discussion? (Would / Could)

12 You _____ bother to come round and tell me – just give me a ring. (needn't / mustn't)

13 John _____ have seen a doctor earlier but he said he was too busy. (may / should)

14 I don't believe you've done that homework – you _____ possibly have finished it so quickly. (mightn't / couldn't)

15 _____ you leave now? It's only ten o'clock! (Must / Would)

16 You _____ have left all that food out – the cat's eaten the lot! (shouldn't / mustn't)

17 I _____ have definitely bought another pair if I had known your size. (would / might)

18 There _____ still be a chance to get tickets, as the group are playing an extra concert. (can / may)

19 You really _____ to look after yourself, you know – you're obviously very run down. (must / need)

20 Personally, I _____ have sent that letter. But you've done it now. (wouldn't / couldn't)

Error correction

Read the sentences and correct any errors. Tick any sentences that are error-free.

21 Aromatherapy uses many of essential oils from plants.

22 Conventional methods have proved as ineffective and they are now experimenting with a radically different treatment.

23 I couldn't whip up any enthusiasm for going out on such a cold night.

24 One vitamin pill a day is the equivalent for drinking two litres of orange juice.

25 Coffee is a stimulus and should not be drunk late at night.

26 Their singing was excruciating and most people left the room.

27 Cantner's Gym has been refurbished and is now open seven days a week.

28 Respiratory unorders such as asthma can be made worse by living near busy roads.

29 It is well-known that smoking can be harmfull to unborn babies.

30 Their exaggerated claims are based on a complete fallacy.

Unit 3 Test

Vocabulary

Choose the best option A, B, C or D.

1 Dominant individuals may use _____ gestures to underline their power.
   A submissive   B expansive
   C flirtatious   D nervous

2 At parties, Jill was always very _____ and talkative.
   A outgoing   B insecure
   C tense   D calm

3 After the match, the two tired lads sat _____ in front of the TV, eating crisps and drinking from cans.
   A cowering   B slouched
   C straight-backed   D stiffly

4 Andrew's _____ was to only tell his mother bad news when she was busy, so that she would have less chance to react.
   A tactics   B intent
   C ploy   D threat

5 Try not to be _____ by the remarks of other more senior people.
   A endangered   B interested
   C intimidated   D faked

6 Melvyn's elder sister has rather _____ views and totally disapproves of his lifestyle.
   A belittling   B rebellious
   C confident   D staid

7 The posters all had the same _____ saying 'Vote Now or Pay Later'.
   A banner   B sign
   C slogan   D flag

8 The elderly are particularly _____ to this form of illness.
   A vulnerable   B weak
   C wimpy   D trivial

9 A few tears were _____ by both parents when Marion finally left home.
   A flowed   B cast
   C sealed   D shed

10 It was Alice's year: a new home, a better job – everything just clicked into _____.
   A place   B position
   C space   D spot

Structure

Fill the gaps in this cloze with one word only.

If women choose to pursue a career once they have children, they often miss (11)_____ on a close relationship with their children. Helen Jamieson is a mother of three who has given up work (12)_____ look after her children full-time. She strongly believes that women are pressurized to do (13)_____ much, driving themselves to the absolute limit. In her own case, after six years of paid employment, Helen finally decided to call it (14)_____ day. She says she initially found (15)_____ hard being at home, (16)_____ she never missed the job itself. She admits that if she had (17)_____ a brilliant career to begin with, she might feel differently now. Financially, she is no worse off (18)_____ before, as the cost of childcare and commuting exceeded her actual income. (19)_____ the government starts to offer tax incentives to working parents, she says she will not return to the workplace (20)_____ her children are grown up.

Error correction

Read the sentences and correct any errors. Tick any sentences that are error-free.

21 If you were in my position, what will you do?
22 If you're feeling nervous during an interview, try to improve your postur.
23 Unless the management finds a solution, there will be a strike on Monday.
24 Even if they take more time off, workaholics would still be unable to relax.
25 Richard's uncle was in an expansively mood and smiled broadly at everyone.
26 If you had warned us about the party beforehand, we wouldn't have mind so much about the noise.
27 Unless the project receives additional support, they won't be able to cope for much longer.
28 You should get back to them, even if you didn't want to accept the job.
29 If a child is rebbelious in school, this may well indicate problems at home.
30 Don't go along with the offer unless you're really sure its what you want.

Unit 4 Test

Vocabulary

Choose the best option A, B, C or D.

1 The light from the car _____ as it receded into the distance.
   A seeped out   B faded away
   C rolled away   D shone out

2 Though tired, she was visibly _____ after the birth of her first child.
   A perplexed   B exhausted
   C unaffected   D elated

3 The old man led a _____ existence after she left and refused even to see his children.
   A reclusive   B deserted
   C remote   D vacant

4 Tickets cost a _____ £6, which for three hours of music is great value for money.
   A few   B small
   C mere   D bit

5 It was so foggy that the climbers couldn't _____ the nearby shelter.
   A make out   B break out
   C take out   D run out

6 Because of his strange story, Richards became a _____ overnight and had a number of requests to appear on TV shows.
   A figure   B character
   C celebrity   D personality

7 A sharp frost _____ the beginning of winter.
   A advertised   B predicted
   C showed   D heralded

8 They are fighting to eradicate the _____ of starvation caused by the civil war.
   A tradition   B legacy
   C leaving   D remains

9 _____, Phil was a gregarious individual who enjoyed the company of others enormously.
   A Socially   B Psychologically
   C Physically   D Technically

10 The teenager took his father's credit card and _____ 7,000 dollars' worth of purchases.
   A made up   B ran up
   C took up   D put up

Structure

Supply the correct past tense in the following sentences, using the verbs in brackets.

11 Helen _____ (work) at the company for three years when the redundancies were announced.

12 David _____ (sleep) on a rug in the garden when a fighter plane suddenly screamed past at low altitude and woke him up.

13 That summer, I _____ (revise) for my exams and I didn't have time for a holiday.

14 A search party _____ (start) at dawn to look for the missing group, but it was abandoned last night because of atrocious weather conditions.

15 Just as he came through the door, the phone _____ (ring).

16 The couple _____ (live) in the house for several months before they noticed anything odd.

17 While I _____ (cook) the supper, the children played chess.

18 Earlier in the year, many employees _____ (start) to take extra work home, but when they heard about the pay cuts, they stopped doing this.

19 In the summer, water supplies _____ (become) dangerously low due to the prolonged hot weather, but are now back to average levels.

20 Alice _____ (try) to interrupt him while he was talking but her efforts were in vain.

Error correction

Correct the following sentences if necessary, by removing any extra words. Tick any sentences that are error-free.

21 The strange incident has occurred in 1947 and it is only now that the true facts are coming out.

22 He was brought up by his grandparents for many years, following on his parents' traumatic divorce.

23 New evidence has thrown a doubt on this hitherto accepted theory.

24 Like any other child, Ruth loved all kinds of sweets and chocolate.

25 I found it very difficult to get used to be drinking tea without milk.

26 It seems that he really was telling the truth about what he did saw.

27 When Henry was younger, he would walk for hours in the forest and quite forget what time it was.

28 By the year 2010 it may be possible to travel faster than the speed of the light.

29 While his subjects were under hypnosis, they appeared to understand all his instructions fully.

30 On looking more closely, they had been found a thin piece of wire connecting the box to the window.

Unit 5 Test

Vocabulary

Choose the best option A, B, C or D.

1 Ken _____ his doctor's advice and continued to overwork.
   A disassociated   B disregarded
   C disowned   D disappointed

2 After a difficult childhood, Jeannie bounced _____ when she was adopted by a caring family.
   A back   B up
   C off   D over

3 Most babies seem to _____ on cow's milk but a few are allergic to it.
   A exist   B live
   C thrive   D benefit

4 Both children exhibited severe _____ problems after their father was sent to prison.
   A behave   B behaved
   C behaving   D behavioural

5 Some people believe that _____ is preferable to punishing offenders.
   A therapy   B commitment
   C change   D sustenance

6 As the fire blazed, fire-fighters pleaded with _____ to keep out of the way.
   A audiences   B crowds
   C onlookers   D groups

7 Shopkeepers have blamed vandals for a _____ of broken windows in the city centre.
   A spate   B run
   C collection   D sequence

8 Social workers admitted feeling utterly _____ when faced with the problem of drugs and violence.
   A aimless   B helpless
   C pointless   D clueless

9 The council will remove any vehicles parked _____.
   A unavoidably   B prohibitively
   C illegally   D unreasonably

10 Tracy said she had been very lonely since _____ up with her boyfriend.
   A finishing   B ending
   C stopping   D splitting

Structure

Report the following sentences using the more suitable verb in brackets.

11 'If I were you, Teresa, I'd make sure I got some qualifications before leaving school.'
   Teresa's father _____. (insisted / advised)

12 'I'm afraid I really can't afford to buy you any new trainers.'
   Ian's mother _____. (explained / wondered)

13 'These two essays are almost identical. You must have copied each other.'
   The teacher _____. (advised / accused)

14 'My boss? He's the man sitting at the next table.'
   Jane _____. (wondered / whispered)

15 'Is there anything I can do to help?'
   My neighbour _____. (asked / suggested)

16 'Don't you understand? I don't want to have dinner with Sam.'
   Sue _____. (insisted / asked)

17 'You never listen when I'm talking to you.'
   John's girlfriend _____. (complained / wondered)

18 'Take one tablet three times a day after meals.'
   His doctor _____. (told / suggested)

19 'Would it be rude to ask her for a lift, do you think?'
   Charlie _____. (suggested / wondered)

20 'Thank you. I'd love a cup of coffee.'
   Mrs Williams _____. (explained / replied)

Error correction

Read the sentences and correct any errors. Tick any sentences that are error-free.

21 The journalist asked the policeman, 'Do you believe there is sufficient evidence to say there is a direct connection between poverty and crime?'

22 You could never accuse Madonna of being shy; she is a very demonstrable person.

23 The couple were having a terrific arguement so they didn't hear me when I walked in.

24 The psychiatrist suggested against allowing Mavis to live with her family.

25 'I don't think there is anything wrong with people begging on the streets, Mrs Blake asserted.

26 Many family breakdowns are due in part to our stressful lifestyles.

27 It's a very small village and there's a great sense of commune.

28 There is no point in trying to win the lottery; it's a hopeful task.

29 Clare suggested to go to the council meeting the following day.

30 The old lady seemed confused and unaware of her suroundings.

Unit 6 Test

Vocabulary

Choose the best option A, B, C or D.

1 The real _____ of the film is caught at the end and finishes up in jail.
   A hero   B protagonist
   C villain   D principal

2 There is a huge amount of _____ associated with children's TV nowadays.
   A manufacturing   B produce
   C merchandising   D sales

3 For me, the plot was utterly _____ and most disappointing.
   A unconvincing   B under-rated
   C intricate   D involved

4 Redman is one of the most _____ saxophonists of his generation and deserves to be better-known.
   A perceptive   B distinguished
   C acclaimed   D applauded

5 The mailing list has done much to _____ the numbers of people attending.
   A lift   B encourage
   C heighten   D boost

6 This rather depressing novel is the product of an extremely _____ period of his life.
   A jaunty   B introspective
   C accessible   D intrusive

7 His plays contain _____ themes of real life that leave a lasting impression on you.
   A compelling   B trivial
   C zany   D phoney

8 The _____ surrounding the band's latest world tour has been ridiculous.
   A advertisement   B campaign
   C promotion   D hype

9 'Dreamtime', an exhibition featuring _____ Aboriginal art, is on until February 20.
   A indigenous   B national
   C resident   D civil

10 Virtual Reality technology is on the _____ of changing the entertainment industry for good.
   A state   B side
   C edge   D verge

Structure

Fill in the gaps in this cloze with one word only.

'Here are some TV highlights for next Thursday evening. (11)_____ you like comedy, you (12)_____ love *The Brittas Empire*. Set in a leisure centre and with Chris Barrie (13)_____ the lead role, this will (14)_____ you crying with laughter from 8.30 to 9.0. Meanwhile, on BBC 2 at the same time, Jackie Bird will (15)_____ investigating the case of a 32-year-old man (16)_____ pretended to be a 17-year-old schoolboy (17)_____ went back to the same school he had attended (18)_____ a teenager. That really is (19)_____ to be essential viewing. Fans of late-night horror films must (20)_____ miss the classic *Dracula: Prince of Darkness* on Sky Movies Gold, at 11.50.'

Error correction

Read the sentences and correct any errors. Tick any sentences that are error-free.

21 The main exhibit was an oval, stunning, turquoise and orange bowl.

22 With the arrival of video on demand, telephone bills will be being astronomical.

23 The Internet will provide access to reference material that most schools could never ordinarily afford.

24 Probably hundreds of people are going to work on space stations in fifty years' time.

25 The idea that all modern art is impenetrable seems quite prepostrous.

26 Society will be having to change radically to keep pace with the technology available.

27 The development of virtual galleries offers new opportunities, predominantly to artists working with computerized images.

28 It seems almost inevitable that the lead actor will be replaced before the show will close.

29 The film has no pace a very thin plot and some very wooden acting.

30 Don't let me disturb you now. I'll be coming back some other time, when you're less busy.

Unit 7 Test

Vocabulary

Choose the best option A, B, C or D.

1   The company had all the necessary _____ for training.
    A   assets   B   resources
    C   supplies   D   riches

2   Suzy has great _____. She'll be snapped up by Hollywood.
    A   potential   B   quality
    C   capacity   D   possibility

3   Philip _____ the whole class and eventually, they were all punished.
    A   kept up   B   stirred up
    C   beat up   D   held up

4   The latest opinion _____ has predicted a new government by next spring.
    A   ballot   B   count
    C   vote   D   poll

5   Brian has done the most _____ jobs from clearing rubbish to washing up.
    A   challenging   B   intellectual
    C   menial   D   creative

6   The job includes a huge amount of day-to-day _____.
    A   administration B   running
    C   provision   D   conduct

7   Once they had booked a suitable _____, the band practised hard for their first ever concert.
    A   room   B   store
    C   venue   D   arena

8   You really must _____ your papers – they're in a real muddle.
    A   send out   B   draw up
    C   clean up   D   sort out

9   I'm glad they've reorganized the groups – I never felt really _____ in that maths class.
    A   pulled   B   strained
    C   stretched   D   pushed

10 After a break of over five years, the actor has made a successful _____.
    A   comeback   B   recovery
    C   revival   D   climbdown

Structure

Complete the following sentences using an appropriate tense of one of the verbs in brackets.

11 That's the doorbell again – I _____ people wouldn't call round at this time of night. (miss / wish)

12 Gareth never _____ his decision to give up music lessons. (regret / wish)

13 I do _____ having Jenny around – when is she coming back? (miss / wish)

14 John will be sadly _____ by all who knew him. (regret / miss)

15 I _____ that the department will not be able to support your claim. (regret / wish)

16 There isn't enough room here! I really _____ moving to a smaller house. (miss / regret)

17 Jackie soon _____ her regular routine and wanted to go back to how things had been. (miss / regret)

18 I really _____ I hadn't told him how I felt. It only made matters worse. (wish / regret)

19 We _____ to have to inform you that there has been an error regarding your account. (regret / wish)

20 Jayne's card says she _____ us all but she's enjoying herself just the same! (miss / regret)

Error correction

Correct the following sentences if necessary, by removing any extra words. Tick any sentences that are error-free.

21 If only that you had said you were unhappy – we could have offered you something different.

22 I wish John didn't smoke as heavily as what he does.

23 You've been so lucky finding that job; everything's fallen into the place.

24 As a youngster, Chris Waddle was spotted as having a strong left foot and quickly earned a place in the team.

25 Sally has achieved herself very good grades and regrets not applying to university.

26 There's a great deal at stake in these negotiations, not just salaries.

27 He was given a high-profile government job but couldn't handle the some stress.

28 With reference to your advertisement, please could you to send me your brochure.

29 I have to confess that I miss the constant sunshine – it's really cold here!

30 My job is so mundane – all I have do is sit in front of that computer screen hitting the keys.

Unit 8 Test

Vocabulary

Choose the best option A, B, C or D.

1 We had a long and exhausting car _____ before reaching our final destination.
    A journey   B trip
    C voyage   D excursion

2 Students frequently accept holiday jobs which offer _____ pay.
    A few   B minimal
    C any   D less

3 When they stopped for a rest, the children wandered down to the beach leaving the adults to _____ the wonderful views.
    A take on   B take up
    C take in   D take over

4 We waited for ages but Jim never _____.
    A showed down   B showed out
    C showed off   D showed up

5 Tricia found the islanders exceptionally _____ and helpful.
    A friendly   B sympathetic
    C affectionate D caring

6 The tourist office was able to recommend several places of _____ interest which we decided to visit.
    A ancient   B historical
    C authentic   D historic

7 The priest offered to _____ us round the church.
    A show   B present
    C exhibit   D demonstrate

8 I like living in George Street; neighbours often _____ for a chat and a cup of tea.
    A drop in   B drop out
    C drop off   D drop down

9 Holiday-makers often suffer from minor _____ such as sunburn and stomach upsets.
    A aches   B disturbances
    C ailments   D diseases

10 When Jill and David drove to the South of France, they _____ more time in the car than they had wanted.
    A drove   B passed
    C stayed   D spent

Structure

Using the information below, write sentences containing relative, noun or adverb clauses.

11 We caught the ferry at Calais. It was packed with holiday makers. (relative)

12 Peter told Gillian. He planned to take her to Paris for the weekend. (noun)

13 stopped in a lay-by   fell into a deep sleep. (adverb)

14 people of all ages on the tour   they all got on very well with each other. (adverb)

15 You will soon find something out. It's more expensive to fly and not always quicker. (noun)

16 I made sure that I had a room in the quiet part of the hotel. I could finish preparing my talk for the conference. (adverb)

17 We jumped on the bus. It was just going to Oxford. (relative)

18 I sold my bicycle to Robert. It was too small for me. (relative)

19 The car engine was making a terrible noise. It might break down at any moment. (adverb)

20 I don't like travelling. I usually have to wait around in airports for hours. (noun)

Error correction

Read the sentences and correct any errors. Tick any sentences that are error-free.

21 The school advised William's parents to let him go on the adventure holiday as it might gain his self-confidence.

22 If you need to keep fit, then why not take on a sport such as squash or tennis?

23 We didn't have a holiday this year but the children went after several school outings.

24 My sister, who is in the travel business, was able to get hold of some cheap tickets.

25 I hate watching the in-flight movie because it's so difficult to ajust the volume.

26 The train journey was long and uncomfortable made Liz feel quite ill.

27 Despite of the freezing temperatures, the Hawker family continued with their walking holiday.

28 We met our friends in Athens a busy place at the best of times who were delighted to see us.

29 Lawrence was unhurt, but the driver who caused the accident didn't even stop.

30 The old lady is desperatly afraid of flying and avoids it at all costs.

Unit 9 Test

Vocabulary

Choose the best option A, B, C or D.

1   It was Paolo's first visit to England and he found most people were very _____ to him.
    A   gentle   B   caring
    C   polite   D   affectionate

2   My father has this annoying _____ of reading his newspaper during a meal.
    A   custom   B   habit
    C   notion   D   style

3   Rachel was _____ when her boyfriend didn't get in touch after the holidays.
    A   degraded   B   distorted
    C   devastated   D   denigrated

4   As it was my mother's birthday, I realized that the music and laughter meant that some sort of _____ was going on.
    A   celebration   B   ritual
    C   anniversary   D   rite

5   Many Australians can trace their _____ back to their arrival as convicts from England.
    A   ancestors   B   relatives
    C   relations   D   families

6   The older inhabitants looked on the festival as an opportunity to bridge the _____ between the newcomers and themselves.
    A   hole   B   gap
    C   blank   D   crevice

7   Emily managed to talk to the politician by _____ herself off as a journalist.
    A   taking   B   putting
    C   calling   D   passing

8   Trying to get to know how other people live can be _____ with difficulty.
    A   full   B   fraught
    C   great   D   loaded

9   The lion ran up to the bars of the cage roaring and _____ its teeth.
    A   showing   B   revealing
    C   baring   D   exposing

10 If I go out in the sun, I come _____ in a rash.
    A   off   B   out
    C   across   D   over

Structure

Complete the sentences below using an appropriate present perfect or past tense of the verb in brackets.

11 Jim and Margaret _____ since 1945. (marry)
12 Since arriving in Jakarta, Marina _____ very good at finding her way around. (become)
13 I think I'll have to go to the doctor as I _____ ill for some days. (feel)
14 The staff at the nursery _____ me that they _____ a hard time persuading my daughter to share her toys. (tell, have)
15 Tom soon _____ he couldn't live as cheaply in England as he had hoped. (realize)
16 For the first time in years Graham _____ his wife's birthday. (remember)
17 The manager claimed she _____ my feelings on the matter but she just _____ agree with me. (respect, can)
18 I don't believe it! It's three in the morning and that party still _____. (finish)
19 I hope Mike _____ his report by the end of this week because I want to check it! (write)
20 Since the end of the conflict, many refugees _____ to stay in the camps for long periods. (force)

Error correction

Read the sentences and correct any errors. Tick any sentences that are error-free.

21 David has been in Bangkok long but he knows it quite well.
22 There was a job going but Alex was turned off when they found out how old he was.
23 Esther hasn't still finished the book I lent her one year ago.
24 We've been trying to ring you since ages.
25 The fact that Tony refused to tell the truth only exacerbated the situation.
26 Peter's teacher never seemed to say anything positive about him and often put him down in front of the class.
27 Adi was unable to take his dependant relatives with him when he emigrated.
28 Mrs Carey hasn't seen them since moving to the country.
29 Marianne cringed with embarassment when James told her he loved her.
30 My brother has been getting so nervous with me recently – I've no idea what's the matter with him.

Unit 10 Test

Vocabulary

Choose the best option A, B, C or D.

1 Many famous people give to charitable _____ because they can afford to.
  A provisions   B causes
  C motives   D cases

2 The politician's wife was able to _____ the information to the press without getting caught.
  A leak   B spread
  C infiltrate   D extend

3 The details about the zoo's closure were obtained from an unnamed _____.
  A origin   B focus
  C source   D store

4 It took several months before the organization was up and _____.
  A ready   B running
  C functioning D about

5 The _____ workers were expecting thousands of refugees to turn up at the camps over the next few weeks.
  A concern   B agency
  C social   D relief

6 Newspapers coined the _____ 'Angel of Africa' to describe the model when she visited the area to make a film.
  A phrase   B saying
  C term   D idea

7 After the concert, everyone had to _____ home through the snow.
  A trace   B tread
  C trudge   D trickle

8 The company was so successful during the 1980s that it _____ 500 new employees in a period of six months.
  A put on   B took on
  C caught on   D laid on

9 The director is totally _____ to promoting the cause of the hungry and homeless.
  A resolute   B committed
  C obliged   D concerned

10 There are insufficient _____ left to pay for medical aid.
  A accounts   B stores
  C funds   D numbers

Structure

Complete the following sentences by inserting the appropriate infinitive, gerund or present participle of the verb in brackets.

11 The minister considered _____ a large sum of money to the restoration fund. (donate)

12 They promised _____ the equipment they had borrowed. (return)

13 If you keep _____ aid to a country, it can become dependent on it. (give)

14 Most people don't need _____ financially once they have found reasonable jobs. (support)

15 What do you feel when you see people _____ in the streets? (beg)

16 The man pretended _____ me the way to my hotel. (show)

17 Many people forget _____ their address on forms. (put)

18 We suggested _____ together to visit the site. (go)

19 As you're so tired, I don't think you need _____ tonight. (come)

20 Wait a minute; I've nearly finished _____ this letter. (write)

Error correction

Read the sentences and correct any errors. Tick any sentences that are error-free.

21 One way to support the needy is through sponsering individual children.

22 More bus services were laid on during the train strike.

23 She abandoned all thoughts of a carreer to become a nun.

24 Very few of us are given the oportunity to become famous.

25 What can you do to help your neighbours.

26 I don't get in with my boss.

27 Remember to check the address before posting the letter on.

28 Were constantly being told to think of others.

29 The whole class has decided to enter in the competition.

30 All donations will directly benifit the charity of your choice.

Unit 11 Test

Vocabulary

Choose the best option A, B, C or D.

1   The Project leader urged everyone to develop a sense of _____ and become aware of the needs of the town's vulnerable citizens.
    A   communication   B   community
    C   commune   D   communicate

2   A simple way to _____ eye diseases amongst children is to provide clean water for washing.
    A   displace   B   improve
    C   combat   D   lower

3   Our cosmetics are designed to _____ your natural beauty.
    A   enhance   B   invest
    C   amend   D   endure

4   After her bike accident, Mrs Edwards was _____ of other cyclists on the road.
    A   caring   B   worried
    C   concerned   D   wary

5   Scientists asked for _____ to test the new drugs.
    A   helpers   B   volunteers
    C   participants   D   members

6   A lot of people are _____ about the benefits of nuclear power.
    A   disbelieving   B   sceptical
    C   incredulous   D   unconvincing

7   My mother poured _____ on the idea that detergents are damaging the environment.
    A   rejection   B   shame
    C   scorn   D   doubt

8   It is unlikely that using vast amounts of pills and _____ will delay the ageing process.
    A   tablets   B   potions
    C   exercise   D   injections

9   The government has decided to _____ a wind farm on the site of the old power station.
    A   construct   B   prepare
    C   structure   D   support

10 The rivers are polluted because we have _____ our environment.
    A   disrupted   B   disordered
    C   neglected   D   negated

Structure

Complete the sentences below using appropriate conditional forms.

11 If you _____ she wasn't going to come tomorrow, you _____ that. (know / buy)
12 If Victoria _____ the correct treatment, she would have recovered sooner. (give)
13 If nuclear power _____ by more natural sources in years to come then the world _____ a better place. (replace / be)
14 If motorists _____ enough incentives in the last budget , they _____ to cut down on their fuel consumption. (offer / try)
15 If farmers _____ on planting so much wheat last winter, there _____ such an enormous surplus now. (insist / be)
16 Supposing that sufficient funds were available, _____ your degree? (finish)
17 If Margaret _____ me she was growing her own vegetables, I _____ from her instead. (tell / buy)
18 If we _____ the problem, we wouldn't have asked for help. (understand)
19 Supposing Dickens _____ a happy childhood, he _____ his novels. (have / write)
20 If the face cream _____ in the cupboard, I would _____ it. (be / see)

Error correction

Read the sentences and correct any errors. Tick any sentences that are error-free.

21 Ken and I talked on the situation and decided to sell the car.
22 It is difficult to know what the affect of so much acid rain will be.
23 The diagnoses was delayed until the result of his blood test.
24 The greyback beetle is one of the worlds most serious pests.
25 Unless you didn't give up eating so much meat, you will continue to feel tired.
26 Wrinkles are usually a sign of getting old.
27 The companies best known invention is referred to as a cosmeceutical.
28 'I hope it isn't true,' she exclaimed, but let's hope nobody finds out.'
29 There is a good deal of unnecessary predjudice against older women.
30 If sales staff had worn white coats, they would have looked more professional.

Unit 12 Test

Vocabulary

Choose the best option A, B, C or D.

1 The manager promised to replace the damaged television free of _____.
   A cost   B charge
   C expense   D price

2 Rosemary was a great friend but at work she was _____ and frequently forgot her appointments.
   A unreliable   B unrecognisable
   C unserviceable D unsolvable

3 The department store will exchange anything you have bought as long as you can produce the _____.
   A account   B ticket
   C receipt   D cheque

4 I don't know how George could ever find anything as his desk was always _____.
   A cluttered   B cramped
   C jumbled   D messed

5 I like shopping in there because the staff are so _____.
   A adaptable   B applicable
   C affordable   D approachable

6 Edward preferred furniture to be _____ rather than luxurious.
   A formed   B functional
   C instrumental   D used

7 The manager complained that unfortunately many people in this country think that serving others is _____ them.
   A underneath   B behind
   C under   D beneath

8 There is a lot to learn about _____ a business successfully.
   A making   B doing
   C setting   D running

9 As Peter had resigned, the company decided to take no further _____ against him.
   A conduct   B deed
   C action   D activity

10 After our disastrous holiday we put in a _____ for compensation.
   A demand   B claim
   C query   D plea

Structure

Complete the sentences below with an appropriate passive form of the verb in brackets.

11 Flexitime _____ by the management next month. (introduce)

12 The Human Resources team _____ two weeks to move into their new offices. (give)

13 The collapse of the company _____ by one irresponsible member of staff. (cause)

14 A series of spot checks _____ before anyone _____ to leave the factory yesterday. (carry out / allow)

15 You should _____ before you go for the interview. (hair cut)

16 Decisions _____ by the senior management team to prevent similar disputes from happening again. (make)

17 To save time, the applicants _____ by a recruitment agency. (select)

18 New equipment _____ for the office when the budget is approved. (order)

19 Sometimes printing errors _____ after the newspaper has been published. (discover)

20 As the main issues _____, the report will be ready for the Annual General Meeting. (settle)

Error Correction

Read the sentences and correct any errors. Tick any sentences that are error-free.

21 The trouble with Mike is that he is uncommunicative so you never know what he's thinking.

22 A successful business encourages staff to be knowledgable and enthusiastic about its products.

23 All staff need training, even those on the very top such as senior managers and directors.

24 John asked if he could be given another week to think about the offer.

25 It is important to balance the amount of time spent at work and to ease down if you feel stressed.

26 Colin a former employee of the company was reinstated as product manager after the take-over.

27 It was suggested that some components were sublevel and should be replaced.

28 Given the strength of our competitors, we believe we must reduce prices.

29 Air-conditioning is installed at the weekend so the office will be closed from Friday to Monday.

30 During the recession the country suffered from high rates of underemployment.

Unit 13 Test

Vocabulary

Choose the best option A, B, C or D.

1 Some witnesses claimed that the police had _____ the violence by their confrontational tactics.
   A   erupted   B   escalated
   C   escaped   D   escorted

2 As the prisoner was led away, he _____ insults at the jury.
   A   hurled   B   cried
   C   forced   D   hustled

3 The headteacher warned that any child who _____ truant would be expelled.
   A   discovered   B   was
   C   played   D   acted

4 William is a very _____ child and cries easily.
   A   sensible   B   sensual
   C   sensitized   D   sensitive

5 Burglars had _____ the flat leaving it in a terrible mess.
   A   ransacked   B   rampaged
   C   rifled   D   ripped

6 Instead of feeling ashamed, many young offenders tend to _____ about their crimes to their friends.
   A   boast   B   support
   C   justify   D   encourage

7 Although it was only a minor _____ she was given a two-year prison sentence.
   A   law   B   offence
   C   term   D   act

8 Terry's father had allowed his son to get _____ with all kinds of bad behaviour at home.
   A   away   B   off
   C   round   D   on

9 Most of the poorer areas are on the _____ of the town, away from the restaurants and fancy shops.
   A   suburbs   B   surroundings
   C   outskirts   D   perimeters

10 Many parents have to work long hours so that even young children are left to their own _____ after school has finished.
   A   concerns   B   activities
   C   affairs   D   devices

Structure

Fill the gaps in this cloze with one word only.

The trouble with prisons is that (11)_____ what some politicians say, they don't turn out good citizens. On the other (12)_____ there is always a balance to be struck (13)_____ what is good for society and what is a good feeling for society. It is common enough for people of sound mind and left-wing tendencies (14)_____ openly admit that revenge is sweet and relish the fact that the kid who broke (15)_____ your car and stole the radio is now languishing in jail. But unfortunately that same kid is (16)_____ only being punished but is also learning how to steal better. (17)_____ he is much older he'll be committing more serious crimes more frequently. This pattern (18)_____ crime is being repeated all over the world especially where young offenders mix freely with hardened criminals. There is no easy solution. (19)_____ by preventing juvenile offenders from being sent to adult prisons is there any hope of reversing the trend. In the (20)_____ way it is vital to remember that the harder we punish the harder the offenders become.

Error correction

Read the sentences and correct any errors. Tick any sentences that are error-free.

21 The judge reccommended that the accused should be sent to a top security unit.
22 No longer they will be able to claim the right to be tried in their own country.
23 Even though the fog I could make out the number plate of the car in front.
24 The lawyer suggested that the two boys had practiced picking pockets at school.
25 The minister promised that those who committed serious crimes would be sent to jail for a long time.
26 One single person could be responsible for the collapse of the bank in no way.
27 Fewer young people are being arrested for possessing drugs not that there are more drugs available.
28 There are many occasions when it would be easier not to say the truth.
29 Assaulting a police officer is a serious offence.
30 It is a well-known fact that newspapers print rarely good news or uplifting stories.

Unit Test 14

Vocabulary

Choose the best option A, B, C or D.

1 Brett's solution to the problem was _____ and brought the project back on course.
   A calculating   B ingenious
   C inadvertent   D shifty

2 Living on a _____ Scottish hillside, he nevertheless manages to work effectively from a home base.
   A separate   B distinct
   C foreign   D remote

3 This report _____ the current problems faced by commuters and suggests a number of improvements.
   A encloses   B inspects
   C encapsulates   D involves

4 New technology is seen as a _____ issue for the next five years and every school will benefit in some way.
   A crucial   B marginal
   C central   D peripheral

5 The Internet has led to the faster and more effective _____ of information.
   A expansion   B coverage
   C spread   D dissemination

6 We are all too dependent _____ our cars and should be encouraged to leave them at home.
   A on   B of
   C to   D in

7 What are the _____ of young people today? Probably the same as they always have been – a job, a steady relationship and somewhere to live.
   A thoughts   B aspirations
   C subjects   D attempts

8 The company seeks to _____ staff and has a generous package of benefits.
   A possess   B own
   C retain   D grasp

9 Flora's limited knowledge of French was a _____ in her work.
   A constraint   B tie
   C deterrent   D bind

10 Let's _____ through the channels and see if any films are on.
   A leaf   B pick
   C thumb   D flick

Structure

Fill the gaps in this cloze with one word only.

Many teleworkers are married women with very young children. (11)_____, there are also a great number of childless couples (12)_____ work from home, as well (13)_____ people with elderly relatives. Sometimes, employees working on-site are asked (14)_____ consider teleworking for a trial period. (15)_____ has its advantages for both employees (16)_____ employers, and is to (17)_____ encouraged. If a person is (18)_____ to being in an office, it is often a huge shock to change (19)_____ an isolated environment. At the same time, many people relish the opportunity to alter (20)_____ lifestyle and end the daily travelling to and from the workplace.

Error correction

Correct the spelling and punctuation errors in these sentences. Tick any sentences that are error-free.

21 People will soon be carrying portable computers for all their retail and business transactions.

22 It will soon be possible to order your weekly shopping and have it, delivered at the pressing of a few buttons.

23 There are many tangable benefits to modern living, particularly in terms of labour-saving appliances.

24 No computer system is necessarily infallible but the number of gaffs caused by this one is incredible.

25 Many multnational companies are opening new branches in this part of the world.

26 Not only is space travel for ordinary people more possible – it is likely to become essential for some.

27 This exhibition really shows the very best state-of the-art technology.

28 Who would have thought thirty years ago that opticle fibres could be used so successfully in operations?

29 If the costs are closely controlled, this can be an effectiv alternative.

30 Scarcely had they left the building when the alarms were activated.

PROGRESS TEST 1 (Units 1–5)

(1 hour 30 minutes)

Reading

Choose the most suitable heading from A–K for 1–8 below.

A   Are my dreams trying to tell me something?
B   Why do I find it hard to remember my dreams?
C   Where is the dream taking place?
D   How do I feel in the dream?
E   Should I tell others about my dreams?
F   What is the action in the dream?
G   Am I active or passive in the dream?
H   Do dreams help me in my waking life?
I   Who else is in the dream?
J   Can I change the dream for the better?
K   Are dreams a form of self-evaluation?

DREAM TIME

Sleep is essential to our health and well-being, and so too is dreaming. Nobody knows quite what function dreams serve, but we do know that someone deprived of dreamtime is said to become confused, irritable and less able to concentrate throughout the day.

1 _____

Scientists view the business of dreaming as a sort of intellectual sorting process for the day's events – our computer-brain getting its files in order for all the information piling in the next day. We store the important stuff and throw out the rest, and this triggers off a nightly cinema show of jumbled images, whether we remember them or not.

2 _____

Others believe that dreams have a supernatural power to predict the future, full of spiritual meaning and messages reflecting our fears and anxieties. Dreams are a signal as to how we should live our lives. They have an individual significance – only you can know what they mean to you.

3 _____

Situations in a dream often mirror something that is happening in life and we may not even know we're worrying about it. You might dream you've failed your exams, even if you passed them years ago – and this could relate to some other 'test' you're facing. Perhaps you've started a new job or a new relationship and you are afraid of not measuring up?

4 _____

Did you feel in control? The most positive dreams are where you feel good about what's happening. However, if you felt out of control, ask yourself whether there's something you feel powerless about – a decision you have to make at work, for example.

5 _____

Were you happy, angry, scared, confused? Push your thoughts further – if you're feeling frustrated and not able to do what you want, this may relate to something you've been prevented from doing in real life. When you trace the emotion back to its source, you could be surprised. You might not even have realised you were frustrated!

6 _____

Do the characters remind you of people in your life? A trait that troubles you about yourself? A dilemma you're facing now? Think about how these people are behaving towards you – everyone who appears in your dream reveals the way you feel about yourself. Even if it's someone you know, you've put the words in their mouths. For example, if someone is angry with you, it may be that you're feeling guilty.

7 _____

Buildings often symbolise yourself, with different rooms representing different aspects of your personality. Is there a wide open space and a sense of freedom or does your dream show you as closed in – in a prison perhaps? Are you feeling trapped in real life? Perhaps you are fed up with a boyfriend, or stuck in a job you hate?

8 _____

The plot contains a lot of clues. Is there a struggle? How does it link up with your everyday life? If you find yourself being chased and not able to escape, you're probably stressed and everything is getting on top of you. Violent dreams often mean you're hiding anger either at yourself or at others. Don't be frightened by the intensity of the dream – maybe you're afraid of expressing anger in real life and are releasing these feelings through your dreams instead.

Vocabulary cloze

Choose the best answer A, B, C or D, for each of the gaps in the text below.

The British, as everybody knows, are dignified and (1)_____, preferring to keep a stiff upper lip. If they seethe with (2)_____, they do so secretly. At a recent international conference, a businessman I knew

(3)_____ the startling observation that the conference (4)_____ from Britain all spent their time (5)_____ covering their papers with doodles – wild circles, spirals, sketchy profiles and flowery shapes blossomed in every bit of white space. Those who were not filling in the capital 'O's and decorating them with (6)_____ of sunlight were scribbling around the titles or drawing little yachts all over the Market (7)_____ section. Some other nations did do the occasional scrawl when listening (8)_____, but the British were undoubtedly the most (9)_____ of all those attending.

Doodles are a secret language which everyone uses to some (10)_____ as soon as they learn to hold a pencil. The pictures, patterns and scrawls have to (11)_____ from the depths of our subconscious and get on to the page without our thinking about them. So, if you want to know someone's deepest feelings about life, never mind (12)_____ – pinch his telephone pad. If you think your boss is behaving a bit strangely, the quickest way to find out is evidently to search the waste-paper basket. (13)_____ those bits of paper with only writing on them and focus on the doodles in between. Heavy, dark lines? He's becoming (14)_____ . Curves, hearts and flowers? There might be a flirtation just around the (15)_____ . But why is there a knife under the flower? Are you sure your working relationship is all it should be?

1	A	close	B	reticent
	C	silent	D	moody
2	A	sensation	B	feeling
	C	fear	D	emotion
3	A	made	B	did
	C	took	D	put
4	A	people	B	members
	C	fellows	D	attendants
5	A	hopefully	B	wildly
	C	fixedly	D	obsessively
6	A	sticks	B	spikes
	C	points	D	pins
7	A	Study	B	Test
	C	Estimate	D	Analysis
8	A	ecstatically	B	calmly
	C	raptly	D	alertly
9	A	compulsive	B	sensitive
	C	sensible	D	controlled
10	A	amount	B	extent
	C	unit	D	stage
11	A	well up	B	pull up
	C	dry up	D	end up
12	A	cure	B	treatment
	C	healing	D	therapy
13	A	Ignore	B	Cast
	C	Pass	D	Reject
14	A	cowering	B	aggressive
	C	offensive	D	slouched
15	A	shoulder	B	bend
	C	corner	D	curve

Grammar cloze

Complete the text below by filling each space with one suitable word.

A recent report by a government department suggests (1)_____ has been a significant rise (2)_____ the number of young people without jobs. Opinions on the reasons for this vary, according (3)_____ the report, but there is general agreement that the situation is (4)_____ worse by employers (5)_____ refuse to take on staff with no experience. Many youngsters still find it impossible to get a job, (6)_____ after undergoing training in their chosen field, (7)_____ often results in frustration and depression. The report also points out that older staff (8)_____ reluctant to make room for younger people, (9)_____ they feel their security is threatened. Although the report is critical (10)_____ many employers, it (11)_____ recognize that some are changing and recommends that (12)_____ attempts are being made to tackle (13)_____ problem, no support should be given. The report emphasizes that young people must (14)_____ prepared to be flexible, accepting jobs they may (15)_____ have originally considered appropriate.

Error correction

Read the following text line by line and find any punctuation errors, writing the correct punctuation in the spaces provided. Tick any lines that are error-free.

Walking in Sicily

1   As a city person, Gill armstrong was looking
2   for a break with a bit of pleasant exercise
3   thrown in when she chose, a seven-day walking
4   holiday close to Mount Etna. The whole thing
5   was pretty relaxed,' she reports 'Although
6   there was an organized walk most days, you
7   weren't ever forced to join in if you didnt
8   want to.' Gills group were based in a small
9   hotel and each evening the leader briefed
10 the group on the next days walk. Usually,
11 the hotel mini-bus would take the walkers
12 to a convenient starting point. That often
13 meant driving us, up the mountain so that
14 we could walk down,' adds Gill 'Although the
15 terrain wasn't that difficult, some of us,
16 did end up with a few blisters. I'd recommend
17 taking a first-aid kit to repair the damage.

1 _____   10 _____

2 _____   11 _____

3 _____   12 _____

4 _____   13 _____

5 _____   14 _____

6 _____   15 _____

7 _____   16 _____

8 _____   17 _____

9 _____

Writing

Choose one of the following tasks. Write your answer in around 250 words.

1   You have just returned from a two-week exchange visit to an English-speaking country, where you stayed with a family. The organizers of the exchange programme would like you to write them a confidential **account** of your stay, mentioning what was good and bad about your accommodation and how you were made welcome.

2   You have seen the following announcement in a magazine and decide to enter the competition:

Calling all readers!

HAPPY AND HEALTHY LIVING

What is your own successful recipe for a fun, healthy lifestyle? Write and tell us – there are six prizes for the most original entries.

   Write your **competition entry**.

3   You have been contacted by an international research company, who are investigating the changing nature of marriage worldwide. Write a **report** on the current situation in your own country, covering the points below:
   - average marrying age
   - family sizes
   - divorce.

PROGRESS TEST 2 (Units 6–10)

(1 hour 30 minutes)

Reading

Read the following newspaper article and then answer questions 1–5.

Customs: old and new

Two small girls stood on the doorstep incompletely disguised as horrible witches. One carried a broomstick, the other a collecting box. They were the perfect embodiment of two separate trends: the rise and rise of events such as Halloween, and the way you nowadays justify any daft, bizarre or preposterous thing you want to do by saying it's all for charity.

Plenty of people resent the fact that Hallowe'en seems to be taking over from good old British Guy Fawkes, but it's OK by me: Bonfire Night itself, after all, was just a rationalisation of earlier pagan flames. And I'd certainly rather see a pumpkin made into a grinning lantern than eat the thing: vegetarians say they would never eat anything with a face, and for me that goes for pumpkins too.

There is, though, a resistance to any growing custom that seems to come from America. But many of their customs catch on here because our own are so often based on an idyllic village life that no longer exists. They don't translate well to town life. But the American ones are rooted in the suburbs where most of us actually live: trick or treat, the neighbourhood cook-in, the barbecue.

All these card and flower occasions like Mother's Day and St Valentine's are often denounced as being purely commercial. And people do make money out of them – as they did at medieval fairs, come to that. But so what? Look how we enjoy sending postcards when we are on holiday just to reassure ourselves that we are still in touch.

I suspect that half the time we are so busy wringing our hands about our declining customs that we hardly notice the new ones coming up. We agonise about those who don't seem to feel the need to get married but don't notice the joyous transformation of the wedding scene for those who do. Stag nights have always been around but now there are serious hen nights too. The video may make three at the altar, which is a pain, but the occasion has changed from a stilted affair in the mid-afternoon to a two-stage occasion. There is a formal part, with food, speeches, aunts; but the young then revert to an older tradition and dance the night away, often playing songs of their own creation.

I feel that an ancient and humane liberal is in a real bind these days. The last thing you want is to come on as an old grouch, disapproving of everything new. Yet there is so much to be appalled by – open any paper. There are serious issues about which it would be supine not to be indignant. So we had better avoid being written off as querulous complainers who just whinge at anything that isn't the way it used to be.

1   How does the writer feel about Hallowe'en?
   A   She prefers it to Bonfire Night.
   B   She thinks it is a charitable cause.
   C   She doesn't really mind it.
   D   She resents that it's becoming too popular.

2   Why are some customs dying out?
   A   They don't make any money.
   B   The older generation complain about them.
   C   Young people have forgotten about them.
   D   They are not so appropriate for city life.

3   What does the writer feel about card and flower occasions?
   A   They are too commercial.
   B   They don't matter very much.
   C   They keep people in touch.
   D   There are too many of them.

4   Some people are worried about the state of marriage today because
   A   girls are holding wild celebrations the night before the ceremony.
   B   the video recording of the ceremony is undignified.
   C   because some couples don't bother to get married.
   D   because the younger people continue to celebrate for hours afterwards.

5   What does the writer say about new customs?
   A   There are more important things to be concerned about.
   B   New customs are more interesting than old ones.
   C   New customs encourage us to be kinder to each other.
   D   There is no difference between old and new customs.

Vocabulary cloze

Choose the best answer A, B, C or D, for each of the gaps in the text below.

Cuba

Here is a wonderful opportunity at a (1)_____ cost to visit the truly remarkable island of Cuba. We have (2)_____ rooms at some of the finest hotels for (3)_____ of 7 and 14 nights. You may (4)_____ your time between relaxing and exploring this beautiful country by taking advantage of our extensive excursion programme.

The (5)_____ of such a small country is amazing and, as it is set in the warm waters of the Caribbean, it is (6)_____ to have one of the most pleasant climates in the world. Cuba, being so small, is not only an ideal country to (7)_____, but is also a place where visitors can relax and (8)_____ in exotic surroundings. Not only has nature (9)_____ Cuba with a magnificent (10)_____ and some fine sandy beaches, but there are also extensive (11)_____ near them. Most beaches are close to important (12)_____ such as the national parks with their (13)_____ wildlife, flora and fauna. Because the south of the island is blessed with being the driest (14)_____ in the country most hotels are situated here. Rain is however (15)_____ in the north from December to July.

1	A	cheap	B	moderate
	C	bargain	D	small
2	A	reserved	B	registered
	C	required	D	retained
3	A	weeks	B	lengths
	C	periods	D	times
4	A	divide	B	pass
	C	extend	D	part
5	A	division	B	diversity
	C	diversion	D	divergence
6	A	suggested	B	hoped
	C	reputed	D	credited
7	A	travel	B	wander
	C	trip	D	tour
8	A	unwind	B	uncoil
	C	unburden	D	unroll
9	A	enhanced	B	endowed
	C	endured	D	enlightened
10	A	beach	B	shore
	C	coast	D	edge
11	A	facilities	B	activities
	C	pursuits	D	sports
12	A	situations	B	sites
	C	districts	D	localities
13	A	huge	B	abundant
	C	great	D	many
14	A	province	B	suburb
	C	region	D	community
15	A	unusual	B	interminable
	C	inevitable	D	unfortunate

Grammar cloze

Complete the text below by filling each space with one suitable word.

Heights of Excellence

It is over one hundred years (1)_____ the German engineer Rudolph Diesel launched his internal combustion engine – just one of the contributions engineering (2)_____ made to every aspect of our world. Engineering, however, means (3)_____ more than engines.

In fact, (4)_____ are dozens of different types of engineering. Civil engineers take care (5)_____ big projects: bridges, roads, railways, airports and tunnels. They also look after the supply and transport of vital resources (6)_____ as water and energy.

The protection of the environment is a crucial part of (7)_____ a civil engineer. Engineers look for ways of reducing harmful emissions from power stations, for example, as (8)_____ as dealing with the disposal of hazardous waste.

One of the giants of the civil engineering profession was Isambard Kingdom Brunel, (9)_____ tunnel under the River Thames, which was finally opened in 1843, is now part of the London Underground system. Brunel possessed a talent which had been passed (10)_____ from father to son, and he went on (11)_____ design the Great Western Railway.

In the latter half of his life, he turned his attention to constructing huge ships, one of (12)_____ was the Great Western, the first steamship to cross the Atlantic, and another the Great Eastern, then the largest vessel (13)_____ built. Today's civil engineers follow Brunel's vision (14)_____ working on huge projects which, in future, will help to make life easier for (15)_____ human race.

Register transfer

Read the following report and use the information to complete the numbered gaps in the letter. **Use no more than two words for each gap.** The exercise begins with an example (0).

Fire Inspector's report

An emergency call was received at 10.45 am on Sunday, 12 May. Two fire engines were on the scene at 11.00 am. The premises consisted of a glass-fronted shop and living accommodation above. The upstairs rooms were blazing and smoke was exiting from the roof. I indicated to the men that they should don breathing apparatus. We endeavoured to enter the building by the back door but access was impossible due to smoke and falling debris. Two men entered through a side door and succeeded in locating two children in the back bedroom who were taken outside to a waiting ambulance. The fire was brought under control and after damping down the fire-engines returned to the station at 3.00 pm.

Dear Katherine

We have had a busy week. On Sunday we were called out to a fire. We managed to (0) <u>get there</u> in 15 minutes. It was awful. There was this shop with a (1) _____ above and smoke was (2) _____ the roof. We were told to (3) _____ our breathing apparatus and then we tried to (4) _____ through the back door. We had to give up because there was too much smoke and stuff was coming down (5) _____ of us. Eventually we (6) _____ through a door round the side. We (7) _____ two children in the back bedroom and managed to (8) _____ to an ambulance. It was (9) _____ by 3 o'clock. But the following morning …

Writing

Choose one of the following tasks. Write your answer in around 250 words.

1   Your teacher has asked you to recommend two international magazines written in English for inclusion in the college library. Write a **review** of the two magazines, giving details of their content and saying why you think other students would benefit from reading them.

2   The tourist office in the town where you live is preparing a guidebook, covering places to visit within an hour's drive of the town. You have been asked to write an **entry** for the guidebook, in which you give details for three different places, one of which should be in the countryside.

3   You have seen this announcement in an international student's magazine:

Traditions and customs – alive and well?

We are preparing a special issue of the magazine on this topic, and we would like to hear about traditions and customs in your country. Write us an article, telling us about one tradition which is still important and one which is no longer observed. You should give your own reasons for why one tradition is alive and well and the other has disappeared.

   Write your **article**.

PROGRESS TEST 3 (Units 11–14)

(1 hour 30 minutes)

Reading

Choose which of the paragraphs A–G match the numbered gaps in the article below. There is one extra paragraph which does not belong in any of the gaps.

Negotiating

Wouldn't it be wonderful if we could all get what we wanted without trying. The truth is that most of us have to learn how to get what we want. Often achieving this at work, whether it's a new job or just an upgrade, depends upon good negotiating skills. We start negotiating when we are little children, and we continue to negotiate throughout our lives. Remember saying something like, 'I promise to be a good girl if …' to your parents?

1 _____

One of the basic principles of negotiation is that you ask for more than you really want so you end up getting what you want or pretty close to it.

2 _____

He or she also completes a form. You both then get together and reach a consensus. You may not always get what you want, but you stand a better chance of doing it this way.

3 _____

You are also negotiating when you send out a CV. Some people send out CVs without covering letters and wonder why they never get a response. Other people send out a CV with the wrong sort of covering letter.

4 _____

When you send out a CV, you want to get 'your foot in the door', so you can have an opportunity to sell yourself.

5 _____

And then you word the letter in such a way that you get what you want: an interview. The letter is then addressed appropriately. Forget about 'To Whom It May Concern' and make sure you address it to 'Dear Mr / Ms X'. This will make much more of an impression.

6 _____

Your tact has helped you get what you want from another. In this instance, an opportunity to get an interview. Any prospective employer realises now that how he deals with your application has an effect on his company's image, and he wants that to be positive.

A This is another example of negotiating in the workplace. This idea works very well where there is an atmosphere of open and honest communication in your organisation.

B A properly conducted performance appraisal is also an exercise in negotiation. The way I recommend is that your boss gives you a blank performance appraisal form and asks you to complete it as you see your performance.

C We negotiated with our friends, 'I'll go to see a film with you tonight if you will play tennis with me on Saturday morning'. You negotiated your terms of employment when you started your job, and this discussion no doubt covered the topic of salary.

D Having received such a letter the recipient is now in the position of having to keep your CV which he will have to refer to when you phone.

E Effective negotiation in these situations requires a little homework. Firstly, you find out the name and title of the person to whom you should be applying for a job.

F They also wonder why they get so few replies. The reason is that they haven't concentrated on what they really want. Always include in your covering letter a sound reason for your application and make sure that you mention the company and know something specific about it.

G The terminology you use provides an indication of your confidence. Your use of appropriate words helps your cause. You should avoid being aggressive, as this turns people off and can be counterproductive.

Vocabulary cloze

Choose the best answer A, B, C or D, for each of the gaps in the text below.

Lately, there has been a dramatic rise in the number of burglaries in the area. John Amos came home to find (1)_____ in his flat. He frightened them off when his car pulled up on the drive but by then the TV and video were gone. Despite their hurry they had the (2)_____ to empty the drawers and cupboards into a heap on the floor and had obviously taken anything of any value.

John (3)_____ local kids who had been pestering him, and (4)_____ insults at him on his way to work. Sometimes they came (5)_____ on his door and yelled at him through the letter box. His neighbours said it was because John was a teacher and the kids were probably (6)_____ truant. They complained to John that kids like that should be put behind (7)_____ and if they were too young for that then they should be sent to secure units as far way as possible.

But John did not bother to call the police. Instead he decided to (8)_____ an alarm system. The advertising blurb claimed that this was no mere burglar alarm but a highly sophisticated (9)_____ system. The equipment included a (10)_____ which would not only warn you that someone was approaching the (11)_____ but would video record them as well. It was expensive but John was keen to (12)_____ even the most determined of burglars.

Somehow word got round that his flat was a fortress and this seemed to incite the kids to (13)_____ him more than ever. Their activities (14)_____ and the attacks became more frequent. John became convinced that the only (15)_____ way of dealing with the situation was to move. The following spring he emigrated to Canada.

1	A	interlopers	B	intruders	
	C	invaders	D	infiltrators	
2	A	audacity	B	rudeness	
	C	bravery	D	enterprise	
3	A	accused	B	presumed	
	C	blamed	D	assumed	
4	A	hurling	B	tossing	
	C	heaving	D	launching	
5	A	hitting	B	crashing	
	C	banging	D	smashing	
6	A	skiving	B	playing	
	C	being	D	doing	
7	A	barriers	B	barricades	
	C	rods	D	bars	
8	A	input	B	install	
	C	institute	D	instigate	
9	A	surveillance	B	inspection	
	C	supervision	D	vigilance	
10	A	catcher	B	observer	
	C	exposer	D	detector	
11	A	establish	B	building site	
	C	premises	D	environment	
12	A	overcome	B	outdo	
	C	outshine	D	override	
13	A	torment	B	tackle	
	C	alarm	D	treat	
14	A	escaped	B	enlarged	
	C	escalated	D	activated	
15	A	adequate	B	satisfactory	
	C	capable	D	passable	

Grammar cloze

Complete the text below by filling each space with one word only.

Prolonging active life

Our health has improved dramatically over the past century. (1)_____ you had been born a male a hundred years ago, you would (2)_____ had a life expectancy of only 44 years – or slightly longer if female. Today the figures are 74 and 78 years respectively.

Thanks to antibiotics and better hygiene, we (3)_____ longer live in fear of infectious diseases. Not only (4)_____ we discovered the importance of a balanced diet, (5)_____ we also have a better understanding of common diseases. Many of these improvements have (6)_____ brought about by medical research. If we fall ill, the treatments (7)_____ likely to be based on scientific principles. A hundred years ago, doctors (8)_____ have relied on guesswork, habit and superstition. However, (9)_____ we are living longer and healthier lives than ever (10)_____ few people enjoy perfect health, especially (11)_____ they get older. Many of the benefits of medical research are costly, and take (12)_____ long time to become available. If future research finds (13)_____ more about what causes common diseases, then we should be able to start looking after ourselves better and have (14)_____ just longer lives – but healthier and happier (15)_____ too.

Phrase Gap

Read the text and complete the gaps by choosing the best phrases from A–J to fill spaces 1–6. Three of the phrases do not fit at all. One answer has been given as an example.

A few years ago one enlightened city decided to ease traffic congestion by (0)__J__. People would just take a bike, ride it to where they were going and leave it (1)_____. The trouble was the citizens naturally found it even more convenient to have their very own free bicycle and (2)_____.

That slight detail of human nature apart, it was a good idea and (3)_____. The electric cars buzzing round the streets of La Rochelle in France are seen as a supplement to conventional cars and, it is claimed, will make it easier (4)_____ within the city centre.

The idea is based on the belief that people like their own space, the freedom to drive a vehicle themselves (5)_____. It's also based on the fact that cars in towns usually carry just one person. In effect, it's (6)_____. At the moment it's a slightly utopian view but the concept has grown out of a practical study.

A   rather than crowd on to a bus or train
B   instead of cars
C   a sort of do-it-yourself taxi
D   for someone else to use
E   stock swiftly dwindled
F   taking the place of bicycles
G   to end the use of private cars
H   it's now the basis of a new scheme
I   to encourage their use
J   supplying sufficient communal bicycles

Writing

Choose one of the following tasks. Write your answer in around 250 words.

1   As a result of falling membership, your local English club has asked you to prepare a **leaflet** to attract new people. Outline what the club has to offer and say how new members can join.

2   Write a **character reference** to support the application of a colleague, who has been short-listed for a job in the finance department of a multinational company.

3   A growing number of people are telecommuting in your area and your college is hoping to obtain a grant to set up a telecottage on its site. You have been asked by the Principal to write a **report** for the grant agency, saying how the grant would be spent and what benefits the college could offer local telecommuters.

Unit test keys

Unit 1 Test

Vocabulary

1	C	2	A	3	D	4	C	5	A
6	B	7	A	8	C	9	D	10	A

Structure

11 Mark 12 Thesaurus' 13 its 14 √
15 doctor, a 16 editor, who 17 London's
18 chessboard. 19 retired, he 20 √
21 (the word 22 'thesaurus' 23 Roget's
24 √ 25 and without

Unit 2 Test

Vocabulary

1	C	2	C	3	D	4	B	5	B
6	C	7	A	8	B	9	D	10	A

Structure

11 Could 12 needn't 13 should 14 couldn't
15 Must 16 shouldn't 17 would 18 may
19 need 20 wouldn't

Error correction

21 many essential 22 proved ineffective
23 √ 24 equivalent of 25 stimulant
26 √ 27 Gym' 28 disorders 29 harmful
30 √

Unit 3 Test

Vocabulary

1	B	2	A	3	B	4	C	5	C
6	D	7	C	8	A	9	D	10	A

Structure

11 out 12 to 13 too 14 a 15 it
16 though 17 had 18 than 19 Unless
20 until

Error correction

21 what would you do? 22 posture 23 √
24 if they took 25 expansive mood
26 have minded 27 √ 28 if you don't want
29 rebellious 30 it's

Unit 4 Test

Vocabulary

1	B	2	D	3	A	4	C	5	A
6	C	7	D	8	B	9	A	10	B

Structure

11 had been working 12 was sleeping
13 was revising 14 started 15 rang
16 had been living / had lived 17 was cooking
18 started 19 became 20 tried

Error correction

21 has 22 on 23 a 24 √ 25 be
26 did 27 √ 28 the (light) 29 √
30 been

Unit 5 Test

Vocabulary

1	B	2	A	3	C	4	D	5	A
6	C	7	A	8	B	9	C	10	D

Structure

11 Teresa's father advised her to get some qualifications before leaving school.
12 Ian's mother explained that she (really) couldn't afford to buy him any new trainers.
13 The teacher accused them / the two students of having copied each other as the two essays were almost identical.
14 Jane whispered that her boss was the man sitting at the next table.
15 My neighbour asked if there was anything she / he could do to help.
16 Sue insisted that she didn't want to have dinner with Sam.
17 John's girlfriend complained that he never listened when she was talking to him.
18 His doctor told him to take one tablet three times a day after meals.
19 Charlie wondered if / whether it would be rude to ask her for a lift.
20 Mrs Williams replied that she would love a cup of coffee.

Error correction

21 and crime?'.
22 demonstrative
23 argument
24 advised / warned against
25 streets,'
26 √
27 community
28 hopeless
29 suggested going to / (that) they went / go to
30 surroundings

Unit 6 Test

Vocabulary

1 C	2 C	3 A	4 B	5 D
6 B	7 A	8 D	9 A	10 D

Structure

11 If   12 will   13 in   14 have
15 be   16 who   17 and   18 as
19 going   20 not

Error correction

21 a stunning oval turquoise and orange bowl.
22 will be astronomical
23 √
24 to be working
25 preposterous
26 will have to
27 √
28 closes
29 no pace, a
30 I'll come back

Unit 7 Test

Vocabulary

1 B	2 A	3 B	4 D	5 C
6 A	7 C	8 D	9 C	10 A

Structure

11 wish   12 regretted   13 miss
14 missed   15 regret   16 regret
17 missed   18 wish   19 regret
20 is missing

Error correction

21 that   22 what   23 the   24 √
25 herself   26 √   27 some   28 to
29 √   30 have

Unit 8 Test

Vocabulary

1 A	2 B	3 C	4 D	5 A
6 B	7 A	8 A	9 C	10 D

Structure

(Suggested answers)
11 We caught the ferry, which was packed with holidaymakers, at Calais.
12 Peter told Gillian that he planned to take her to Paris for the weekend.
13 When / As soon as we stopped in a lay-by we fell into a deep sleep.
14 Although there were people of all ages on the tour, they got on very well with each other.
or Despite the fact that there were…

15 What you soon find out is that it is more expensive to fly and not always quicker.
16 I made sure that I had a room in the quiet part of the hotel so that I could finish preparing my talk for the conference.
17 We jumped on the bus which was just going to Oxford.
18 I sold my bicycle, which was too small for me, to Robert.
19 The car engine was making a terrible noise as if it might break down at any moment.
20 What I don't like about travelling is that I usually have to wait around in airports for hours.

Error correction

21 develop   22 take up   23 went on   24 √
25 adjust   26 … ,which was long and uncomfortable, …   27 Despite the …   28 … , a busy place at the best of times, …   29 √   30 desperately

Unit 9 Test

Vocabulary

1 C	2 B	3 C	4 A	5 A
6 B	7 D	8 B	9 C	10 B

Structure

11 have been married
12 has become
13 have been feeling
14 told / have told   had / have been having
15 realized
16 remembered / has remembered
17 respected   could not
18 hasn't finished
19 will have written
20 have been forced

Error correction

21 hasn't been in Bangkok long
22 turned down   23 still hasn't
24 for ages   25 √   26 √   27 dependent
28 √   29 embarrassment   30 irritable

Unit 10 Test

Vocabulary

1 B	2 A	3 C	4 B	5 D
6 A	7 C	8 B	9 B	10 C

Structure

11 donating   12 to return   13 giving
14 supporting   15 begging   16 to show
17 to put   18 going   19 to come
20 writing

Error correction

21 sponsoring   22 √   23 career
24 opportunity   25 insert ? at the end
26 get *on* with   27 omit *on*   28 We're
29 omit *in*   30 benefit

Unit 11 Test

Vocabulary

1	B	2	C	3	A	4	D	5	B
6	B	7	C	8	B	9	A	10	C

Structure

11 had known   wouldn't have bought
12 had been given
13 is / was replaced   will / would be
14 had been offered   would have tried
15 hadn't insisted   wouldn't be
16 would you finish
17 had told   would have bought
18 had understood
19 had had   might / would not have written
20 had been / was   would have seen / would see

Error correction

21 talked over   22 effect   23 diagnosis
24 world's   25 omit *didn't*   26 √
27 company's   28 'but let's …
29 prejudice   30 √

Unit 12 Test

Vocabulary

1	B	2	A	3	C	4	A	5	D
6	B	7	D	8	D	9	C	10	B

Structure

11 will be / is being / is going to be introduced
12 has been given / will be given / was given
13 was / has been caused
14 were carried out   was allowed
15 have / get your hair cut
16 have been made / will be / were made
17 have been / were
18 will be ordered
19 are discovered
20 have been settled

Error correction

21 √   22 knowledgeable
23 at the very top   24 √   25 ease up
26 Colin, a former employee of the company,
27 substandard   28 √   29 is being installed
30 unemployment

Unit 13 Test

Vocabulary

1	B	2	A	3	C	4	D	5	A
6	A	7	B	8	A	9	C	10	D

Structure

11 despite   12 hand   13 between   14 to
15 into   16 not   17 Before   18 of
19 Only   20 same

Error correction

21 recommended
22 No longer will they …
23 In spite of / Despite the fog …
24 practised
25 √
26 In no way could one person be responsible for …
27 even though (instead of *not that*)
28 tell the truth
29 √
30 … newspapers rarely print …

Unit 14 Test

Vocabulary

1	B	2	D	3	C	4	A	5	D
6	A	7	B	8	C	9	A	10	D

Structure

11 However   12 who   13 as   14 to
15 This   16 and   17 be   18 used
19 to   20 their

Error correction

21 √   22 it delivered   23 tangible
24 gaffes   25 multinational   26 √
27 state-of-the-art   28 optical   29 effective
30 √

Progress test keys

Progress Test 1

Reading
1 H   2 A   3 K   4 G   5 D
6 I   7 C   8 F

Vocabulary cloze
1 B   2 D   3 A   4 B   5 D
6 B   7 D   8 C   9 A   10 B
11 A   12 D   13 A   14 B   15 C

Grammar cloze
1 there   2 in   3 to   4 made   5 who
6 even   7 which   8 are
9 as / because   10 of   11 does
12 unless   13 the   14 be   15 not

Error correction
1 Armstrong   2 √   3 chose a   4 'The
5 reports.   6 √   7 didn't   8 Gill's
9 √   10 day's   11 √   12 'That
13 us up   14 Gill.   15 us did   16 √
17 damage.'

Progress Test 2

Reading
1 C   2 D   3 C   4 C   5 A

Vocabulary cloze
1 B   2 A   3 C   4 A   5 B
6 C   7 D   8 A   9 B   10 C
11 A   12 B   13 B   14 C   15 C

Grammar cloze
1 since   2 has   3 far / much   4 there
5 of   6 such   7 being   8 well
9 whose   10 down / on   11 to
12 which   13 ever   14 by   15 the

Register transfer
1 flat   2 coming / pouring from
3 put on   4 get in   5 on top
6 got in   7 found   8 get them
9 all over / all finished

Progress Test 3

Reading
1 C   2 B   3 A   4 F   5 E   6 D

Vocabulary cloze
1 B   2 A   3 C   4 A   5 C
6 B   7 D   8 B   9 A   10 D
11 C   12 B   13 A   14 C   15 B

Grammar cloze
1 If   2 have   3 no   4 have   5 but
6 been   7 are   8 would   9 although
10 before   11 when / as   12 a   13 out
14 not   15 ones

Phrase gap
1 D   2 E   3 H   4 G   5 A   6 C

TS

Exploring Science

The Exploring Science series is designed to meet all the Attainment Targets in the National Science Curriculum for levels 3 to 6. The topics in each book are divided into knowledge and understanding sections, followed by exploration. Carefully planned Test Yourself questions at the end of each topic ensure that the student has mastered the appropriate level of attainment specified in the Curriculum.